A DAUGHTER'S DEADLY DECEPTION

A DAUGHTER'S DEADLY DECEPTION

THE JENNIFER PAN STORY

Jeremy Grimaldi

DUNDURN
TORONTO

To protect identities, some names in this book have been changed.

Printer: Webcom
Cover image: High-school portrait of Jennifer Pan.

Library and Archives Canada Cataloguing in Publication

Grimaldi, Jeremy, author
    A daughter's deadly deception : the Jennifer Pan story / Jeremy Grimaldi.

Includes bibliographical references.
Issued in print and electronic formats.

ISBN 978-1-4597-3524-8 (paperback).--ISBN 978-1-4597-3525-5 (pdf).-- ISBN 978-1-4597-3526-2 (epub)

1. Pan, Jennifer. 2. Deception--Ontario--Case studies. 3. Murder for hire--Ontario--Case studies. 4. Murder--Ontario--Case studies. I. Title.

HV6535.C32O65 2016b   364.152'309713   C2016-905288-5
                                                  C2016-905289-3

1   2   3   4   5   20   19   18   17   16

  Conseil des Arts du Canada / Canada Council for the Arts  Canada   ONTARIO ARTS COUNCIL / CONSEIL DES ARTS DE L'ONTARIO / an Ontario government agency / un organisme du gouvernement de l'Ontario

We acknowledge the support of the **Canada Council for the Arts** and the **Ontario Arts Council** for our publishing program. We also acknowledge the financial support of the **Government of Ontario**, through the **Ontario Book Publishing Tax Credit** and the **Ontario Media Development Corporation**, and the **Government of Canada**.

Care has been taken to trace the ownership of copyright material used in this book. The author and the publisher welcome any information enabling them to rectify any references or credits in subsequent editions.

— *J. Kirk Howard, President*

The publisher is not responsible for websites or their content unless they are owned by the publisher.

Printed and bound in Canada.

VISIT US AT

dundurn.com | @dundurnpress | dundurnpress | dundurnpress

Dundurn
3 Church Street, Suite 500
Toronto, Ontario, Canada
M5E 1M2

CONTENTS

PART THREE: HOW COULD THIS HAPPEN?

PART FOUR: CONCLUSIONS

PROLOGUE

It has to be a nightmare.

"Where's the fucking money?" the voice asks.

The hushed tones of the intruder are followed by a silent, visceral threat — the cold metal of a handgun against his cheek. As the father of two lifts his gaze, quivering with fear, the man speaks again: "Where's the fucking money? I said."

What is happening? The man is in his own bed, in his own home, sleeping soundly after a long day of work. He attempts to shake off the grogginess of his deep slumber, to understand exactly what's transpiring. The intruder standing over him doesn't have time for his attempts at comprehension; he has his orders, now he needs to execute. Today is payday. He grabs fifty-seven-year-old Hann Pan roughly by the scruff of the neck. If Hann had time to put on his glasses, he would be able to see into his assailant's eyes, though they're largely hidden beneath a baseball cap that is pulled down low on his forehead. The man leads him downstairs, the gun pressed firmly to the back of his head. As they descend the semicircular staircase, the scale of the threat to Hann and his family is revealed one horrifying step at a time. Downstairs, another masked man, also wearing a flat-brimmed baseball cap, stands over Hann's wife, Bich-Ha, a gun to her neck.

Bich's feet are still soaking in a bucket of water after her weekly line-dancing class. She timidly looks up and asks her husband, in

Cantonese, her voice cracking with fright, "How did they get in?"

"I don't know," he answers. "I was sleeping."

Impatient, one of the men shouts, "Shut up! You talk too much." He turns to Hann and repeats, this time slower, his voice seething with rage: *"Where's the fucking money?"*

Hann, believing the men only want to rob him, not hurt his wife or him, obliges. The problem is that since the Pans were robbed years ago when they lived in Scarborough — a rough area he moved his family out of to avoid this sort of confrontation — they no longer keep large amounts of money at home. "I have $60 in my pants upstairs, but my possessions are worth plenty," he tells his tormentor.

"Liar! I need the fucking money, nothing else."

Hann suddenly feels a searing pain in the back of his head. He falls to the floor. A gush of blood cascades over the living room couch.

"Get up!"

As he and his wife are led into the basement of their middle-class suburban home, true fear begins to rise to the surface of Hann's mind. Still, he can't imagine the scale of violence and horror that is about to descend upon his home and family this unseasonably warm November night.

It's different for Hann's wife. She senses the imminent danger. She blurts out a panicked plea: "You can hurt us, but please don't hurt my daughter." Her mind is racing, frantic, wondering why they're being taken downstairs. She begins to plead with the intruders, whimpering and begging them to take pity on her humble family.

In the basement, the couple is ordered to sit on the couch, the same place where their daughter Jennifer lounged, watching her weekly sitcoms, just hours earlier. The men throw blankets over the couple's heads, blankets that keep the family members warm in the often-frigid basement. Hann remains calm, resigned to his fate; his wife is hysterical. The assailant readies himself, aims, and fires. One bullet rips through Hann's face, fracturing the bone near the inside corner of his right eye, grazing his carotid artery. A second bullet hits him in the right shoulder, exiting out the back of the top of his shoulder.

The men turn their attention to his screaming wife. The initial blast from the firearm pierces the base of her neck. A second shot tears through her upper-right shoulder. And a final bullet, this time fired at closer range, enters and swiftly exits her skull: a fatal shot.

Daughter Jennifer, who is later discovered by the police tied to the upstairs banister, recounts the sound of "four or five pops" and then an unknown number of footfalls before the intruders leave the house.

When Hann slowly regains consciousness and opens his eyes, he is gripped with terror as he comes to realize that the last eight minutes of his life have not been a gruesome nightmare but instead a terrifying reality. As the details of the break-in race through his mind, he looks beside him, where the love of his life lies, bloodied; her body has slumped to the floor. He crawls to her, wincing in pain, blood dripping from wounds in his shoulder and head. He shakes her, calls out her name, once, twice, three times — no response. The life has already left his wife of thirty years. He begins to howl in agony, a pain both physical and emotional. As he lurches upstairs, his desperate screams and moans are clearly audible to the 911 operators fielding his daughter Jennifer's panicked call for assistance. Hann reaches the main floor and staggers to the front door. Outside, he collapses in front of a neighbour who is on his way to an early shift at work.

"Dad?" his daughter Jennifer yells down to him. "I'm calling 911 … I'm okay."

But her father doesn't hear her. He is racked by pain in his own world of dread.

PART ONE

SHATTERED DREAMS

The names of some persons have been
changed to protect their identities.

1

THE INVESTIGATION BEGINS

"Nine-one-one. Do you require —?"

Before the operator can get all the words out of her mouth she hears a young woman's frenzied cries for assistance: "Help me, please! I need help … I don't know where my parents are …"

"Ma'am, ma'am, calm down. What's going on?" asks the operator.

"Some people just broke into our house and they just stole all our money!" the girl screams. "I just heard shots, pops. I'm tied upstairs. I had my hands tied behind my back. I had my cellphone in my pocket. Please come … help!"

"What did they look like?"

"I'm not sure … the guy who was with me, he was a male … one of them had a hoodie. They had most of the lights off before they left. I think he was black, I think, I'm not sure. They didn't hurt me.… They had guns and they were holding me at gunpoint.… They took my parents downstairs and I heard pops.… All they said was 'You're not co-operating.'" The woman is calling from a live crime scene.

In the background a blood-curdling howl is heard.

"Dad …? I'm calling 911 … I'm okay!" the caller yells out.

"Do you hear [your] mom anywhere downstairs?"

"I don't hear her anymore …" The girl's voice trails off and cracks with emotion. She sounds petrified and begs the operator to remain on the phone with her until the police arrive.

Moments later, sirens and loud shouting can be heard as police officers arrive on the scene.

THREE MEN JUMP out of the cruisers and take in the gruesome scene, their eyes struggling to grasp what lies before them. Two men, one partially dressed and dishevelled, are in the driveway of 240 Helen Avenue. Neighbour Peter Chung stands worriedly beside Hann Pan, who screams about the pain in his face in broken English. His clothes are drenched in blood, a "thick red liquid dripping from his nose." When Constable Mike Stesco approaches, he hears the confusing cries of Hann, but quickly realizes that gunmen have robbed the home when Hann motions with his fingers in the shape of a gun. Hann manages to get across that the intruders shot him and his wife and left his daughter inside the house.

Nothing is further from York Regional Constable Mason Baines's mind than murder as he drives around the peaceful city of Markham, Ontario, in his cruiser that night. After hearing the gun call on his CB, he races over to Helen Avenue, breaking the posted limit and covering the mile and a quarter in two minutes flat. When he gets out of his car and draws close to the door of the house, he recalls from his training what to do when faced with a gun call — hit the wall, draw your pistol, check that the coast is clear.

The young uniformed officer glances down and notices blood droplets leading to the front door. Following them inside and through the home's dining room, he calls out, trying to locate the person yelling from within. A panicked female voice answers, telling him that she's "upstairs."

"I'm okay!" she cries, but says something is wrong with her mother, who's in the basement and has been shot.

Baines makes his way through the house and is confronted with an eerily calm scene. The trail of blood leads him slowly forward. Other than the red drops that stain the hardwood, the rest of the main floor seems in order.

Mike Stesco, along with rookie partner Brian Darroch, follows Baines. He later notes: "Everything in the house seemed to be where it should be. Obviously, we've done home invasions in the past where the house had been ransacked, but [in this case], nothing was out of place, nothing taken."

The basement crime scene.

When the three officers descend into the basement, Baines recoils at the sight before him. The body of Bich-Ha Pan lies face down in front of a sectional leather couch. She is wearing green silky Winnie-the-Pooh pajamas. Her feet are still wet from the water they were soaking in mere minutes earlier.

Stesco later describes the scene: "There was a lot of blood. It was a real dark sort of thick-coloured blood. It wasn't like the trail we followed down, light sort of splatter, it was thicker. It was by her head and then she had a blue towel over her head."

At the scene, Stesco speaks to the woman but knows deep down it's pointless. There is no response. Baines checks her pulse, then notices two shots to her neck and back. Darroch notices Bich's legs are discoloured in pale shades of grey.

Four paramedics rush in soon after and flip over the lifeless body. They try to revive her, but it is a useless exercise.

Stesco tells his partner to head upstairs to secure the young woman. Darroch, his gun drawn, moves cautiously up through the house. As he approaches the home's final victim, he starts to holster his weapon. When he calls out, Jennifer tells him she's unsure if the assailants are actually gone. Darroch grips his service pistol again and quickly raises it. Peering through the gun's sight finder, he acknowledges Jennifer, then proceeds to clear all the rooms. The master bedroom is in shambles, the mattress flipped, the drawers — clearly rifled through — lie broken and empty, the contents spilling across the floor. The others appear in order.

Satisfied that no intruders are still present, Darroch returns to Jennifer. Later, the constable, a Scotsman and new to Canada, says the young woman's position on the floor reminded him of Copenhagen's *Little Mermaid* statue. Her ankles are to her side, her bound wrists able to move away from the banister about eight inches. Darroch retrieves a pair of scissors from Jennifer's bedroom and cuts the bootlace binding her tiny wrists. Noticing her panic, he tries to soothe her with his deep Glaswegian voice. Once she's free, he immediately ushers her out the front door, noting no redness or bruising on her wrists.

When Darroch sees Jennifer shiver, either because of nerves or the brisk night air, he covers her with his police jacket and delivers her to the waiting paramedics, implying that he is worried she might have been sexually assaulted by the men. Later, he says: "I asked them to have a look at the young lady. Sometimes things happen to ladies that they don't want to divulge to men, so I just wanted to make sure that she was okay."

As paramedics load Hann onto a stretcher and begin working on him, Peter Chung — the neighbour Hann implored to call 911 as his blood seeped onto the driveway — watches helplessly along with several other neighbours and a solitary cameraman, all witnesses to the ghastly results of gun violence.

Also being treated by paramedics, a worried Jennifer yells, "Daddy, are you okay?" These are the last words Hann hears before the doors are shut and his ambulance speeds off to the hospital.

Ever the gentleman, Darroch accompanies Jennifer to the hospital in her ambulance. It is only when she inquires about the well-being of both her parents that he breaks the news to her that her mother is dead. He asks her what she can remember from the night. Not much, she replies. There were three men — one was smaller than the rest and another had dreadlocks. It was too dark in the house during the invasion to catch sight of the men, she tells Darroch. The only light that shone occurred when the thieves opened the refrigerator while searching for her mother's purse.

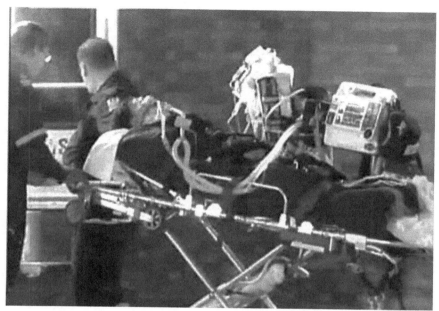

Hann Pan is placed into an ambulance at the scene of the home invasion. He would be transported to nearby Markham Stouffville Hospital in serious condition.

When Jennifer finally walks through the doors of Markham Stouffville Hospital, she is soon informed of the severity of her father's injuries. Many people seem surprised he's even alive. Hann wasn't able to speak as doctors worked furiously to save his life.

As the anguish of what has just occurred sinks in, Jennifer begins to fall apart when she acknowledges her new reality: life without her mom and possibly her dad. She reaches out to crisis workers at the hospital and is seen by them at 11:15 p.m. An anti-anxiety medication is prescribed for her to calm her badly frayed nerves. Outside, Darroch stands guard.

Finally, Jennifer is released back into Darroch's custody. It is now 1:31 a.m. on November 9. Before the pair get into Darroch's cruiser to drive to the Markham police station, Jennifer's Rogers Samsung phone is seized as part of the impending murder investigation.

2

INTERVIEW ONE

Just four hours after the double homicide attempt, with her father still clinging to life, twenty-four-year-old Jennifer Pan is led to an interview room at the Markham police station where she will be questioned by York Regional Police Detective Randy Slade, a veteran of the homicide unit. It is 2:45 a.m. on November 9. The interview will last two hours.

Faced with an obviously broken young woman who has just been left motherless by armed thugs, Detective Slade does his best to deliver his questions with kid gloves. The young woman before him is wearing glasses, and a French braid hangs down over her left shoulder. She's dressed in an oversized figure skating club sweater, black yoga pants, and a pair of bright blue–bowed Asian-style slippers.

Slade gently explains to Jennifer that the sworn video statement caution form sitting between them is not accusatory. It's a guarantee that she swears to tell the whole truth. To this she nods in understanding. However, as he carries on, pointing out that this is a homicide investigation and laying out the penalties for dishonesty, her head moves up and down far more pensively. When she's informed that the jail term for lying is fourteen years, Jennifer grows nervous, fidgeting and rubbing her legs before placing a delicate hand over her heart. Slade leaves the room briefly to get a Bible for her to swear on. Jennifer appears startled when he returns. Despite the anti-anxiety drugs now coursing through her system, she seems awfully jumpy.

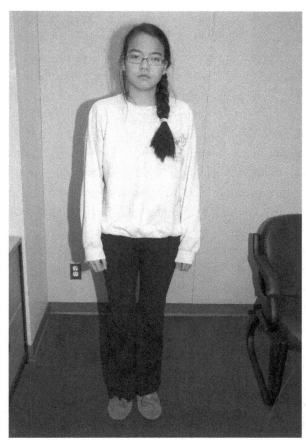

Jennifer is photographed during her first interview with police the night of her mother's murder.

Promising to tell the truth, the whole truth, and nothing but the truth, so help her God, the young woman with perfect posture then blurts out "As much as I can remember" as her bottom lip quivers.

"That's all I ask for," a concerned Slade responds. "This form, please don't take it personal, okay? But it's something we go through with everyone."

It's only when the murder of her mother is mentioned that Jennifer begins to display intense emotion — bowing her head and sobbing uncontrollably. Her heartache appears so great, she struggles to pronounce her mother's name, eventually sounding out the correct pronunciation — *Bick-Ha Pan* — before turning her face away and weeping. It doesn't take long before Detective Al Cooke, observing from an adjacent room, notices something troubling. When Jennifer is given a tissue, it comes away dry — there are no tears. "When she came in to her first interview, obviously, yes, we were watching," he says. "She wasn't crying. She wasn't very upset. She could have been in shock, so you can't rely on that as a piece of evidence. It's just something you look at, and maybe it'll mean something later."

Detective Slade and the other investigators, watching the interview via outdated recording equipment, listen intently as Jennifer begins to explain what transpired that November night. She recounts an incredible story. Her family home was raided by three gunmen who grew so enraged by the lack of spoils and her parents' uncooperative behaviour that they shot them both in the head.

Slade's first order of business was nailing down the assailants' descriptions. The first, Jennifer tells him, was black with a medium build and dreadlocks that "flopped" over his face so that she couldn't make out his features. He was between twenty-eight and thirty-three, about five feet six inches tall, and "seemed to be the one in charge." (Oddly, Jennifer refers to him using the term *gentleman*.) When asked about his facial hair, she motions with her hand around her chin, saying "I think …" before her first utterance of a phrase that would become a recurring theme throughout the interview: "I don't want to say something wrong." She says the man — who she describes as "Number One" — carried a handgun, wore black leather gloves, and sounded as though he was born in Canada. Her description of him is quite vague, even contradictory — his face, she tells Slade, had a "roundish, squarish" quality.

"Number Two," who she says was running back and forth between the other two men, assisting, had a long, oval face and was wearing a dark hoodie. A bandana covered his nose and he never spoke, only taking orders from others and nodding.

Although she states she didn't get much of a look at "Number Three," who was holding her parents at gunpoint, she said he had a Caribbean accent, resembling the way her high school friend's Guyanese parents spoke.

When Slade asks her to take him through the day leading up to the murder, Jennifer starts on the morning of November 8. The day began with an odd occurrence in the normally peaceful neighbourhood. When they were leaving the house, Jennifer and her mother saw that police had cordoned off part of their street. They were told they couldn't leave due to a gas leak nearby. Once police lifted the order, Jennifer told Slade, she decided to stay home and practise piano instead of going out with her mother. The day then unfolded in a routine sort of way, with Bich running errands before returning home in the mid-afternoon. Jennifer and her mother sat down for dinner together; Hann ate alone before retiring to his study to read the Vietnamese news, as was his habit. Jennifer's brother, Felix, she explained, was in Hamilton, about forty-five minutes away, where he was attending McMaster University, studying engineering.

After supper, Jennifer's friend, Adrian Tymkewycz, dropped by and the pair watched their favourite television shows: *How I Met Your Mother* and *Gossip Girl*. When he left, Jennifer retired to her bedroom, turned on the TV, watched *The Amazing Race*, and chatted on the phone with Edward Pacificador, another friend. She said she heard her mother return home at about 9:30 p.m. from her weekly line dancing session held at a Toronto church — something her mother did each Monday.

Upon hearing Bich "rummaging" around downstairs, Jennifer was startled to hear her mother yell upstairs for Hann to come down. It was the language she used — English — which sparked concern, prompting Jennifer to hang up the phone and sit in silence. Bich rarely used anything other than Vietnamese or her native Cantonese inside the home. Jennifer sat "frozen" in place, she says, listening to strange and muffled voices coming from inside her home. "The voices weren't any voices I was familiar with, and so I was scared ... I couldn't move. I just sat in my room for a while and then I thought I heard them all leave the top floor." When Jennifer finally opened the door and peered out into the dark hallway, she saw the man she refers to as Number One walking toward her with a string in his hands. He grabbed her and tied her hands behind her. "I have a gun behind your back. Do what I say," she was told. "If you do what I say then no one will get hurt. Where is the money? Show me where your money is."

Jennifer says she obliged, showing the man where she kept $2,000 in cash, which she'd been saving to buy the new iPhone. The men then "pushed" her to her parents' bedroom across the hall at gunpoint. Number One and Number Two asked her where her parents kept the money. She didn't know, so the men ransacked the room and discovered some cash in her mother's bedside table. They proceeded to "drag" Jennifer downstairs and ordered her to kneel on the floor and keep her eyes on the ground. Although she says she only saw Number Three's shadow, she heard him engage her mother in an angry confrontation, demanding her wallet and yelling orders that confused Bich. "My mom kept trying to get up and they kept telling her to sit down," she tells Slade in a weeping tone. "They were trying to find her wallet, but her English isn't very good, so she kept saying *purse*." When Bich tried to stand up one last time, Jennifer says she was shoved back onto the couch. "I didn't want her to get hurt, so I told her to sit down," she adds before beginning to sob and losing control of her emotions.

"Take your time," the detective tells her soothingly. "All this is very important, so take your time."

When Hann told the "gentlemen" that his wallet, containing $60, was upstairs in his bedroom, the men brought Jennifer back upstairs and found the money. Next Number One asked Number Two to get a string from "Cuzy." When he returned, Number One used it to tie Jennifer to the upstairs banister. The next thing she remembers is her parents being led to the basement. "The last thing I heard them [the intruders] say was 'You lied. You lied to us,' and then I heard two pops," a despondent Jennifer recalls. "My mom screamed, I yelled out for her, and [I heard] a couple more pops and I think I heard my mom say or moan or something. They did one more [shot] and one of the guys says 'We have to go now, it's been too long,' and then they ran out the front door."

By the time Jennifer was able to access her phone to call the police, she began to hear her father's voice coming from downstairs. "I still hadn't heard anything from my mom, and all I could hear was my dad running [out onto] the street, moaning," she adds.

Once Jennifer's initial account is complete, Detective Slade says he is intent on retracing the events with her one more time, but this time under his own methodical questioning: "We're going to go back clinically. Put yourself now as a figure looking down at what you saw."

While the telling and retelling of an event can help victims remember small details, it can also give investigators an opportunity to catch any inconsistencies in the witness's story. Jennifer remains composed and relatively concise during the recounting of the details, but there are key differences in her second version of events that catch the attention of investigators. Initially, she didn't see her mother after she returned home, but

The main floor and staircase leading to the second floor at the Pan home.

The upstairs landing, where Jennifer was bound to the railing with string. An officer cut her loose with the scissors shown.

in her second telling she descends the stairs to greet her. Her first account also involved a man coming toward her with a string, but in her retelling she claims Number One showed her his gun "in a holster" before ordering her to sit on the bed and grabbing the money — this time $2,500 rather than $2,000. In this version, she says she wasn't tied up until Number Two brought Number One a shoelace. "He had pulled really, really tight, and I guess he felt me flinch and that's when he tied the second knot," she says.

When she was led downstairs, she was told to sit on the floor (in the first account she said she was ordered to kneel). She then recalls something new: a critical moment. It was at this point, Jennifer says, that she disobeyed the assailant's orders to keep her eyes on the floor and looked up, noticing that Number Three was of thin build. She also observed that he was pointing a "revolver" at her father — something she says she could tell because of the gun's "rotating cylinder." In this version, though, she tells Slade that the men found substantially more of her parent's money — which she now recalls was $1,100 of unspent American dollars from a recent trip to the United States. During this second version, the men fail to locate the wallet and castigate her father for his perceived dishonesty (a comment Jennifer would repeat a number of times): "You lied to us. You lied to us. You just had to co-operate."

In a distressed, almost whiny voice, Jennifer then works her way through the terrifying end to her mother's life: "I think I hear[d] my parents going down the stairs, and my mom was asking them for me to come with them, but they wouldn't let me — 'I want my daughter. Why can't my daughter come, too? I want my daughter,'" she says, pausing, before breathing out heavily and continuing haltingly. "I heard two pops ... my mom scream ... I yelled out for her, and [heard] a couple more pops.... And I think I heard my mom say or moan something and then they did one more [shot]. One of the guys said, 'We have to go now. It's been too long.' And then they ran out the door."

A few minutes after this, when she was on the phone with the 911 operator, Jennifer recalls hearing her father groaning as he fled the house. "My dad was outside," she says, sobbing again. "I was yelling at him, but he wouldn't come in. I don't know if he didn't hear me, but he didn't come in. I think he went to look for help. And I didn't get to see my dad ... until before I left the hospital just now."

It is this detail that Detective Bill Courtice's mind refuses to let go, turning it over and over as he watches the interview, wondering why a father would bolt from the house, injury or not, knowing his daughter is still inside. "Dad is shot downstairs. He has a fatal injury. Some parents might go up because of their concern for their child," he later says, referencing cases where parents run into burning buildings to save their children. "In this case here, he exits stage left very quickly. He hears her screaming and he doesn't stop." Detective Courtice (pronounced *Curtis*), though, says he put his doubts to one side for the moment. "But at [that] point ... we took her comments at face value."

As questions turn to her situation at home, Jennifer gives Slade little to go on, explaining that her family "needed [her] home for a while." When he quizzes her about her professional circumstances and how she got the sort of money she handed to the thieves, she says she earned it teaching piano for family friends. When Slade inquires about her education, she mentions nothing about her past, only discussing her future plans: "I'm going back to school in January," she tells him. "To study biotechnology engineering." And when questioned about whether anything odd happened in the lead-up to the murder, she gives Slade the most vanilla of responses: "We live a straightforward, almost routine life."

Jennifer once again grows agitated when Slade nonchalantly tells her that her brother, Felix, is being interviewed in the room next door. Rather than asking how her baby brother is feeling or if she can speak to him, Jennifer seems more concerned with the police inquiries. Apparently unaware that a murder investigation, especially one as detailed as this would be, can involve hundreds of interviews, Jennifer breathlessly asks: "Oh, he has to be interviewed, too?"

"Just because, you never know," Slade replies, allaying her fears, suggesting police are just going through the motions by speaking to him. "It's more of an administration."

The news of her sibling's presence seems to be the precursor to something far more intriguing. When Slade eventually leaves the room to discuss what he's uncovered so far with his colleagues, we begin to see wild fluctuations in Jennifer's behaviour. The video footage shows her taking a swig of water before placing her head in her hand, her thumb and her forefinger on her temples. Her two hands eventually cover her face before she sits up and places her hand over her stomach. She stands up, appearing dizzy and disoriented, at one point even regaining her balance on the wall and then her chair before almost fainting as she paces around the room, one hand always on the wall. She begins to shake her hands and then places her forehead against the wall. When Slade re-enters twenty excruciating minutes later, he shares with her some of what the investigative team might have been contemplating. "It doesn't take a rocket scientist to figure out [the intruders might] have been drawn to [your mother] because of the type of car she is driving and where she's driving to," he says. "It's something we have to explore."

It is with the utterance of this theory that Jennifer comes alive once again, seemingly more at ease with the new line of discussion. She's questioned about whether a potential motive for the crime could have been what Jennifer calls the family's wealthy "aesthetics." Jennifer enthusiastically responds that her mother does drive a Lexus. When asked about her father's car, she responds with a wry smile: "He drives a Mercedes, and he loves that baby."

However, this mood doesn't last, and her emotions start to shift as police focus on her electronic communication. Jennifer appears to flinch when Slade mentions "time stamping" events using data collected from her cellphone. "I just don't, like, I talk to people on the phone, but I don't —" She hesitates.

Slade interrupts her with a response that seems to worry her even more. "The unfortunate thing is that Edward [Pacificador] and Adrian [Tymkewycz] are probably going to have to be interviewed because they were in the house and on the phone with you," he explains. The distressing news doesn't stop there. Detective Slade advises her exactly what to expect from the media whirlwind that is likely to follow a murder of this type. "I'm telling you that the media is going to be around this case," he explains. "We have no control over what they say and they do. My only advice to you is, don't read the papers and turn the TVs off. Home-invasion-type robberies where someone is murdered can become very big news and people ... hang on it."

Jennifer takes it all in with her hands crossed, again over her chest, on the verge of tears. Investigators then ask her to sign over her consent for access to calls and texts from her Rogers Samsung phone between November 1 and 9. She manages to muster enough intestinal fortitude to question exactly who will be contacted. "How ... deep into this will they look …?" she asks. "Just regular phone calls …? It's only because some-times I phone [piano] teachers and stuff like that."

When Slade mentions just how vital her cellphone information will be to catch the murderers, Jennifer appears surprised the police won't simply take her word for what happened in that house. In today's cellular world, Slade says, corresponding cell towers track mobile phone usage, and this information can become central to any homicide investigation. "Towers become relevant in this case because of where you are when the phone call comes in," he explains to Jennifer. "It firms your story to say 'I was in my room when the calls came in.' That will show up on the tower site informa-tion. It also may turn out that [in the lead-up] you were targeted and you were in an area, and towers enable us to go back and try to look for cameras [in those areas]. Not saying it's going to happen in your case, but … tower sites always show where and [at what time] you're on the phone making calls. If you're lying as a part of this whole process, telling us fictitious information, now the records can also be used against you. We have to let you know [that] by law we can use these against you if you're lying to us."

Clearly shocked by where this investigation might be headed, Jennifer tries to salvage her sense of control over what might occur next. "Will I be informed of who, if anyone, is contacted on that?" she inquires. But Slade won't budge. She'll be left in the dark from here on in.

Jennifer leaves the station at around 5:00 a.m.

It is during the meat of this conversation that, just a few miles away, the decision is made to airlift Jennifer's father from Markham Stouffville Hospital to a central Toronto trauma centre. Doctors make the difficult decision to place Hann in an induced coma.

3

A CRACK SQUAD

The brutal nature of this particular crime prompts some investigators to consider the possibility that Hann and Bich may have been involved in the underworld — gambling and drugs can't be ruled out. During her first interview, the subject of illegal gambling is raised with Jennifer when she is asked if her parents are known to keep large sums of money in the house. However, this line of questioning is soon abandoned. Although detectives don't like to dismiss motive without firm evidence, the clues left behind at the crime scene reveal a very different story. The reality is that fifty-seven-year-old Hann and fifty-three-year-old Bich couldn't be more straitlaced: these Vietnamese residents were just hard-working, middle-class parents.

But something clearly doesn't fit. The idea that Hann and Bich are two entirely innocent victims runs counter to everything detectives surveying the scene know from experience. Why would thieves intent on plundering a home of its wealth complicate a quick payday by resorting to such violence? It is completely out of the ordinary. A random home invasion, one in which criminals drive down a street and indiscriminately select a home based on appeal or assumed riches, may be widely feared by the public, but in police circles it's virtually unheard of. Any seasoned investigator will tell you that in 99 percent of cases there is a distinct motive, a reason — a tip about a safe bursting with cash, rumours of jewellery, thousands of dollars under the mattress, or top-of-the-line sports cars. However, in all these instances the motive is material benefit, and those willing to take part would ensure the home is empty. After all, those who steal possessions can expect six months or less in prison; murder, on the other hand, can land you in prison for life.

Otherwise, a victim might have links to the underworld. In this case, the motive might switch to payback for an assumed wrongdoing, or to send a signal if someone is trying to muscle in on your turf.

Regardless of the guidelines investigators are meant to follow — rules intended to avoid a phenomenon called "confirmation bias," which occurs when detectives seek out information that confirms their existing beliefs about a case — they still have instincts. Even the 911 operator started asking questions during Jennifer's frantic eight-minute call to police: "Do they know your parents, anything like that? Any relation to them?" she questions, perplexed. "They just came and tied you up?"

THE NOVEMBER 9 story in the *National Post* properly describes the shock and surprise felt by many upon hearing about the brazen killing: "The quiet streets of suburban Markham are rarely the setting for random violence … [but on this night] they left one woman dead, her husband seriously wounded, and their daughter bound and terrorized. They also left a neighbourhood in fear, wondering what might have prompted such an attack on a family with no apparent links to crime."

As far as suburbs go in Canada, York Region, with just over one million people, of which the City of Markham makes up about one-third, is as safe as it gets. The entire region only experienced fourteen home invasions — which involved criminals breaking into a residence expecting to commit violence — the year before (2009). Markham had only six. "This appears, from our early investigation, to be … random," then York Police Chief Armand La Barge advises the media. The crime is so heinous on its face — the matriarch of a "normal" family killed in the safety of her own home — it prompts the chief to label the crime "despicable." La Barge promises to bring "all hands on deck" to find those responsible — resulting in some twenty-four officers being assigned to the case, a number that quickly dwindles as information begins to roll in. One lawyer involved in the case says this approach stands in contrast to other Canadian police forces with fewer resources, which often begin with few officers and then more are added when and if required.

The Pans' Markham home on Helen Avenue.

In the aftermath of incidents like this one, where a murder, serious sexual assault, or abduction leaves an "intense public demand for identification, apprehension, and prosecution," Canadian police forces pull together what's known in law enforcement as a Major Case Management unit. It involves a team of three experienced investigators forming a "command triangle," intent on giving officers three sets of eyes and ears, not only for logical decisions and strategies but in order to lead a large group of officers in the field.

In this case, the senior investigating officer responsible for the direction of the investigation is Detective Sergeant Larry Wilson. He is the major case manager — the most experienced of the three — and is well versed in significant homicide probes. The primary investigator running the day-to-day tactical strategy is Detective Bill Courtice. Up to that point, Courtice took the lead in five homicides but was part of some eighty murder investigations in all, including one of Markham's most infamous, involving convicted murderer Chris Little. He has been described as a difficult investigator to get along with by more than a few of his colleagues, in part because of his blunt honesty and hard-nosed pursuit of the truth, sparing little concern for people's feelings. The number three, the file coordinator, is Detective Constable Alan Cooke, a former drugs and vice detective who also worked in the intelligence bureau. He makes up for his lack of experience in homicide by his history of undercover work with traditional Mafia figures, specifically 'Ndrangheta, the Calabrian Mafia. Others might have difficulties working with Courtice, but not Cooke, known as "Cookie" around the office. During the years-long investigation, the two grow as thick as thieves and remain so to this day. The hours are long and arduous, with the pair clocking the first forty-eight hours awake and together.

The initial police inquiry divides investigators into two camps: some quite simply find the circumstances of Bich's murder, Jennifer's subsequent behaviour, and the storyline she provides too fishy, too arbitrary; others, faced with this angelic girl, simply can't fathom that she could have any involvement in such a devious and gruesome murder.

Detective Sergeant Wilson, the most analytical of the three investigators, is unwilling at this point to begin formulating theories. He remains on the proverbial fence, awaiting more information. Detective Courtice, a gruff former military man with a rosy complexion, also very rule-orientated in his thinking, chooses the "wait and see" approach, as well, harbouring suspicions but unwilling to commit to a theory. Although there are troubling inconsistencies, the well-dressed chain-smoker wants more. "Every officer is going to have differing opinions," he later tells me, denying the men would often engage in shouting matches about what really occurred on that night, as reported by other investigators. "We weren't having arguments, [but] certainly discussions. That's what we do. We critically view what we have and we come to a direction."

Detective Cooke, a cop's cop, a personable sort of investigator skilled in understanding and relating with a wide range of characters, says he knew something was up from the get-go and was willing to stake his claim on that side of the debate. "I knew it was an inside job," he tells me. "I always thought she was part of it. You don't break into a house, shoot, and kill two people [at this point it was unclear if Hann would survive], and then leave a witness tied up. I mean, they tied her up. It's not like she hid from them. She's tied up, but other people are subject to being shot, yet not this person. Why not?" He then lists the countless reasons why random home invasions are so rare. "Someone might be home when you don't expect it. They might have no money. They might have a gun. It goes against everything we know. It just doesn't make sense."

The reality is that investigators, like everyone else, can be either trusting or skeptical. Either you believe in a person's capability for mass deception, or you don't. Although Detective Slade insists he was intent on remaining completely impartial during the interviews in order to allow the facts to bear themselves out without bias, interviews appear to show that he believes Jennifer. However, it's not quite that simple. Another investigator, speaking on condition of anonymity, makes it clear that "believing" someone, especially in the initial stages of an interview, can be the ideal technique. "Sometimes getting people to talk is the best way," he says. "A lie told is better than nothing spoken, because lies can be disproven. When nothing is said, the investigation ... suffers. [And that] all depends on the interviewee...."

THE DAY AFTER the murder, November 9, the media turns out in droves at police headquarters in Newmarket for a hastily assembled press conference. As Slade predicted, this story is going to get plenty of traction. Mounting the makeshift stage with media satellites beaming the press conference to the four corners of the nation, Chief Armand La Barge is solemn in his delivery, clearly disturbed by the case. "Given the very brutal nature of this crime, it goes without saying that the individuals that are responsible for the home invasion and the murder last night pose a very real danger to our community," he says. "These are, for all intents and purposes, residents that were just enjoying a nice night [when] suddenly three individuals burst into their home and terrorized them. In ... other home invasions ... there's some criminal activity involved.... But in this particular situation, there is absolutely no evidence [of criminal activity] ...."

He continues, stating, "This is a very lucky man ... and if not for the grace of God, we could have been dealing with two homicides here. To shoot an innocent woman and to shoot an innocent man, I mean, that's troubling."

Police say they believe the murderers may have been attracted to the home because of the family's high-end vehicles; however, they note that neither vehicle was taken as part of the robbery. For any seasoned crime reporter, this is a disquieting contradiction. The next admission could go either way. Although investigators refuse to divulge how much money was taken as part of the invasion, they make it clear there was no sign of forced entry, meaning the home's door was unlocked. What reporters aren't told is that police discovered $240 in Bich's purse, $60 in Hann's wallet, and £20 in Jennifer's wallet, completely untouched. The suspects' descriptions released that day are precisely based on Jennifer's account:

> **Number One:** Male, black, twenty-eight to thirty-three years old, five feet seven inches tall, with a medium build.
> **Number Two:** Male, black, thirty-one years old, five feet eight inches tall, with a thin build, wearing a dark hood and a bandana over his face.
> **Number Three:** Male, thin build, with a Caribbean accent.

Neighbours share their fear with reporters who descend on the street soon after the press conference. Mamh Lang, who lives across the street, is terrified. "I feel nervous now. I can't sleep," he says. "This happened to a good family, you know."

Concern is so high that security firms blitz the neighbourhood in the following days, hoping to land big sales of home security systems. But it isn't only the neighbours who are frightened by the details coming out of Markham. Canadian newspapers plaster their front pages with shocking headlines the day after, the details scary enough to put any family reading them on alert: "Woman Murdered in a 'Random' Home Invasion."

4

AN ANONYMOUS INFORMANT

As the news begins to hit the streets, it doesn't take long for Jennifer's closest friends to learn the grim details — prompting a flurry of communication to her cellphone:

Jen, just saw the news. Is that ur house? Are u okay? Let me know if u need anything. with love, C.

Hey Jen, just wanted to say that you are an awesome person, just like your mom and that she would only want you to grow stronger right now. I believe tha.

Hey girl? I hear that it was your family that was involved in the home invasion!! I am very sorry for ur loss!! Please call me if u need anything at all!! All my love is with u!!! Love ya … btw it's J!

As he drives to work the next morning, Daniel Wong, Jennifer's ex-boyfriend, says he's gobsmacked to hear the news on the radio. "Jen's mom is dead and her dad fighting for his life?" He quickly picks up his phone just before 9:00 a.m. and, like so many of her other friends, writes her a quick text: *If u need I'm here for u.* He later responds to Jennifer's reply, giving insight into her own emotional state at the time: *Just hang in there and try to eat.*

Five hours after her interview ends, Jennifer is still awake, gathered with her family around her comatose father's bedside in the intensive care unit at Toronto's Sunnybrook Hospital, one of Canada's foremost trauma centres. When the doctor enters, the grief-stricken family hangs on his every word as he fills them in on Hann's dire but miraculous condition. Apparently, one bullet entered his face and travelled down, shattering his neck bone and lodging itself in his neck. The doctor explains that Hann still has bullet fragments in his face, but that somehow the bullet missed a vital artery, the source of oxygenated blood for the brain and head. Had that been hit, he would have been dead. But, as it stands, it looks as if he is going to pull through. The news comes as a great relief to Hann's siblings and the other family members in the room.

Beneath her smile, though, Jennifer's mind is likely reeling. She asks the doctor if the bullet lodged in Hann's neck could cause an infection. "No," he assures her.

As the machines beep and flash, drowned out by the jubilant chatter of her family, Jennifer asks if anyone has change so she can make a phone call, explaining that her cellphone has died. When her uncle, Juann Pan, Hann's brother, offers her his mobile, she rejects it and repeats her request for fifty cents. After he hands her two quarters, Jennifer gets up and goes into the hallway where the pay phones are located. At 10:40 a.m. on November 9, the day after her parents were shot, Jennifer calls a number she knows by heart — that of Daniel Wong. The call goes to voice mail.

BACK AT HELEN Avenue in Markham, the police continue their inquiries. As part of the early investigation, two detectives are tasked with canvassing hundreds of homes in the neighbourhood. As the officers sit in their mobile police vehicle, trying to figure out just how they are going to possibly visit all four hundred homes, they hear a knock on the steel door of their "command post" vehicle, a small RV of sorts. They are about to be gifted the first break in the case.

Once inside the vehicle, the anonymous informant, a young man, tells the officers that Daniel Wong, Jennifer's boyfriend, is a drug dealer and that she is his delivery person. A cursory check of police records shows that Daniel Wong does, in fact, have drug convictions on record in Toronto years before. In a case where police know next to nothing, this information is treated with the utmost diligence.

THE FOLLOWING DAY, November 10, Daniel walks into Markham police station at 4:00 p.m., accompanied by a girl named Katrina Villanueva. Sporting a black fleece sweater and glasses, his hair black and unkempt, Daniel takes a seat in the interrogation room, apparently fighting a head cold and sniffling regularly. He is interviewed by Detective Robert Milligan.

Unlike Jennifer during her interview, the twenty-five-year-old remains a sea of calm as he is questioned, betraying little to Milligan. At one point he even manages to fall asleep when left alone. Daniel doesn't only come across as relaxed, but also respectful, friendly, and willing to engage. While Jennifer could be described as circumspect in her interview, Daniel is freewheeling.

Detective Milligan knows the optics might not appear great from Daniel's position, especially considering boyfriends and ex-boyfriends are usually the first suspects in any murder investigation involving young women. So, before the interview even begins, Milligan — keen to garner as much as possible from this individual — attempts to allay any fears Daniel may have that he's under suspicion by the police. "Just so you know, we interview everybody," Milligan assures him. "Everybody who has known the family at some point in the last ten, fifteen years, so we can say we interviewed everybody. So you're not anything special compared to everybody else."

The two quickly build a rapport as Daniel runs through a brief history of his life. He explains how he attended York University, where he studied music (he played the trumpet), before quitting to work full-time at Boston Pizza, a popular sports bar and restaurant chain. Daniel proudly tells Milligan how quickly he was promoted from his lowly starting position in the kitchen.

It doesn't take long for the conversation to turn to Daniel's private life. But Milligan is deliberate in his questioning, betraying little of the information he already knows. He waits for Daniel to tell him the extent of his relationship with Jennifer, to see if he is willing to lie about it. But Daniel does not. When asked if he has a girlfriend, he says, "I'm seeing someone," referring to Katrina Villanueva, the woman he arrived with. When he's asked about his relationship with Jennifer, he flinches and rubs his nose.

"I'm actually her *ex*-boyfriend," he begins. "We had a relationship at the end of high school and we sort of continued it until about two years ago."

What comes next, within the first three minutes of the interview, marks a significant turning point in the investigation. Daniel's revelations will show that Jennifer's "routine life," which she worked so hard to portray to Detective Slade, was not in the least bit routine. He tells Milligan how they were a couple for seven years, all behind her parents' backs. Jennifer, coming from a strict Asian home, was not allowed to date boys. "She was a figure skater and she also played piano," Daniel says. "That's why in high school she really had no time for a relationship. It would be early-morning skating and then school and then piano or skating again [after school]. Her parents pretty much drove her to the path where there was no time for a relationship."

Daniel Wong, Jennifer's ex-boyfriend, is interviewed by police.

Daniel wastes no time implicating Jennifer in plenty of bizarre behaviour. As part of their forbidden love, Jennifer, he says, fabricated a separate existence for herself, one in which her parents believed she was attending university and even working as a pharmacist. Yet, all the while, she was actually employed as a server at East Side Mario's, then later at Boston Pizza alongside Daniel. He reveals that three days a week Jennifer slept at Daniel's family home, located in the town of Ajax, a suburban neighbourhood east of Toronto. Her parents had no clue, since Jennifer told them she was living with Topaz, her best friend, in Topaz's downtown Toronto apartment so she could maximize her study time and be closer to the university campus.

Although they contemplated tying the knot, Daniel says he was honest with himself from the beginning. "Yes [there was talk of getting married] ... well, there was not real talk of getting married because I was afraid of commitment," he tells Milligan.

The police detective then ribs Daniel, quipping, "Hey ... a lot of guys are. You're still young." Winking, he gives Daniel a nudge, prompting smiles from both men.

"There were times when I started to get serious about her," Daniel admits. "But I knew, in the back of my mind ... we've been together for seven years and I haven't formally sat down and met her parents or just [eaten] dinner with them, [or] anything like that. The only thing has been 'Hi, how are you?' [I couldn't] call her house looking for her. I'd have to always call her cellphone. I didn't want to call because then they might yell at me."

Daniel claims that once Hann and Bich knew about the couple's relationship, they took issue with it, despite Jennifer trying to endear him to the family by telling them that he graduated university with an engineering degree. As far as he knows, her parents told her he wasn't making enough money at Boston Pizza to support a family of his own. "They're like 'Oh, why did he finish engineering and just work at Boston Pizza? Why doesn't he go make $60,000 or $70,000 being an engineer?'"

Another time, he says, she told him Hann and Bich took issue with his ethnicity, commenting on the fact that he was only half Chinese. "The next time I asked her, she said it's not even about how much money you make, it's the fact that you're [part] Filipino." Whether or not the couple wanted to marry eventually became irrelevant, since the house of lies Jennifer had built up so that she could be with Daniel eventually came crashing down with exceptional force. "We were planning to stay together," Daniel says, "but there was a big issue with her and her parents. They basically said 'choose us or him.' When she stopped seeing me and quit all her jobs and went home, basically choosing her family, they pulled everything from her." He tells Milligan how this meant that Jennifer's laptop, money, and cellphones were confiscated and she was forced to quit her jobs and return home for good. "When stuff hit the fan, they said 'You're not allowed to work there, you're not allowed to work, period,'" he adds. "So obviously, I said go with your parents, try to work it out, and we'll see what happens."

This, more than anything, Daniel says, spelled the end of the couple's relationship. "Afterward, her parents didn't let her out of the house," he tells Milligan. "She was a prisoner…. It was hard." As a result, the couple became estranged ever since their breakup in April 2009, he says, except perhaps one visit or the odd phone call. "She tries to call me. If I answer, I answer," he says. "Or I'll call her, sort of thing, just to see how she's doing."

When Milligan's attention turns to questions about Hann and Bich, Daniel pleads ignorance. "In all honesty I don't really know much about her parents except for what she tells me." He explains that throughout their seven-year relationship he was only at her house a handful of times. However, he does divulge some of the "unique" parts of the family relationship Jennifer described to him. "From what she's been telling me, they never slept in the same bed," he says. "Her mother often slept in the basement and her father slept in the room upstairs. They'd often get into fights. What it seemed like was her father took everything for granted and her mother worked for everything." Daniel also drops details about a renovation the couple did to their home, paying a contractor some $30,000 in cash. It isn't long before the questions came back to why Jennifer's parents didn't like Daniel, as Milligan tries to steer the conversation toward Daniel's run-ins with police. But Daniel denies they were aware of his criminal past. (He was busted the first time after he was stopped by Toronto cops, who found a pound of marijuana in his car — a quantity he estimates would be worth between $1,000 and $4,000 on the street.)

His second run-in with the law wasn't his fault, Daniel claims, referring to the time a friend borrowed his car and got pulled over and charged with possession. After this, he says, he got out of the drug game for good, finding it too risky. "I didn't want to be to the point where you're always looking over your shoulder; what's going to happen or [thinking about a] competitor or anything like that."

Daniel adamantly denies Jennifer was ever involved in his dealing, though. "At one point you were trafficking, and I don't care about that. We're over that," says Milligan. "And at some point, because you dated so long, Jen probably helped you with that, and that's understandable."

"I told her never to touch it," Daniel replies. "Because I [didn't] want her to get involved in it."

The conversation then turns to the subject of several bizarre communications to Daniel's cellphone since his breakup with Jennifer, including a series of mysterious calls and texts. "Lately it's just been happening more and more," he tells Milligan. "[An unknown person would] call and I'd answer and it would just go quiet for ten seconds and then they'd hang up. It would happen over and over, and when I would [not answer] it would get worse and worse. It got ridiculous. It was up to a hundred times a night."

Over time, Daniel says he began receiving text messages of a more threatening nature, texts like: *ha ha ha, bang bang bang.* And he says he wasn't the only one receiving these anonymous communications. Jennifer said she, too, was receiving hateful messages calling her "ugly" and "stupid" and questioning why Daniel would ever want to date a girl like her. His new girlfriend, Katrina, wasn't spared the torment, either, and her phone was inundated with texts accusing Daniel of sabotaging their relationship by continuously contacting Jennifer: *Doesn't he want you to be happy?*

The odd happenings reached a crisis point, he says, after Jennifer's cellphone went missing and then turned up in her mailbox sitting in a bag containing a white residue. Jennifer even received a bullet in the mail, Daniel says, and was raped by a gang of five Asian men.

An interesting exchange occurs when Milligan repeatedly implies that Daniel's drug dealing might have sparked the home invasion that resulted in Jennifer's mother's death. "Could it be a competitor?" Milligan asks. "[One who] doesn't like you?"

Confronted with this line of questioning, Daniel responds by steering the conversation back to the anonymous communications. "It's actually the phone calls and the other things that I think it's related to," he suggests. "I'm more than 95 to 99 percent sure it has nothing to do with my drug dealing back then. There's nothing [for a competitor] to compete with. For marijuana, no one is going to shoot you over a gram [of weed]." He insists he limited his drug business to a small and intimate circle of customers, then doubles down on his theory, muddying the possible link between drugs and the murder. "Yeah, I am [worried for my safety]," he says. "I haven't slept … because I don't know who it is, if it's [the crank callers], they call my house private, they call my cellphone, so they have my address. It's pretty obvious … if they got access to finding her address through her phone number they can find my address through my phone number. My mom couldn't sleep, either. It kept going through my head: *Who could it be? Who is it? Is it really just a random break and enter?* It's actually the phone calls and the other stuff that I think it's related to."

From an investigative standpoint, though, it is Daniel's revelation that Jennifer has a second cellphone — a Bell Mobility iPhone — that sparks the most interest. "One was her own personal phone [the Rogers cell] that her parents would take away from her, and then there was another phone that I gave her so I could contact her," he says.

After his initial denials about their ongoing relationship, the question has to be asked: Just how "broken up" were the two?

"We were close friends," Daniel says. "Seven years was a long time, and I appreciated what she did for me, and we were best friends right after [the breakup]." However, Daniel's most shocking statement comes as the interview wraps up. The stunning proclamation caps a masterful bit of interrogation by the charismatic Milligan as he asks nonchalantly what it costs to have someone taken out. "In the industry, what would you kill somebody [for]? Give me a number."

"Any amount," Daniel says. "If someone is desperate enough, they'll do it. If someone were to … it would probably have to be around $10,000. I'd be pretty sure for $10,000 someone would do something like that."

It is around the time Daniel walks out of the Markham police station — two and a half hours after he arrived — that Jennifer and her family are struck by a further twist of fate. In front of media waiting outside the hospital for Jennifer's arrival, at least one scribe hears her receive a call as she stands near the elevators. At one point in the conversation Jennifer cries out and begins to sob, quickly seeking the comfort of those around her. As Jennifer and her family continue their vigil at Hann's bedside, relatives explain to the reporter that Jennifer's grandfather, Bich's father, has just died.

5

"THAT HASN'T GONE UNNOTICED"

From the moment Jennifer left her home that fateful night in November, 238 Helen Avenue became a sealed crime scene. Consequently, she is forced to stay with her cousin, Michelle Luong, and her aunt and uncle, whose home is less than a mile away. This isn't easy on Jennifer. She not only has to borrow clothing from relatives but is forced to live under a cloud of suspicion from her own family as the questions mount. The media are hungry for news about the uninjured girl at the centre of the bizarre home invasion. The public openly speculates about her role in the case. And living in close quarters with her mother's relatives will result in further aspersions being cast on her by police.

On November 10 at 9:10 p.m., Michelle, Jennifer's cousin, is interviewed by police. Michelle informs investigators that hours before her interview, Jennifer specifically told her she and Daniel had broken up. Jennifer also said she was receiving threatening messages on her cellphone. When asked about the comments in a later interview, Jennifer obfuscates, telling investigators she was simply trying to soothe a "nervous" Michelle, only advising her to "tell the truth." It is clear, though, that the police have grown more skeptical.

But it isn't just Michelle; other family members have also noticed Jennifer's odd behaviour. Her Uncle Juann, for example, confronts Jennifer, alleging that he saw her one day in the months preceding the murder at a Tim Hortons coffee shop accompanied by a black male. There are ongoing questions about who Jennifer called from the pay phone at the hospital and why the call was placed from that particular phone at that particular time. Although it may have been easy for Jennifer, the much-heralded victim, to brush off suspicions at this early juncture, as the days wear on, her family's misgivings about her increase.

THE NEXT MORNING, at 9:43 a.m. (November 11), Jennifer looks utterly petrified as she arrives for her second interview at the Markham police station. Video footage from the detachment shows a solitary Jennifer sitting in the interview room like a caged animal. She wrings her hands and cracks her knuckles. During what becomes a four-hour interview, she knows — based solely on the information Daniel shared with the police, which one might assume was relayed to her — that she will have to do plenty of backpedalling.

"Do you, Jennifer Pan, swear that the evidence that you give in this investigation shall be the truth, the whole truth, and nothing but the truth, so help you God?" asks the commissioner of oaths.

"Yes," she replies. Her hair is pulled back in a tight ponytail, and she sports an outdated knee-length grey cardigan and a form-fitting shirt. On her nose sit her trademark glasses, which she often has to push back into place. She's done away with her blue slippers and now wears oversized running shoes — footwear no doubt borrowed from a family member.

"Do you suffer from any mental illness?" Slade asks. "Have you been drinking? Did you take any drugs?"

Jennifer omits one key detail from her reply. "No drugs, no drinking," she says before an unwitting Slade moves on.

The detective has barely taken his seat before Jennifer attempts to manipulate him. "I'm very nervous," she states, trying to explain away the "mistakes" she fears she will make during the upcoming interview. "I don't want to say the wrong things, because that day was a lot and I've been scattered, and so bits and pieces are here and some pieces aren't here. I'm getting the last few days mixed up together."

His response is simple and concise, providing a window into the focus of the interview by day three of the investigation: "Truth is always the best way to relieve anxiety."

When Jennifer is asked once again to explain exactly what happened at her home the night of November 8, she knows something is up. Her leg begins to quake uncontrollably, the fabric of her jeans briskly rubbing together, the sound clearly audible on the recording.

After first being forced to admit that her education ended after high school, Slade explains to Jennifer that there are multiple questions about the first interview that he wants to ask her about. Sensing her emotionally elevated state, Slade takes Jennifer through some relaxation techniques before the pair delves back in to that horrific day. Jennifer's hunch is right: her third recounting will contain plenty more glaring "mistakes." She explains how she sat "frozen" on her bed upon hearing her mother call up to her father in Vietnamese (not English as she previously said). Jennifer recounts how, after peering out of her bedroom door, she was shocked to see Number One coming toward her with his gun drawn (in the first interview, she stated he was carrying a string). Flustered and frightened, she then fails to mention the $1,100 taken from her parents' bedroom. "I didn't see them recover anything, no," she says.

"Are you sure?" Slade presses. "Because when we spoke the last time there was some mention of some other money." At this point she recalls that a "couple of hundred" dollars in U.S. currency was found by the intruders.

It's not long before she apologizes anew. "I'm sorry," she says, weeping, her legs still quaking. "I don't remember everything."

"Don't apologize. The only reason you'd apologize is if you've lied to me," says Slade.

"No" is her response, delivered in a barely audible whisper, her hands in prayer position in front of her mouth.

She's left even more vulnerable when Slade questions why she thought the intruders didn't ask for the combination to the plainly visible safe in her parents' bedroom closet.

One of the names Jennifer likely never intended to mention to police is then uttered for the first time — Andrew Montemayor. She tells Slade how he called her prior to the murder and wanted to meet up. But she was forced to tell him no, explaining to him for the first time how she wasn't able to leave her house.

Slade makes it very clear to her that he knows a lot more than he did just two short days ago. "We'll go in later to your past, to talk about why you couldn't leave the house," he says. "That hasn't gone unnoticed."

The Bell iPhone she failed to mention previously is the next subject on tap. Jennifer explains to Slade that her "friend," Daniel, gave her the phone and was paying the bills. When he asks her where the cell is, she pleads ignorance, stating she hid it to avoid her parents' detection. "I don't remember the last time I used it," she says. "I had it in my jacket pocket, but I don't know now." The last time she spoke to Daniel was a week ago, Jennifer adds.

Jennifer's physiological anguish is only just beginning. Slade then demands she stand up and show him how she managed to call 911 on her cellphone with her hands tied behind her back. "It's obviously very relevant. We know you made the phone call, but questions are obviously going to be raised that if my hands are bound and I'm against a railing, how do I talk to a 911 operator?" Slade explains as Jennifer nods, appearing to wince in pain.

The details of that phone call are very important to Detective Courtice, who later says he questioned how a device could be tucked in the back of Jennifer's yoga pants without it falling out and without the intruders noticing it. "The phone was supposed to be tucked in the Lulu Lemon pants. Well, wouldn't it fall down into them? We know she was up there by herself, yet she doesn't place the phone call until everyone leaves?"

Whimpering and hesitating, clearly not wanting to oblige Slade's request, Jennifer takes a large gulp of water, removes her sweater, and puts the dummy phone he's given her in her waistband. Jennifer slowly rises before somehow managing to contort her body through a plausible display of how she pulled her phone out while her wrists were bound. How she could make the call in this state is another matter. With her head bent toward the phone and her hands bound with imaginary string, she reaches for her ear, but the two remain a significant distance apart.

"How do you make the phone call," Slade quizzes her.

"I'm yelling at the phone like this," she replies, her dainty wrists glued together, the phone about a foot and a half from her ear. When he asks her how she can hear, she appears to panic momentarily, pausing, before conjuring up a response. "I turned the volume on max," she responds.

Her disgust at the insinuation that she's lying is dramatically revealed by her body language, which speaks volumes. She recoils from Slade, acting as though she has been violated by his request for demonstration. She manages to make the veteran officer uncomfortable. Slade, the eternal gentleman, gauges her emotions before he attempts to help her back into her

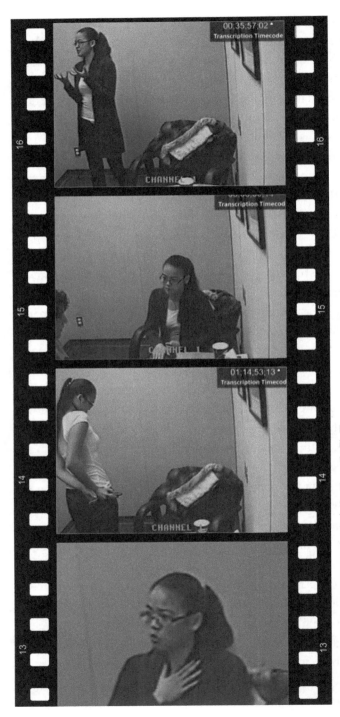

In her second interview, Jennifer is more animated.
1. She asks about the investigation and the officer attempts to reassure her.
2. She swears to tell the whole truth.
3. The inspector asks her to demonstrate how she was able to make the 911 call while her hands were bound behind her back. She reluctantly obliges.
4. Jennifer repeatedly denies any involvement in the plot.

sweater. She refuses his help. Taking hold of her sweater, she stays a healthy distance away. Slade, wanting to coax her back into his realm of trust, asks her if she wants more water and then seems to apologize for requesting the demonstration. "I really appreciate that," he starts. "Obviously, it's very important to see it because we can't put you back in the same position, but we just needed to see how you got the phone out and made the call."

When his questioning returns to the scene of the crime, Jennifer tries to beef up her story about why the intruders left her alive. First she injects a new comment from Number One, stating that he told her: "You obeyed" (by handing over money). Conversely, she notes that Number Three shouted at her father, angry about his disobedience: "Where's the rest of the money? You lied. There's more. Where is it? You lied."

Just as the distraught Jennifer appears as if she can take no more, Slade heaps more pressure on her, asking her to recount the events once again, but this time backward. Jennifer's leg starts to quiver anew, uncontrollably now. As her stress level increases, a division develops between the physical and mental, with Jennifer failing to notice how her behaviour might appear to those observing her. With long pauses between each step, once even whispering to herself *Am I missing something?* she recounts the invasion from end to beginning. Gripping her grumbling stomach throughout, her intestinal gas gets so bad at one point that she passes wind, apologizing to Slade. Astonishingly, though, she once more pulls it off before sheepishly asking, as if she has just taken an oral exam, "Is that okay?"

The investigators watching the interview later insist that, despite her behaviour, they kept an open mind. As such, Detective Cooke explains that the lead detectives watched her behaviour with a keen eye. "She was holding her stomach like she might throw up," he says. "There were a lot of inconsistencies in her story from the first one. You always have a suspicion. You may say, 'Okay, that person is exhibiting these factors,' but you lead by the evidence. You can't have tunnel vision." He says that what investigators are particularly interested in are a person's reactions to being caught in a lie, seeking out what poker players call tells. "We all do it in our everyday lives," Cooke adds. "You can tell when someone's lying."

Finally, Jennifer is given a breather, and she seems relieved, her demeanour growing calmer when Slade explains that they will now be moving on to talking about her past. The shift in her behaviour at this point in the interview is dramatic. As if she's lying on a therapist's couch, she begins for the first time in her life to describe the true story of her past as well as her relationship with Daniel, the love of her life. She starts at the beginning, reminiscing about how she and Daniel first started dating and fell in love, all under her parents' noses. "It just happened. We started going out — well, saying we were going out — but I didn't really get to see him much," she says. "I wasn't allowed to have a boyfriend. I was seventeen." She explains how it was her father who was against her having a boyfriend and that her mother took a back seat to his opinion.

Jennifer concedes that she still has feelings for Daniel as the questions slowly shift, dredging up the uglier parts of her past. She admits to the fraudulent university career and all that went with it. "My father was very adamant [that I do] something in the medical field. He wanted me to become a pharmacist."

"What do you do for the next few years?" Slade asks, seemingly shocked by the extent of her deceit. "While your dad [wants] you to get into the medical field, what do you do?"

"I lied to him. [I told him] that I was going to school for my bachelor of science," she continues, explaining how instead of attending class at two separate institutions — Ryerson University and the University of Toronto — she was actually going to the library to falsify notes. She also worked as a server at the time, studied piano, and lived with Daniel three days a week.

"You would have had bills. How were these bills being paid?" Slade asks, still trying to wrap his mind around how someone could manage this sort of deceit.

"I was working at East Side Mario's and I took care of myself," she says. "Financially, my father never took a hand in [paying] bills."

"Both your parents thought you had gone to university?" he asks.

Jennifer nods.

"Do they still to this point think you [went] to university for sciences?"

Glancing at her hands like an ashamed daughter caught red-handed by her father, she softly responds, "Yes."

"How did you feel about that? How did you feel about having to lie to your parents?"

Jennifer responds by explaining that, although she felt guilty, there was so much expectation from her parents that she simply chose to power through rather than disappoint them. Perhaps most shocking of all, Jennifer goes on to plead with Slade not to expose her lies to her father, insisting that, although he caught her lying about some of her schooling and living at Daniel's home, Hann still believed she attended one of the two universities. It's during this line of questioning that it becomes clear how much the opinion of her parents still means to Jennifer. By this point, her mother's murder takes a back seat, her reputation the front, as she grows consumed by the idea of her family uncovering the last vestige of her lies. Seemingly oblivious to the fact that she might be on her way to becoming a suspect in the murder of her own mother, it is this deception, the one she managed to maintain all those years, that she is still determined to keep from her parents. "I don't want to disappoint my mother. They don't know about that university stuff, and I don't want people who saw my mother as a good person to think wrongly of her," she says. "She was such a good mom and I don't want that to change because of my decision."

With disbelief at the sheer number and scope of the lies this bewitching young woman who sits before him has told, Slade inquires over and over again how she managed to pull the wool over her father's eyes regarding so many details. While Slade refuses to pass judgment on her behaviour because of the restrictions she was living under, he does appear perturbed by her actions, perhaps imagining his own daughters trying to pull off this level of deception.

Jennifer explains to him how her life during the time spent at home consisted of waking up, playing piano, helping with chores, going to music lessons, and returning home again. She recounts for him the only time she left the house at night over the past few months was on her birthday when she went skating with her friend, Topaz. That night, she says, her parents confirmed directly with Topaz before Jennifer left the house, and they secured Topaz's cellphone number so they could check in on them throughout the night. Even with those restrictions, she explains, she had to be home before 9:00 p.m. This, she says, was a strict curfew in place since high school and was only relaxed once — for a close friend's wedding reception. Clearly not wanting to lie to Slade when she didn't have to, whether for fear of incriminating herself or betraying the bond they've developed, Jennifer opts to skirt his next question.

"Did you have any resentment toward [your parents] for this?"

Her response shows how a devious Jennifer fooled so many for so long, obfuscating when possible, only lying when absolutely necessary. "I chose what I chose," she says, shaking her head. "But in the end I chose my family."

When the questions move to her alleged involvement in the drug trade alongside Daniel, she insists over and over again that she was never involved. However, when Slade asks about whether her parents were involved in either gambling or drugs, she leaves the door open ever so slightly. "Not that I know of," she says.

She further implicates her father with a rambling and intricate story implying that he was engaged in an extramarital affair with a "Chinese-speaking woman." "My father doesn't even know I was on the line ... it was a lady's voice I have never heard before ... this woman was saying, 'You have to come over right away, right away,'" she says. "My father kept saying, 'I can't come over. No.'" Soon after that, she says, her father left the house, telling Jennifer he had to go to the Luongs' house (Jennifer's aunt and uncle) to help them with some housework. It was at this point, Jennifer says, that she caught her father lying. When she confided in Michelle about the conversation and his hasty departure from the home, she was told that Hann had indeed come over, but that it hadn't been until much later.

When the landline at the Pan home received another private call soon after, Jennifer says she became enraged and yelled into the phone. "These phone calls were happening periodically.... My mother and I answered and they'd hang up on us," she adds, noting this took place in late August, early September, of 2010. "A few days later, I was home by myself and I got a private call, and I didn't hear them hang up, so I yelled in Chinese: 'Do not ever call this number ever again!' They called probably one time after that and then the private calls stopped."

Whether Detective Slade's departure from the interrogation room at this point is a strategic move to see how Jennifer will react, or just an appropriate time to speak to his colleagues, is unclear, but it certainly causes a stir. Although Slade leaves the door open a crack, trying to ease Jennifer's concerns about being left alone, it does nothing to calm her. She begins to lose control very quickly during the ensuing half-hour.

Watching the tape is like witnessing a train wreck; one is unable to look away. Jennifer begins breathing heavily and pacing back and forth before sitting back down, her stomach clearly convulsing. Detective Constable Deborah Gladding, who is sitting in a neighbouring room watching this young woman in clear distress, walks in and attempts to ease her anxiety. She gives her some water and then clears the hallway to give Jennifer a washroom break. When Jennifer returns to the room a few minutes later, she starts to sway, putting all her weight on one foot before switching to the next. Before long she begins to pace back and forth — all while facing Gladding, who is still in the room — thoughts no doubt rippling through her mind. Her obsessive movements eventually morph, and she begins to manically stroke her ponytail.

Jennifer then begins to speak, a litany of words tumbling from her lips. "I'm just beating myself up," she says as she continues to pace back and forth, as if she's on amphetamines. "He's asking me these questions like I should have been more attentive, but it just happened so fast, and it's like … and I can't give him the answers I don't know."

"You don't want to make up something —" Gladding starts to say.

But Jennifer interrupts her. "No, I'm not, it's not that," she says, continuing to stroke her hair. "I wish I was able to answer. I want to be able to answer it, so it would help."

"But if you don't know, you don't know," Gladding states matter-of-factly. "That's the bottom line. Who are we to say? We weren't there. You're the one that went through this."

Jennifer then inquires about how the investigation is going. "Have they been able to find out anything? Do they have any leads or suspects? Does anyone know where the car went after?"

Once again Jennifer is so caught up keeping herself from emotional breakdown that she fails to realize she's giving the investigators watching in the next room a front-row seat to a meltdown of epic proportions. After Gladding watches Jennifer appear to grow dizzy then steady herself on the wall, she asks if Jennifer wants some food, noting that she can hear her stomach grumbling. "That's your stomach saying you're hungry," the detective implores. Despite Gladding practically begging her to have chips, a bagel, or a chocolate bar, Jennifer refuses, clearly too agitated and nauseated to eat. The detective then pleads with Jennifer to take a seat because she's doing so much pacing. When she sits down, Jennifer grips the arm of the chair tightly before assuming the fetal position, her head between her knees, something that will become normal practice for her over the next few years. She then covers her face and weeps.

When Detective Slade finally returns to the interview room, he attempts to calm Jennifer. Referring to her emotions as "survivor's guilt," he tells her it's something she will have to work through with the help of therapy. "It's a long road. What you're feeling," he says, "I hate to say it's normal, but it is. It's something that a lot of people who are in the same circumstance will feel."

This apparent sympathy for Jennifer's situation doesn't last long as the seasoned detective gradually takes up an accusatory style of interrogation, first using the media as cover to suggest that it's her association to the drug underworld that might have led to the murder. "[The media are] bad. They can be very bad when they start to sniff around and they sense something," he tells her. "And I can tell you that the media is portraying [this as] some sort of drug-related thing: that you guys weren't a random target; that you guys were a targeted house because of drug activity. Is it possible that you were being mistaken somehow of being involved with [Daniel's] life in those things?"

Jennifer continues to deny that she was involved with the business of marijuana. "I wanted nothing to do with it, so I refused to know what [Daniel] was doing," she says.

Slade seems to take her protestations at face value before continuing. "I don't know if that's, in fact, what happened," he tells her, exasperated. "I'm trying to find a rhyme or reason for why your house was targeted. I'm still trying to figure out how they got in your house. You didn't hear a doorbell. You didn't hear a ... knock. You didn't hear a door kicked in. Somehow they got into your house by getting through your mom, down on the lower level. So it's very confusing. Generally random events are not, in most cases, random."

Then Slade gets down to business, something the other investigators have long been encouraging him to do. "So you're telling me you had no involvement in what happened? You had no involvement in any type of illegal activity that would have drawn ... attention [to] you? To have bad people come to your house looking for large sums of money? You're not involved in this any which way?"

Again, choosing not to speak, Jennifer shakes her head, her bottom lip quivering.

"Because the question obviously stands, Jennifer; you're upstairs and they're downstairs, so it's a natural concern. Why would they leave you alone? Why would they not do the same to you?"

Jennifer continues to shake her head before going back to her faithful line. "The only thing I can say is that he said I co-operated," she insists, weeping. "But I asked him to take me with my mom."

"You've admittedly lied. Not to me," Slade continues unabated. "You've lied to your parents. Who's to say this whole thing isn't a lie? That what you're telling me is a lie? Because if you are lying, it's the most cold-blooded thing I've ever faced in my life."

A wily Jennifer stares at him as if he's just put a dagger through her heart. The silence hangs thick in the air as the two contemplate each other. Eventually, Jennifer glances down and away and resumes shaking her head.

Slade speaks first, inquiring if Hann and Bich had life insurance policies.

"I think. I don't know," Jennifer responds.

"Back to another very difficult question, but if I don't ask it … it's an obvious one," he says. "The resentment that you may have had toward your parents for the interference in your relationship, in your life, and essentially locking you down in your house …"

"At the end of the day, I love my parents," she responds, once again skirting the crux of his query. "And I chose to be with them. If I wanted to, I could have just left, but I didn't. I wanted to stay with them. And take care of them."

"So this wasn't some evil plot that you thought of to —"

Her hand on her chest and a shocked expression on her face, she interjects indignantly, "Oh, my God, no!" Her eyes remain fixed on his, not blinking.

"You didn't have anything to do with this whatsoever?" Slade asks again.

"No" is the response.

"Because you know it will be a very easy thing to discredit you on, right?" Slade says. "It'll be very easy to find flaws in what you've said, which then again turns the focus back to you. It's a natural thing that investigators do. We eliminate people or draw our attention to them. It's a natural thing. It's not brain surgery."

A knock at the door draws Slade back into the hallway. Jennifer's leg begins to shake again, moving so forcefully this time that her hand and arm rattle the rest of her torso. "Can anyone come in?" she requests in a petrified child's voice.

Gladding responds, "I'm here," but without entering the room. Jennifer returns to the fetal position, rocking back and forth.

"You really scared me," she scolds Slade when he returns. "It's hard to take. I'm just afraid, because I know everything is just pointing negatively right now and I don't understand why. I feel the way you're speaking to me it's kind of like … I know you said you had to say those things … there's like ideas in my head. And I'm afraid to say it out loud."

"The fact that you've lied to your parents over a long period of time … that is disturbing," Slade says. "At times we have to point the finger … and provoke you and see what you're going to do, how you're going to respond. It's only a question and it's been answered, and if you've been truthful, you have nothing to fear." After a moment, he asks, "Is there anything [in your account] you think you want to change?"

"Now I feel like I've said something wrong," she responds.

Slade then tries the direct approach. "Could you be lying to me?"

"I can't," Jennifer insists.

"Why?"

"Because you're scaring me," she finally says.

Slade tries to reassure her. "In a case that makes no sense, that may be the only sense we get out of the investigation, is that strange things happen. Right now there [are] no fingers being directed at anyone. You're our only link … until your dad is able to be spoken to. You're our only link to this case."

After four hours, the interview is finally over and Jennifer walks out of the Markham police station at 2:00 p.m.

IN ADDITION TO the question of Jennifer's behaviour in the interview room and why her life was spared by the intruders (she wasn't injured at all during the attack, nor was she sexually assaulted), Detective Cooke's inquisitive mind swirls around another question he's contemplated from the start: *Just how inept can the thieves involved in this robbery be? Is it possible to have been so unprepared?* After all, Cooke is being asked to believe that a group of three grown men would break into a house look-ing for money without any tools to jimmy open the door and no bags to carry the loot. Furthermore, by that point, investigators have figured out that the string used to bind Jennifer to the banister came from her mother's sewing kit. The men didn't even have duct tape or rope to tie up the victims. "What do they leave the house with?" he asks. "They have [almost] nothing." But this isn't all. His suspicions about what led criminals to the home in the first place persist. "They [aren't] even busi-ness owners, they're nobodies. Why choose this house? That's what kept running through my head."

6

HANN SPEAKS

When the interview is finished, Jennifer ventures dutifully back to the hospital, keeping vigil at her father's bedside, wanting to be the first person he sees should he open his eyes. But returning to the same place over and over leaves Jennifer exposed to those attempting to capture the images of the young woman everyone is talking about. On this day it is CTV News cameras that chase her through the parking lot. In the ensuing moments, younger brother Felix is forced to partially shield Jennifer from the prying lenses as she traipses through the blowing cold of the hospital campus. She masks her face and head underneath the hood of her winter jacket but is forced to look up in order to see where she is going. Until a photo from Bich's funeral replaces it, this is the go-to image for anyone wanting to gawk at the young woman who managed to escape a murderous home invasion unscathed. Of course, shielding her face from the cameras does little to help the presumption of innocence that all Canadians enjoy. Later that day, Jennifer thinks she is being followed in her car. Panicked, and unaware if it is reporters or assailants, she calls police for an escort.

On November 12, Hann comes out of his coma, but Jennifer is not allowed near him without someone peering over her shoulder. "Not only was my father in the hospital, but there was always supervision," she says. "I couldn't … speak to him alone." Jennifer is not permitted to see him until the police are done with their interviews.

Hann's awakening is greeted with jubilation by the rest of his family, and they do their best to comfort him as he deals with his raw emotions.

For Jennifer, however, her father's revival sparks another "breakdown" after which she once again seeks out a hospital therapist. It is during this meeting that Jennifer's mental health issues, which will be discussed later in the book, first become apparent to others. Just days after her mother's murder and hours after her father awakes from a coma, one might expect her concerns to be about her grief over her mother or ongoing concern for her father. Instead, it seems that Jennifer's overriding torment is how the situation is affecting her. She is worried about what is being written about her in the press — more specifically speculation in the media regarding her personal problems. The entirety of Jennifer's medical records are tightly sealed; however, this morsel, garnered via a source close to the case, gives as clear an indication as possible of her self-absorption at this time, repeatedly putting herself first, suffering mental anguish over her own security and reputation rather than her family's well-being.

HANN REMAINS IN stable condition, but with a bullet lodged in his neck he suffers great pain. A support device is used to prop him up in bed. At first he can't speak and is forced to breathe through his mouth with an apparatus fixed around his lips. He also still has bullet fragments in his face, which the doctors are never able to completely remove. "My neck was very painful, my eyes were droopy because I was shot in the face," he later tells the court. "My neck bone shattered."

Hann has little time to mourn his wife and visit with his family before the police initiate an interview. But before they arrive, his siblings fill him in on what has transpired since the murder. Jennifer's pay-phone call is one of the first things they share with Hann.

When Detectives Marco Napoleoni and David MacDonald enter the hospital room, they find a broken man — one who has awakened to discover that a most horrific nightmare is, in fact, a grim reality. His wife is dead, and the officers can sense that he feels his daughter is involved. The two investigators begin questioning Hann about what he remembers from that night.

Hann tells them that two black men and one white broke into his home. They were tall, he says, each about six feet, and they were wearing turtlenecks — possibly, the detectives ask, to hide tattoos? And, finally, Hann tells them that the black clothing they wore appeared to have brown splotches on it. After completing his description, Hann suffers through what must be the most excruciating conversation of his life. He reveals to the officers that, while he and Bich were being "terrorized" under the threat of gunfire, his daughter was "comfortable" and "freely moving around the house."

It is after this lengthy conversation focusing on Jennifer that Hann remarks that it is very important to him that the police catch those responsible. As Hann stares into the eyes of the interviewing detectives, it is this comment that sticks with them long after they leave the man's bedside. "Use your police tactics to find out who did this," says Hann, an unspoken accusation that everyone in the room understands.

Although Hann specifically tells his family that he doesn't want to see his daughter, Jennifer manages to get to his bedside on Saturday, November 13, after police finish interviewing him for the second day in a row. It is the first time Jennifer isn't under constant supervision around her father, as well as the first time she is free from the sedatives the doctor prescribed to her immediately following the murder.

Although not bold enough to accuse his daughter to her face, Hann does ask her if she thinks Daniel was behind the murder. "I don't know 100 percent, but I don't think he [was]," she tells her father. She later explains to police why she thought he was suspicious of Daniel. "He thinks that we still talk and [Daniel] would go to any length to be with me. I think [Daniel has] moved on so I don't think he'd go to any lengths to be with me. I don't think he knows anyone [who could do this]."

Hann also asks Jennifer if it was "Danny" who she called from the pay phone right after she discovered he was going to survive. Jennifer admits to the call but says it was only to share the good news. (A central tenet of the defence later contends that the call, which was made without the use of her police-monitored cellphone, was intended to be a warning to Daniel that their plan was falling apart. Lawyers showed the court that despite claiming her phone was dead, Jennifer used her mobile soon before and soon after the payphone call to Daniel.) With unrivalled chutzpah, Jennifer then asks her father for $1,200, claiming it is for college tuition.

That day, Detective Courtice officially makes Jennifer a suspect in the investigation. It doesn't take long before Jennifer's relationship with her family grows too tenuous to bear. Although no one is comfortable with her staying in their home, she is, after all, blood, and she has nowhere else to go.

"No one was particularly happy about it, but there was an obligation there," one investigator says. "They are family, and until they know for sure ..."

It is Hann's family who are the most suspicious. Jennifer's Uncle Juinn first confronts her and then even threatens to call the police on her. He wants her to go and speak to the investigators, knowing police want Jennifer in for another interview, but she resists under cover of organizing her mother's and grandfather's funerals. Later, Juinn also advises the police that, at one point Jennifer told him that she managed to survive the home invasion because the men "liked her."

"My family, on my dad's side, who [were] never really a part of my life, became a part of my life," Jennifer says. "But then, suddenly, I felt that they started pulling away again."

Two days later, on November 15, Jennifer attends her mother's funeral, something she later complains her father left her to organize all by herself. In Chinese culture, the older members of the family are buried first, according to Jennifer, so the funeral for Bich's father was held days before. Jennifer then begins picking caskets, clothing, and special blankets for Bich's Buddhist ceremony, which will follow. She is laid to rest four days later, according to Jennifer's testimony.

Jennifer Pan and her brother Felix leave their mother's funeral. Their father, Hann, was not well enough to attend.

Police and another attendee describe Jennifer's behaviour at her mother's funeral as "remarkable." A Buddhist monk presides over the ceremony, which takes place in front of about one hundred mourners inside Scarborough's Ogden Chapel. Jennifer stands at the front alongside her brother and beside her mother's casket. Police later say they attended not only to observe Jennifer's actions, but also to pay their respects, insisting they were deeply disturbed by what they saw. "She's up there rubbing her eyes, then looking up at us, then rubbing her eyes again, but never crying," one police officer says. "That funeral really got to me. Don't be looking at us when you're paying your respects to your mom who was just killed." The police aren't the only ones to report this sort of behaviour. Jennifer's former long-time piano teacher, Ewa Krajewska, similarly states that while many in the chapel are awash in tears, Jennifer remains dry-eyed: "She wasn't crying, her head was down, it was like she was crying, but with no tears."

Jennifer bemoans how she "had to make out on her own" after Felix returned to school to complete his exams. She also displays her tactlessness once again when she says how disappointed she is that, despite her father being cleared by doctors to go, he chooses not to attend his late wife's funeral.

A picture is snapped by a photographer from the Chinese *Sing Tao Daily* when Jennifer and her brother leave the chapel.

On November 17, surgeons remove some of the bullet fragments from Hann's face, seal them in a bag, and send them off for analysis to Canada's Centre of Forensic Sciences in Toronto.

Three days after burying her mother, on November 22, Jennifer receives a phone call from her Victim Services liaison informing her that she has to come in again to speak with the police. Jennifer resists, but she is overruled and advised that there is little option but to attend. "I had family over, I was grieving," she later says. "There was so much going on. I wasn't mentally prepared. I had just buried my mother and I [thought] they could just give me a day. She insisted it was [important] that I come in."

A WIDELY HELD perception among many Canadian citizens is that police are obliged by law to tell the truth. Jennifer counts herself as one of those people. However, this is far from reality. In 2000, the Supreme Court of Canada ruled that police are allowed to lie not only about evidence but tactics, as well. The decision in R v. Oickle sets out four factors that should be considered when judging whether a police confession is voluntary: whether there are threats or promises made by police; whether the oppression to gain a confession is "distasteful or inhumane"; whether the suspect is aware of what they're saying and who they're saying it to; and the level of trickery, whether it's so egregious it "shocks the community." Outside those tenets, police can pretty much say what they like, truth or fiction. In the Oickle case, although he passed a lie detector test, police told him he had failed in order to obtain a confession. They also neglected to mention that the results of a polygraph test are inadmissible in court. Police often use this interrogation method under the guidance of something called the Reid Technique, a common police confessionary tactic that involves interrogators flipping the founding principle of Canada's justice system — "innocent until proven guilty" — on its head. It hinges on the interrogator implying guilt from the beginning of the interview and is often conducted as a monologue by the friendly, patient, and seemingly understanding interviewer. Eventually, the suspect is offered an "out," with the interrogator offering psychological justification for the crime.

The method, which has been banned in many countries, involves an implicit assumption of guilt without evidence that might go something like this: "Can we locate the body by you telling us where it is, or will you have to show us?" It's this, detractors say, that can lead to false confessions, much like what occurs in the case of Steven Avery's nephew Brendan Dassey in the true-crime documentary *Making a Murderer*, or a premature narrowing of the investigation, reinforcing assumptions of investigators. An investigator with the York Regional Police, speaking on condition of anonymity, says the Reid Technique is widely used in the service; however, it is rarely done in textbook fashion, since officers develop their own styles and methods. Some, he says, don't like to lie, others prefer to use the practice in tandem with the fabled "good cop, bad cop" technique. He says, at the core of the method are "themes" explaining that everyone has a "weak spot" that must be exploited. The first step involves direct confrontation. The second step tries to shift the blame from the suspect onto others. Three discourages the denial of guilt, which if uttered, can make the process more difficult for the interrogator. Four involves turning a reason why the suspect didn't commit the crime into a confession, and on it goes until number nine.

7

"WHAT HAPPENS TO ME?"

On November 22, 2010, a taxi is sent to pick up Jennifer (paid for by police) and drops her off at the police station around 2:00 p.m. Jennifer must know something has to give. On top of staying with a family that suspects her of killing her own mother, she also contends with intense police scrutiny coupled with media speculation that is becoming too acute to bear.

When Jennifer walks in and takes her seat in the interrogation room, there appears to be previously unseen resignation in her behaviour. There are remnants of the damsel-in-distress persona she has used so effectively with Detective Slade; however, she now seems to be a more solemn and lonely figure. Her manic demeanour and constant fidgeting are still present to a degree, but as the interview wears on, they're supplanted with more insular behaviour as she replaces her nervous tics with a complete shut-down — often descending into the fetal position and resting her face in her hands. In short, although Jennifer hasn't entirely given up hope of a resolution, she now appears to grasp the gravity of the situation. In her pocket she carries two crisp hundred-dollar bills and sanitary pads, fighting not only the ensuing emotional roller coaster but menstrual cramps, it seems, as well.

At this point, two weeks after the murder, Jennifer has ditched her over-sized running shoes, arriving well dressed after perhaps gaining access to someone's closet. Of course, she now appears to have money, so she might have purchased them. Her ill-fitting footwear has been replaced with black European-style runners, while her raggedy plaid winter jacket has been swapped for a stylish thigh-length black coat. Underneath, Jennifer sports black slacks and a black V-neck cardigan over a collared white shirt, which initially masks a vertically striped back-and-white t-shirt.

This interview is going to be much different than her last one. She is no longer a victim in the eyes of the police; rather, she's their lead suspect.

Faced with a new interrogator, Detective Bill Goetz (pronounced *Gates*), Jennifer is about to be confronted by a dramatic shift in interview style. Detective Goetz is not a homicide investigator; he's a seasoned interrogator and polygraph expert. The "truth-verification expert," as he calls himself, will come across as far less paternal than Slade, who has taken over another murder case and is no longer available. There will be little comfort for Jennifer this time around. Goetz — or "Gator" as he's known around the force — is cold and calculating from the get-go. He clearly means business and is in no mood for Jennifer's manipulative tendencies. A burly and imposing figure with grey hair in a military-style crewcut, he strikes an unsympathetic figure, playing both good cop and bad cop with Jennifer, a role with which he seems entirely at ease. His interview will contain a series of outright lies as part of the Reid Technique. (A number of suspects and witnesses involved in the Pan case would later complain before judge and jury that the police were dishonest with them.)

When Jennifer sits down to begin, Detective Goetz makes it clear he's in no mood for her diversions. His questions are direct and delivered without sympathy. He initially asks her if she knows why they are here today.

"To discuss stuff," she says reluctantly.

"Regarding what?" he asks bluntly.

After a short pause in which she stares at the ground, she purses her lips and says, "About what happened at my home." Then she looks up to see his expression, but quickly bows her head.

"As a result of that home invasion your father was actually shot and your mother Bich-Ha was actually killed," Goetz says. "Is that correct?"

With her eyes closed and head down, she nods.

"You'll have to speak up."

"Sorry ... yes," she replies softly, wiping her eyes. This time, no tissue is offered. When the audio equipment fails, forcing them into another room, Jennifer tells Goetz she doesn't want to be left alone when he steps out. But instead of getting an officer to sit with her, he simply tells her to "hang on."

Once they're settled in the new room, Goetz begins by reading Jennifer her rights, signalling her responses will now present her with a real and present danger of legal repercussions. "If you had any involvement in that home invasion, then you could be facing charges of murder and attempted murder," he informs her. "Anything you do say to us regarding that home invasion is being recorded and could be used as evidence in court. You understood that?"

Jennifer's jet-black mane of hair, neatly braided, has but one strand loose that she repeatedly places behind her left ear before she answers "Yes."

As they continue, Jennifer's responses are muffled by sobbing each time her mother is mentioned, but rather than console her, Goetz nonchalantly but sternly tells her to speak up.

Goetz is not only an expert at detecting deception, he says, but is also well versed at coaxing information from those who otherwise try to deceive the police. In Jennifer's case, he spends the next two hours gaining her trust. Once that stage is complete, he turns the tables, using the goodwill and familiarity he's built with her to secure a confession.

After his initial bluntness, Goetz changes tack. He eases back in his chair, dropping the cop-speak and focusing his attention solely on Jennifer, prompting her bleak outlook to appear rosier. He begins by asking about her love of piano, figure skating, and her friends. In response, she almost immediately switches from despondency to a sunnier disposition. However, each time her mother is mentioned, her head bows and she starts to weep again. This affects Goetz little as he trundles on, seemingly unaffected by her emotional outbursts. He does his best to keep the interview light and breezy, many times laughing out loud as they chit-chat about Jennifer's personality, qualities, and upbringing.

The Reid Technique requires officers to "reinforce sincerity" to ensure the suspect is receptive to their overtures. Hence, Goetz shares with Jennifer his own experiences. When he reminisces about his time playing piano, he inaccurately refers to the ballet *Swan Lake* as "Swans on the Lake," prompting a smile from Jennifer. He then asks her if she switched jobs from East Side Mario's to Boston Pizza for "better tips," again drawing a smile from Jennifer, who seems to somewhat enjoy the attention being lavished on her. The conversation focuses not only on her achievements but her struggles, as if she's reminiscing with someone who really understands what she's been through. The "scheduled" existence she claims to have suffered through as a child and teenager takes centre stage.

Jennifer remarks how little time there was for anything other than school, competitive skating, and piano lessons. Her parents constantly comparing her to her classmates, teammates, and cousins also affected her negatively, she says. And when Goetz suggests that Jennifer never thought of herself as being "as smart" as Hann and Bich imagined, Jennifer agrees. At one point she tells the detective that she was under so much pressure during her teenage years that she was compelled to forge high school report cards to mask her average grades, turning them into exceptional ones. Her lies multiplied from there, she confesses, morphing into a bogus university career after her applications to higher learning were rejected.

But the threat that she'd be caught was ever-present. In a bid to keep her dishonesty from her parents, Jennifer continued to forge report cards and even student loans. "When [my parents] asked for something, I would try and make a document for them," she says. "It was really hard. I wanted to tell them, but it's just, they always looked down in disappointment."

It was more than just her schooling that she'd end up lying about, though. Jennifer tells Goetz she dated Daniel without their knowledge or consent for seven years. "I hid it from my parents at first because they didn't agree with me having a boyfriend," she says. "Once they found out, they didn't like the fact that he was of mixed race and they told me to stop seeing him." She tried to keep her separation from Daniel permanent, but somehow she'd always end up back in his arms. "He was the person who filled an empty void," she says. "So [when we broke up], I felt that a part of me was missing."

Eventually, though, the option to run back to Daniel was wrenched from her grasp. Her parents offered Jennifer an ultimatum after she was caught lying one final time: stay with the family or go with Daniel and never return.

Jennifer chose her family and was subsequently kept at home, rarely let out of her parents' sights, she contends. This is when Daniel decided to move on with another woman, Katrina Villanueva. "It made me feel that I wasn't good enough to wait for," she tells Goetz. The breakup with Daniel, coupled with a life under almost constant supervision, resulted in a dark period in her life, just as she'd faced years before. "I wasn't happy with any part of my life," she admits. "I regretted not going to school; my piano wasn't going as fast as I [would have liked]; my friends were moving on with their lives. It felt like I wasn't going anywhere. It felt like I was left behind. I didn't understand why at twenty-one ... I had to be at home

During her third police interview, on November 22, 2016, Jennifer opens up to Detective Goetz about her past and admits to deceiving her parents for years. She also often hides her face in her hands or puts her head down on her knees.

[for curfew] at nine o'clock." Jennifer explains how depression eventually led to cutting, and then finally a failed suicide attempt. "I cut myself, on my wrist. I had to hide it, so never twice in the same spot," she says. She admits to Goetz that she wanted to kill herself.

Her difficult life at home was compounded, she says, by the fact that, although her parents "put on a front," the reality was that "there was not much of a relationship" between them. She explains that her parents were fighting "every day" and that she was forced to become the "mediator." This, she claims, became more pronounced after Felix left for school, leaving her without an ally in the home. "They just haven't really been getting along. [They fight] about my dad being loud and noisy and inconsiderate, my mom nagging, and my dad not doing enough housework and not caring enough. [She believed] he had all these ideas about other people's houses, but he doesn't do anything for our house — decorating, upgrading. [She feels] that he doesn't care about the house, the family." The exchange is perhaps most interesting because of the dynamic it creates between the two, with Jennifer growing increasingly comfortable and relaxed as she shares countless private details for the first time in her life, while Goetz shrewdly collects information that he'll soon use against her.

As for how she felt having to remain home under strict guidelines for some eighteen months after she was given the ultimatum, Jennifer says it was difficult, but that it was her choice. "[The choice was] living out on my own with Daniel [or] staying home with my parents," she says. "[Living like that] was okay. It wasn't the best feeling in the world because I always felt trapped. But it's what I chose: to be with my family. Family always comes first."

In response, Goetz empathizes with Jennifer, at one point even giggling at her deceit. Justifying her behaviour, he even labels Hann and Bich's treatment of their daughter "abuse," suggesting their expectations were just too high. "I get that feeling: it's pretty tough to live up to their expectations," he notes after Jennifer tells him that if she could, she'd become a piano teacher. "Your dad would ultimately like you to be a doctor, that type of thing, but maybe you can't do it. Those are pretty high standards for anybody ... few people would be able to reach that expectation. Not everybody can be a doctor, but they may have acted like you could have done it no problem."

But his empathy doesn't last. Now that he's gained the personal knowledge required to implement his technique, the conversation slowly shifts back to her behaviour in the lead-up to and the night of the murder. Goetz asks Jennifer if she told a family member that the intruders "liked her" and that's why they kept her alive.

"I didn't say that," she insists after a moment. "I asked them [the intruders] why I couldn't be with them [her parents], and they're just, like, 'You co-operated. Keep co-operating.'"

Goetz then asks Jennifer to list the African-Canadian males she knows, explaining that the police have a photo of her speaking with a black man in a café. She names only two men, identifying the male she met in a café months before the murder only as "Ric."

"He's not really a friend. He's more of a friend of mine's roommate," Jennifer contends. "But I did meet up with him once." It's at this point that she admits to lending "Ric" $1,100 because he and his roommate, Andrew Montemayor, were having rent problems.

Goetz asks if this was the same Andrew she spoke with the night of the murder.

Jennifer says that it was.

These two admissions signal an interlude as Goetz shifts his tactics anew, heaping further pressure on Jennifer. Suddenly, he sheds his friendly and engaging demeanour and begins to sow strife between them. Step One of the Reid Technique: direct confrontation.

"Would it make sense for someone that was going to kill somebody to leave a witness behind that could describe them? Does that make ... sense, for killers?" he asks. "Do you think that was a mistake they made then? You must think about this."

"I still do, and I've spoken to a therapist about it," Jennifer responds before repeating her well-worn line that she "co-operated" and that the men kept saying it was "taking too long," implying they had no time to shoot her because they were forced to flee. To Jennifer's dismay, Goetz then recounts the sequence of events once more. "I don't want to go through this again," she tells him, weeping.

When Goetz gets up and leaves to get some water, Jennifer curls back up into the fetal position, gripping her head tightly. As silence fills the room, she begins to make noises that sound like squeals. When he returns, Goetz asks her to recount the denominations of the bills that made up the $2,500 she handed over to Number One. How long was the cash in her night table? How big was the stack? These probing questions continue until Goetz enters the penultimate phase of the interview: "In my experience as a police officer, no matter what the case is, people make mistakes, as in they don't always tell the truth," he says as she strokes her braid, repeatedly winding the tip between her fingers. "They may tell *some* of the truth, but they don't always tell *all* of the truth. You're well aware of what half-truths mean, right? Withholding information is not telling the truth. It's purposeful deception."

During the speech that follows, Goetz uses the trickery that Jennifer has honed for so many years against her. In this case, Goetz goes at her whole hog. "We have computer programs," he says. "We feed everything into the computer and it analyzes what a person has said. It will tell us where the areas of deception are, areas of concern, and areas that are flat out not truthful; you come back with a result that says, 'Not possible.' Do you watch *CSI* at all?" he suddenly asks her, his questions turning the interview into one long monologue peppered with only occasional responses from Jennifer.

"A little," she replies quietly.

"[The police] are going over that house with a fine-tooth comb. They're going over every hair fibre, every skin cell, every bit of blood. You know what DNA is, right? A person cannot go in or out of anywhere without leaving a part of themselves behind. [Your] doorknob is very important. We're looking for who was the last one who touched that door lock. We would get fingerprints of one person locking it and then overlapped by the person that unlocked it." He swiftly moves on to just how high-tech murder investigations have become since the old days. "We have to reach out to modern technology, so another thing we utilize is satellites. The satellite is a twenty-four-hour video that's going on. It's recording information … the military uses it for precision bombing. We're able to go back and review that. It's like an X-ray. We're able to tell … are the people in the positions that the witness is telling us they were in or are they different? Another thing we do is talk to a lot of people … we don't leave any rock unturned. You've heard of Crime Stoppers, right? When you get a case like this, people want to help. It's in the papers; it's everywhere. So people end up coming to us to help us out with the case. Three people are inside the house. Somebody always tells somebody else. Suddenly, we get people calling in. They want to help. You don't know how many people call in on their friends ... they want that money. They get greedy."

The Reid Technique clearly states that an interrogator must try to discourage the suspect from denying his or her guilt. True to form, Goetz refuses to let Jennifer get a word in edgewise — she speaks little for the following sixty minutes — but he eventually offers her a way out. "Nothing surprises me in this job. I am well aware that anyone on this Earth is capable of making a mistake," he tells her as she bows her head. "I don't care if they're a priest or a schoolteacher. One thing that you have to remember is that your dad was there and your dad had a front-row seat to all of this. Your dad's a very smart man and he has a very clear perception of what's going on. A lot of the things you told the police didn't happen. It doesn't match at all ..."

After alleging guilt and implying that police have proof of such guilt, Goetz now seamlessly shifts his attention to Step Two of the Reid Technique: shifting the blame away from the suspect, justifying her behaviour, and excusing the crime. "You've spent a considerable amount of time over the past seven years telling half-truths, and I can understand why. You've had a tough life. What's happened to you, to me, equates to abuse. Now you're under a tremendous amount of stress. You're involved in this. I know that. You've lived your whole life trying to live up to expectations that you can't make. You're a twenty-four-year-old woman being treated like a fifteen-year-old. You're not the first person [to lie about] dating a guy, because in your culture they don't accept it." Then he offers her a chance to confess. "Who else is involved in this?"

"I don't know," Jennifer manages to say, still stroking her hair but listening intently.

Using Hann's description of a white male in the house, Goetz accuses Jennifer of falsifying Number One's description entirely. He then moves back into the accusatory stage, treating her guilt as a fact they've already established before justifying it. "We know that you were involved, but we also know that you're a good person that's made a mistake here," he adds. "You got involved with the wrong people. You don't want to keep living this lie. Everyone knows, and you're getting that feeling. Nobody is surprised here. You were a prisoner in your own house. You were living someone else's expectations. No matter how much they love you, they're taking away Jen. The Jen that just wanted to be a piano teacher. Why is that not good enough? Why not just be a lab technician? Why a doctor? Why does it always have to be something bigger?"

For the first time Jennifer appears calm. But there's a storm on the horizon. At this point she seems to have made a decision about her next steps. Sitting with her hands in her lap and staring at Goetz, she bows her head and weeps.

"The tension built up to a point ... it's like an animal that gets cornered," Goetz continues. "At some point even the nicest dog when it's cornered bites back. It's called self-preservation. Eighteen months ago you chose your family over Daniel, but you gave up Jen. Jen was in a state of depression, backed into a corner. Why you froze there on your bed was because the plan was in motion, there was no turning back. And I know right now you wish you could turn it back, right?

"It was a form of abuse," he continues. "You can't do that to a person. This is Canada. We're in the twenty-first century here. It's like your dad fixing everybody else's home but not his own. It's the same with you. He was trying to make a future for you bigger than it should have been. In the process of his love for you, he made the mistake of actually pushing you away. All his good intentions went the other way. The good thing is that you didn't shoot anyone here. You couldn't do that. You're not that type of person, right?"

As part of the Reid Technique, the investigator must be seated in a wheeled chair and the suspect in a fixed one. This is so that the interrogator can wheel close, either to show sympathy or make the suspect feel she is cornered. As Goetz begins to accuse Jennifer, he inches his chair closer and closer to her until the pair are almost touching, his burly stature bearing down on her. "You're involved in this. I know that," he tells her as she continues to fiddle with her hair. "There's no question about it. The only question right now is: Are you going to keep making mistakes?" Just before the three-hour mark, after about forty-five minutes of Goetz droning on in this vein, Jennifer finally starts to crack. After barely a peep for so long, she utters a muffled, inaudible sentence. She repeats it, this time loud enough for Goetz and the audio system to pick up.

"What happens to me?"

8

"IT WAS FOR ME"

Police in Canada might be allowed to lie to suspects about the evidence they have collected, but they're not able to speak on behalf of the judicial system or the courts and are strictly prohibited from making threats, deals, or promises in regard to how a suspect will be treated. Only the judicial arm of the province, the Crown, can do that. This becomes a problem for Detective Goetz when Jennifer openly wonders what kind of fate awaits her should she confess to her involvement in the murder. Although Jennifer repeats the same question multiple times — "What happens to me?" — the officer's hands are tied, so he puts her off. "I don't know the details, so I can't even say," he repeats on three separate occasions. "We're going to have to deal with this one step at a time. You've got to be honest with me and then you and I are going to work through this together. But I need to hear it."

Jennifer eventually relents and moves forward with a new version of events. "I wanted it to stop," she says.

"I know you did ... but once they came in you couldn't stop it, could ya?" Goetz responds in a comforting tone.

"I didn't know who they were," she says, giving a window into her eventual defence.

"Are you sorry for what happened?" Goetz asks. "Do you wish you could take it back?"

Jennifer, her head clenched tightly between her knees, finally says yes.

Goetz, leaning forward in his chair, thinks he's finally getting somewhere. "That's good, that's positive. You wish it didn't happen. He places a hand on her back and rubs her shoulder, sensing a full confession is coming. "I know this has been hell for you ... all you were looking for is a break, a chance to be on your own, to make your own decisions. How did it start? What was your plan? We know you were involved from the start. Over three hundred kids in North America every year are involved in their parents' deaths. And when we look into those cases, there's always a common factor. In those cases, those kids [had] to live up to expectations. The house rules were just so out of whack."

Jennifer approaches the cliff three hours and fourteen minutes into the interrogation, telling Goetz again, "If I could have stopped it, I would have stopped it." Moments later she takes the plunge, her face in her hands.

Although Jennifer's next words are inaudible on the tape, it is clear she has thrown Goetz a curveball. He repeats what she appears to have whispered to him. "They were supposed to take you...? Why? They were supposed to take the whole family out?"

"No, just me, because I didn't want to be here anymore. I'm such a disappointment," she says petulantly.

"It wasn't supposed to be Mom, is that what you're telling me? What about your dad?"

"It was supposed to be me, so they could be free from me," she insists. "I was a disappointment in everything. [Even] when I tried suicide I failed."

"Who did you get to do this, then?" an audibly exasperated Goetz asks.

"I don't know who he is. I just got his number," Jennifer says, advising him she's doubtful police will find her cellphone to corroborate her statement and that she doesn't know where its SIM card is, anyway. "[The order was] 'come in and take me out.' [They'd know it was me because] I was the only girl in the house." Jennifer goes on to explain that she set the plot up with a man named Homeboy after Ric gave her his number (notably leaving Daniel out of the equation). According to her, the job was to cost $2,000, a price she and Homeboy agreed on about two months before the shooting. If she wanted to be killed, Homeboy said she was to have the money ready for the men when they arrived. A frustrated Goetz, who thought he was getting to the meat and potatoes, continues to question why Jennifer would ever engage in such a "crazy" scheme. Jennifer forges on, explaining how she made the decision after her father accused her of seeing Daniel when she hadn't. She says, prior to entry on the night of November 8, the men texted her the message "Game on."

"What you've just told me is half the truth," Goetz tells Jennifer, asking her to sit up and look him in the eyes. "What I do believe is that you went to somebody, and I do believe that night you paid them the $2,000. That's the true part. But what's not true is that it was never for you. The job was for your parents."

Jennifer strengthens her story, insisting that she was using two phones that night, her Rogers Samsung phone to call her friends, and her Bell iPhone to speak to the murderers. After receiving the request for "VIP access" via text from Homeboy — texts she deleted afterward — she then says she made sure the door was unlocked.

Goetz is growing annoyed now. "Your dad wasn't supposed to live, but when he did live he was able to tell us what happened that night, which was in conflict with what you told us," he says. "This is how you deal with stress. You give half and you keep half. That's your stress mechanism. That's what you've been trained to do. No one thinks bad of you here … everybody in this police department feels sorry for you… basically it's like a volcano and at one point it was just too much and you erupted."

"Is that what you want me to say?" Jennifer asks. "But that's not what happened."

Goetz continues to push for the next forty-five minutes. And Jennifer continues to refute. "This is not going to go anywhere, because I wanted them to kill me," she insists testily.

After leaving the room to seek advice from his colleagues, Goetz returns before calmly stating, "I need you to listen close, okay, Jen? At this point of the investigation I will be arresting you for murder, also attempted murder and conspiracy to commit murder. Do you understand?"

Jennifer bows her head once more and begins to cry, covering her ears.

"You have to listen, so can you take your hands off your ears?"

Four hours and twenty-five minutes into the interview, Jennifer makes her last pitch for freedom. When asked if she wishes to say anything in response to the charges, she displays her sense of betrayal. "I thought you were on my side," she says.

This moment signals the end of Jennifer's freedom, the end of the road after more than a decade worth of lies and deceit perpetrated against every single person in her life. Those lies will result in plenty of fights, ultimatums, emotional heartache, and family dysfunction. But none of that will compare to her new reality — when her mountain of duplicity finally comes crashing down. Hunched over her knee on the faux leather police chair, she sobs as her leg shakes.

As Goetz enters and exits the room, trying to get her paperwork in order, Jennifer once again asks for his company. "Do you have to leave?"

Goetz responds, "We have to take care of the lawyers. That's the priority right now."

9

PANIC SETS IN

A mere nineteen miles away from Helen Avenue's tree-lined, middle-class streets live three of four men whose identities will soon become of great interest to the police. Despite their relative proximity, though, their lives greatly contrast with Jennifer's. Whereas she has lived in a plush Markham home, complete with two high-end vehicles, each with their own garage space, with two income-earning parents, both of whom spent much of her life focused on ensuring her success, countless children in Toronto's forgotten enclave of Rexdale are lucky to get even a semblance of this sort of upbringing. Of course, parents do their best all over the city, but if we are truly products of our environments, then it's easy to see why there are still so many social problems plaguing this area northwest of the Toronto core.

Granted, Jennifer and Daniel both spent their childhoods living in a similarly rough neighbourhood in Scarborough in Toronto's east end; however, they both benefited from secure, closely knit families, with a wealth of resources at their disposal.

While countless success stories have blossomed from the concrete used to pave over farmland in Rexdale in the 1950s, there remain to this day significant social issues in the area. Inside the residences in this part of the city, about a quarter of households are led by a single parent. Outside on the streets, the negative influences are plentiful. Respected Toronto urban landscape journalist Christopher Hume describes the intense feeling of isolation one might sense growing up among Rexdale's "patchwork of precincts" connected by expressways.

"There are many Rexdales," writes the *Toronto Star*'s Hume. "They can be found across North America, clustered on the fringes of the cities that spawned them.... [Rexdale] has become shorthand for suburban blight, social breakdown and gang violence ... a grey landscape of highways and highrises, shopping malls and churches. And for the kids that live there — the subject of much concern and study — the common complaint is that there's nothing to do. Wandering around the anonymous streets of this place, that's not hard to believe." He argues that Rexdale was built for people with vehicles, yet when industry dwindled and workers moved on, residents who were left were forced to survive without. Without subways, many have to travel by foot or take buses to their destinations.

One campaigner, Reverend Walter McIntyre, outreach pastor at the Kipling Avenue Baptist Church, says that, without the appropriate community hubs, it's a struggle to keep kids away from drugs and gangs. While there is an issue regarding financial resources and public projects reaching Rexdale — which has a community makeup of 30 percent South Asian households, 26 percent Caucasian, and 20 percent black, according to 2011 statistics — there have been plenty of police resources spent trying to clean up the mess left behind, often with a firm hand rather than a helping one. Outrage was sparked throughout the community and the city in mid-2016 after pregnant mother Candice Rochelle Bobb was killed, her car sprayed with bullets on Jamestown Crescent. Her baby boy, who had spent five months in the womb, survived for three weeks after doctors performed an emergency C-section. Tragically, the child later died in hospital.

During much of the 2000s, there were running battles between two gang-infused parts of the area, on streets like Jamestown Crescent and Mount Olive Drive. In 2013 Rexdale hit the headlines and was subsequently caught up in the raging news story of now-deceased former Toronto Mayor Rob Ford. After Ford — adored by many in the community — was photographed outside a neighbourhood crack house, a man tried to sell the video of him allegedly smoking the drug to the media. One of the men pictured with Ford was later shot and killed outside a Toronto nightclub. Following this, police executed raids in Rexdale, arresting forty-three people during an investigation related to murder, guns, and drug trafficking (of drugs that included heroin, cocaine, and marijuana). The investigation focused on the Dixon City Bloods, a.k.a. the Dixon Goonies, and $3 million worth of drugs, $500,000 in cash, and forty guns were seized. Among the men arrested were Mohamed Siad, a.k.a. "Soya," who tried to sell the Ford video, and Liban Siyad, a.k.a. "Gully," who was allegedly later extorted for the tape's return by a Ford associate.

This street term *gully* will turn up in the Pan investigation.

Eric Carty spent much of his youth in Rexdale at apartment buildings along Kipling Avenue — a road sometimes called "Cripling" in reference to local gang, the Crips (who are not affiliated with the notorious Los Angeles gang). Always a little shorter than his classmates, Eric was the eldest of a family of six children. Growing up, he was a good student until about grade ten. He was described by his track coach as a "quiet and reserved" young man who was pleasant to be around. Although, like Jennifer, he suffered from asthma that would affect his health, especially later in life, he was also plenty quick and athletic as a youth. "He was a quiet, quiet little guy. He just blended in with the rest," says Earl Letford, founder of the area's Flying Angels Track and Field Club, which has seen many of its members head to the United States on scholarships. "Some of the kids take it serious and go deep into it. But they usually have plenty of family backing and support. I get them when they're young and get them on a good path."

Although Letford has no idea what happened to cause Eric to stop coming out for practice, he was shocked to hear that Eric resorted to a life of crime. However, Letford adds that his limited knowledge of Eric's life appears to have been consistent with the young man's loss of a male role model, a trend he's well acquainted with. "He was a very well-mannered kid and very nice," he insists, noting that he remembers Eric as a "follower" in his youth. Although he's seen more of his fair share of "tough guys" in his time, he says Eric wasn't like that.

Eric's demeanour soon changed, and by the time he was in his thirties he was being described as the exact opposite of a follower. One man who knew him characterized him as the epitome of a leader, in charge in almost every relationship he was involved in. But others, often the ladies in his life, revealed his softer side, noting that he not only had big dreams, but that he was also very loving and supportive of his children. He was the kind of person who was not only very personable but also dependable, often sharing advice and going out of his way to help those closest to him. And when it came time to unwind? Well, Eric was the life of the party.

But episodes in his life show that, starting in his mid to late teenage years, he displayed a keen sense of revenge. It was likely the ability to put getting even with his enemies above his freedom that won him the respect and fear of his associates. At the tender age of fifteen Eric lost his hero, his dad, in a tragic car crash. This event would alter his life forever. Soon after this tragedy, Eric fell into a criminal lifestyle, and just a year after his father's death, when Eric was only sixteen, he had his first significant run-in with the police. Two years later, in 1998, he was charged with uttering threats.

In 1999, he made his first lengthy visit to the penitentiary, convicted of carrying a prohibited weapon and discharging a firearm to endanger life. The charges stemmed from an incident on July 12, 1998, a hot summer's day, when Eric and his friends went to Brampton's Wild Water Kingdom. In-between the waterslides and bathing-suit-clad children dashing about getting soaked, Eric and his friends got embroiled in a fight with two other teens. After being escorted from the park by employees, Eric hopped in a friend's car and confronted the two teens who were driving another vehicle. As the car he was riding in slowly pulled up beside the other car, Eric pulled out a .22 calibre sawed-off shotgun. From about six feet away, hanging out of the window, eighteen-year-old Eric took a shot, piercing the window's moulding and striking the passenger in the vehicle in the left eye. Luckily for both men, the bullet didn't penetrate the victim's skull, but the man was badly injured.

Three days later Eric was arrested. He was held in jail for six months until he finally relented and pleaded guilty to the charges. As he had committed the crime one month after his eighteenth birthday — making him an adult in the eyes of the law — he was sentenced to five years in prison.

The incident at Wild Water Kingdom went down in infamy among Eric's friends and earned him the nickname "Snypa," which he later tattooed on his leg beside an image of an AK-47. On his neck he has a tattoo that reads GOD BLESS and on his right forearm the term SOULJA. His other nicknames include his middle name, Shawn, and "S."

When Eric was eventually freed, his behaviour didn't improve; instead, it escalated until it became a lifestyle. Rarely, if ever, did Eric hold down a job, and his source of income was often from the proceeds of crime, the government, or one of the many women in his life. After his release, he racked up charges for everything from cocaine trafficking to marijuana possession and assaulting a witness in a robbery investigation. But he was astute and managed to evade conviction in all those cases.

Although Eric Carty has been linked to gang violence — including allegedly being stopped by police while in a car seated beside a supposed member of the Hells Angels — those who know him reject the idea that he was involved in any serious gang-related activity. One man, speaking on condition of anonymity, describes Eric as a "lone wolf," a "middle-level drug-dealer" — a lifestyle that inevitably comes with a certain level of violence. Despite Eric's reputation, the man characterizes him as "very jovial" and extremely loyal and dedicated to his friends — of whom there were plenty. However, he also says that a friendship with Eric came at a cost, considering how dangerous it was to be around him at certain times. He was sometimes wanted by the police and often relied on those closest to him to help him out when trying to avoid police capture, something that could bring the heat down on those housing him. "He's very smart and a leader, no doubt," the anonymous associate says. "Everyone is a brother or a cousin to him. He's bubbly, but very demanding. A very good friend to friends, but that probably comes at a high cost. Just being around him comes at a high cost."

Much of Eric's free time was spent pursuing two of his favourite things, according to another friend — ladies and partying. He was known to be dating and staying with at least five women at the same time (police said the number could have been closer to ten), including more than one of his children's mothers. One good friend says he was a magnet for women: "Listen, ladies love this guy. Every time I see this guy he has a new girl." There was one woman, though, Leesha Pompei, the mother of two of his children, who more than the rest, remained a constant in Eric's life.

By the time he was an adult, fully immersed in a criminal lifestyle, Eric got the body art to prove it. On one arm he has the word OUTLAW emblazoned. On the underside of his left forearm is written RIDE WITH US OR COLLIDE WITH US. Eric rarely went by his "government name," preferring to call himself "S" or "Snypa."

Using nicknames, of course, can be a good-natured way to interact, but for many can also be used to keep one's identity secret to avoid the police.

One of Eric's good friends who was a business associate of his in the marijuana trade, was Lenford Crawford. Eric and Lenford hung out and smoked weed, drank, partied, and flirted with girls. But Lenford didn't grow up in Rexdale; in fact, he didn't even grow up in Canada.

Lenford was born in Kingston, Jamaica, on June 2, 1982, to Megreta and Lenford Crawford, Sr. He had one sister. Soon after Lenford was born, his father was sponsored to come to Canada, and he jumped at the opportunity, leaving a young family behind. Lenford's father later married his sponsor and had children with her, settling in Vancouver, British Columbia. With his father gone and the family suffering from a severely reduced income, Lenford, his mother, and his sister soon moved out of expensive Kingston and back to the countryside to Megreta's home parish of Clarendon. It was there, among the peaceful and agrarian Jamaican plains dotted with fields of tobacco, cotton farms, and banana, coffee, and cocoa crops, that Lenford spent his youth.

The quiet boy was always willing to lend a hand to his mother, doing the dishes and never shirking his chores, and he performed well at school. For his mother, one thing that struck her was his dependability. He was always a very calm and relaxed child, something that would stay with him into adulthood. "He would always come with me and help me sell things at the market," she told me. "He was a kind sort of boy. You could depend on him. He would do the shopping for me. He was the kind of guy who you could call when you needed help, and he'd always be there for you. If he had a dollar in his pocket and you needed it, he'd give it over without even thinking about it. He was not lazy; he was not idle."

Megreta soon met another man, Albert Anderson, whose surname she now shares. It was in 1994 that Megreta decided to send Lenford to Canada to live with his father to ensure her boy a better education. "That was my mistake," she says, describing Lenford at that point as easy to influence, or as she puts it, "humble and willing." She says that, in the town where he grew up, there were few negative influences for a young boy. He was introduced to the street life much later in his existence when he moved to urban Vancouver. Although she has no idea what occurred when he arrived as a teenager, she remembers distinctly getting a call from a tenant living below the home where Lenford was residing. "He said to me: 'Please, this is a good kid. I don't want to see him getting mashed up.

Keep him away from these influences,'" she says, explaining that the man had no relation to her or her family, but said he called out of the goodness of his heart after noticing the types of people Lenford was befriending.

Soon after, Lenford, who she says was the youngest of the bunch, was nabbed by police as a young offender after getting involved with drugs. Megreta knew then that she, too, had to make her way to Canada. Her husband, Albert, was eventually sponsored, and Megreta followed him north to Toronto and was reunited with her son in 1999.

Keen on his success, Albert helped Lenford, now seventeen, get night-shift work with him at a pastry manufacturer cleaning machinery in Toronto. Lenford also went to school in the city for body work and mechanics and soon started doing oil changes, brakes, and tires at a local garage before eventually getting a factory job at Rexdale's Kik Custom Products, a manufacturer of bottled household products.

Although it's unclear how Daniel Wong and Lenford Crawford met, many say it was through their respective love of cars. Like Daniel, Lenford was a hard worker who got promoted quickly. He joined Kik Custom as a stock boy, and three months later when managers noted his dedication to the job, he was promoted to line mechanic, not only operating machinery but repairing it when it went down. Lenford was making about $17 an hour, often worked overtime, and owned his own car. He rarely took vacations and, at times, worked seven days a week, according to his mother. "He's not a troublemaker; he's not a gangster," she insists. "He's a hard-working guy. He's never even been on welfare." True to her words, life for Lenford was routine to the point of appearing downright dull, with him usually going to work between 3:30 p.m. and midnight and then going home to his mother's Rexdale home or to his girlfriend's place in Brampton where they often stayed together with their young son. For his age (he was now twenty-seven), Lenford was a very dedicated father and held plenty of love both for his girlfriend and son, his mother adds.

In his new city, Lenford set about making a place for himself, meeting new people and earning extra money by selling marijuana. It's unclear exactly how he met Eric, but police say they were introduced through the drug trade. To his friends, Lenford was known by a number of names, including his middle name Roy and also "Columbia" and "Columbs," because of his link to British Columbia. Over the years, he called Toronto's challenged neighbourhoods of Rexdale and Jane-Finch home, and also lived in the nearby city of Brampton. Lenford said he'd known Eric long enough to have met his "whole family," and he regularly referred to Eric as "fam" — in other words, the pair were close friends. According to Lenford, the pair got to know each other through several young women they both knew.

While Lenford's hard work paid off — he had a steady job, a car, and money in his pocket — Eric struggled financially. Historically, he came into large sums of money often, but by late 2009, because of extenuating circumstances, he was only getting by with the help of the women in his life, at whose homes he'd spend his nights.

Another of Eric's good friends was a man from Rexdale named David Mylvaganam. David was born in Montreal to a Sri Lankan father and a Jamaican mother. David eventually split his time between living in Quebec with his father and in Toronto with his mother. He grew up near Eric Carty and his girlfriend, Leesha Pompei. Leesha says she remembers him as "just some little kid running around the neighbourhood."

But as David grew up, he allegedly got involved in a number of criminal endeavours, including the sale of guns, although he managed to stay largely out of trouble with the police. His nicknames included his middle name Ramu as well as "Rambo," "Indian," and "Coolie." When he was in his early twenties, David fancied himself a rapper and used his nicknames as aliases in his music videos, some of which are credited to "Mad Indian." He has two sons with two different women.

David, like Lenford and Eric, was very close to his kids and cared deeply for them. When a picture of his son and the child's mother, Denise Brown, was later shown in court, he welled up. However, the couple's relationship eventually grew strained because of what she called his immaturity. Bearing in mind that he was just twenty-two at that point, Denise says he was not only more involved with his friends than his young family, but also unfaithful and irresponsible with money. As a result, she broke off the relationship.

Lenford eventually introduced Eric and Daniel to each other, which led to a newfound partnership between the three. Daniel and Lenford were close friends, as were Lenford and Eric. But three's a crowd, as they say, and Eric and Daniel didn't see eye to eye on a number of issues. Eric didn't consider Daniel experienced enough for the drug trade. As in most of his relationships, Eric was the senior partner in the triumvirate, with Lenford in the middle, and finally Daniel, the junior partner — this despite Daniel providing many of the drug contacts for the trio. At various points throughout their relationships, Daniel and Lenford spent a considerable amount of time trying to show just how "street" they were to those they were attempting to impress — Daniel to Lenford and Lenford to Eric.

Although up until that point, Daniel was relatively well versed in the small-time drug trade, meeting Lenford heralded an introduction into new partnerships, larger quantities, more money, and an expanded clientele. Daniel became Lenford's understudy, taking up the role of his little brother as he introduced him to bigger deals. But larger quantities and new colleagues bring with them new dangers that Daniel either didn't realize or chose to ignore. Although it's unclear exactly how much weed the trio was selling each week, they were allegedly regularly purchasing half pounds, paying $2,700 for higher-quality weed and $1,900 for bottom-end stuff. In the lead-up to the Pan murder, Lenford and Daniel spent much of their time working or hanging out with their girlfriends. More than Daniel, Lenford and Eric passed much of their time smoking pot. However, both were very highly functioning: being high was both a lifestyle and a leisure activity.

10

AN EARLY CHRISTMAS PRESENT

On November 23, 2010, at three o'clock in the afternoon, television crews, newspaper reporters, and radio journalists, all with microphones in hand, crowd into York Police Headquarters in Newmarket to find out the latest on a case that many in the media — a skeptical bunch at the best of times — had more than an inkling of suspicion about to start with.

This story, as reporters put it, has "legs." The crime was not only committed in the middle of an upper-middle-class suburban neighbourhood, but it involved a young, attractive female and two hard-working parents who were caught off guard while relaxing in their home. But unlike so many murder investigations, this one ensnared both sexes as well as people from a vast array of the cultural backgrounds and ethnicities that make up Toronto's diverse diaspora.

Simply put, the case has all the hallmarks of intrigue, from horror to passion and, from the public's point of view, the seduction of a "whodunit." But at its core, this is a tragic tale of the destruction of an innocent family.

This big public reveal comes the day after Jennifer Pan's arrest. During the press conference, Chief La Barge — who only two short weeks earlier told reporters the Pans were attacked "for absolutely no particular reason" — alters the public's view of the investigation with one statement: "We had nothing to indicate what the motive was.... That changed."

When the first press conference took place two weeks earlier, Hann Pan was "in no way, shape, or form prepared to be interviewed" by investigators. Since then, he has spoken to officers and is being held, police say, at an undisclosed location. Detective Sergeant Larry Wilson admits that it was after interviewing Hann that the focus of the investigation began to shift to the victims' daughter, twenty-four-year-old Jennifer. Although the police remain tight-lipped about the possible motives, the media are able to garner some nuggets of information from the press conference.

Hann is now the "key person" and is providing police with a new description of the men being sought. This indicates to everyone that Jennifer lied in her initial description of the intruders. Newspapers discover from anonymous family members that Jennifer was living at home with her parents and didn't work. Furthermore, the fact that Jennifer has been charged with first-degree murder means the police believe "some planning and deliberation" occurred between her and the shooters.

After Jennifer's arrest, police attention shifts to the others involved: a male, black, twenty to twenty-five, six feet two inches tall, with muscular build; a male, black, twenty to twenty-five, between six feet and six feet two inches tall, with skinnier build; and a male, white, twenty to twenty-five, six feet tall with heavier build and a round face.

When they return to their desks after the press conference, homicide detectives say their phones are inundated with calls from reporters.

The local impact of the murder is also deeply felt, with parents worried for the safety of their families. "I'm glad that there is some kind of closure to this, because people in the neighbourhood were really concerned that it was a random ... act," says Aurelia Fernandez, one of the Pans' neighbours. However, as with many cases that evolve over time, new information does little to dispel the feeling of insecurity many feel in modern society. "I don't think you'll ever be safe in a world like this one," Fernandez adds.

News of Jennifer's arrest is broadcast on news channels across the city, province, and country. This is an unwelcome development for the others involved in the crime, and they all respond to the news differently. For three of the men who will eventually end up the subject of police inquiries, one detail looms larger than their freedom: money. The actions they take at this point in time will make this quite clear.

FOR POLICE, JENNIFER'S arrest is the easy part. Now the real work begins — trying to find the men who were in the tinted-windowed late-model Acura that zoomed down Helen Avenue at 10:30 p.m. on November 8. But finding men intent on not being discovered and then proving they're responsible is no simple task. This is especially true when all you have to work with are a couple of phone numbers.

Two days after Jennifer's arrest, on November 25, Detectives Courtice and Cooke receive a "snapshot" from the call logs on Jennifer's Bell iPhone. The first thing they discover as they scan the information it provides, is that Daniel was deceitful with them. Despite the fact that he told Detective Milligan he hadn't "spoken with [Jennifer] recently" — on November 8 alone, he engaged in thirty-six text messages and fourteen calls with her.

In addition, there were numerous suspicious calls and texts that day to and from other numbers. But these weren't your typical phone numbers registered to named individuals with cell contracts and credit card information. These were from prepaid phones — called "burners" on the street — that are often used by drug dealers. They are simple to buy, burn through, dump, and repeat. In the case of several of these phones, the users had cheek, and in one case, at least, they seemed to be clearly taunting police — using as an alias the name of a man with a blatant hatred for law enforcement. Detective Al Cooke says that on top of having no forensic evidence from the crime scene, most of the phones in this case were assigned to people who didn't exist. "It [very quickly] became a phone case," he says. "It's very frustrating. Everybody has a phone or two or three phones in different names."

Investigators initially focus on the last four numbers to call Jennifer on her iPhone before the murder. One call, which came in at 6:12 p.m. on November 8, draws their particular attention. This number includes the digits 8 and 5 and has a Toronto area code, just as Jennifer told them Homeboy's did. But at that point, police aren't sure what parts of Jennifer's statement they can believe. Another call came in at 8:16 p.m. and lasted twenty-eight seconds, and yet another at 9:34 p.m. — this one a minute and forty-two seconds in duration. The last call was received at 10:05 p.m. This time the two parties talked for three minutes and twenty-three seconds. The home invasion occurred five minutes after this conversation ended, at 10:13 p.m.

The records for these phones and the corresponding tower information attached to them are requested immediately by police, in the form of a warrant, but it can take up to thirty days to receive the information once requests have been signed off by a judge. While waiting for that data, the police decide to take a chance and call the numbers. All but one let the calls ring right through. The only number where they get an answer is the one that called Jennifer at 8:16 p.m. on the night of the murder. The phone, of course, is registered under a bogus name, James Anderson. The owner, it turns out, is a real joker — Demetrius Mables, who later describes the initial phone conversation he engaged in with police on November 26 as one of mystery. "At first I didn't know it was the police. They were talking to me like they were trying to do me something," he says. "I'm like, I'm not going to tell you who I am, and I don't even know who you [are]. When he told me it was an investigation of a homicide, I'm like *What the hell?*"

When Mables rejects the police's assertion he had anything to do with the murder, Detective Courtice conveys his frustration. "Mr. Bloodpressure [Courtice] came and picked me up and told me how I'm getting his blood pressure high," Mables later says. "'What am I doing? What am I talking about?' I came over and co-operated with him because I know I'm innocent. We went to his car, we sat down in his car, he put on his little microphone, and he started talking."

Detective David MacDonald, meanwhile, has an even harder time while trying to reach the owner of the investigation's target phone — the one that called six minutes before the entry — but no one answers. So he throws a Hail Mary pass and texts the phone: *Hello, it's the police, please call me back as soon as possible. Det. MacDonald.*

He receives no response.

The phone goes silent from then on, but police are far from done with it. The following day, the police attempt another long shot and drive out to Brampton to knock on the door of the address listed on the phone they now know is registered to a Peter Robinson. Detective MacDonald's heart sinks when an elderly male answers, completely mystified as to why a homicide detective is on his doorstep. MacDonald might have suspected as much, considering Peter Robinson is the name of the former mayor of Brampton.

Later that day, though, Detective MacDonald, who's been working for months on-shift from 8:00 a.m. to 1:00 a.m. without a day off, catches a break. The clean-cut former military man, who rose through the York Regional Police ranks quickly to become a detective in homicide that year, raps on the door of Lenford Crawford's family home in Rexdale, the only legitimate address listed on any of the phones that called Jennifer's iPhone that day (at 10 a.m. and 6:12 p.m.). Lenford's parents are none too pleased to find police searching for their boy; it's unclear how they would have reacted if MacDonald told them he was from homicide. Rousing him from his slumber, a seemingly relaxed Lenford agrees to be interviewed at the police station as long as officers promise to get him to work on time for his shift. But despite granting them an interview and showing police plenty of respect during it, he doesn't give them much in terms of information. After a lolling but friendly description of his work, family, and personal life, during which he details his attempts to mend his relationship with the mother of his child, the conversation eventually turns to Daniel Wong — a man Lenford knows by the nickname "Bruce."

"I used to hang out with my friends," he says, referring to Daniel and others. "[But] I don't really have time to talk to them anymore because of my son." It is at this moment that Detective MacDonald drops his unassuming, pleasant demeanour, his expression growing dour. It signals a shift from pleasantries to business.

"How do you know Jennifer Pan?" he asks point-blank, staring right into Lenford's eyes. Seemingly unfazed, Lenford continues to plead ignorance. Once pressed though, he admits he might have spoken to Jennifer while trying to get hold of Daniel. But he denies having a conversation with her. "What did you guys talk about at 10:00 a.m. [on November 8]?" Detective MacDonald asks.

"It would have to be about [Daniel] or me trying to get hold of him," Lenford replies.

MacDonald, sensing he's being misled, warns him not to play with the police. "I want to make sure you understand the gravity of this," he tells Lenford. "It's important it's truthful. When you're talking to me straight, you're looking at me in the eyes. When you don't talk to me straight, you're looking somewhere else. Tell me the truth … that's what we're after."

Lenford doesn't bite and remains balanced, entering into a long, drawn-out story about being owed money by Daniel's friend. He says the man's name is Vince, a "drug addict" who owes him $500. Before long MacDonald goes at Lenford again, this time directly asking if he was involved in Bich's murder, but the young man insists it wasn't him: "I wasn't involved, absolutely not."

Unsatisfied with the response, MacDonald presents Lenford with a scenario. "A guy who was short of cash, finding the pinch of life was closing in on him, and was offered money in order to do a job, then finds himself in over his head, and ends up having to deal with the consequences even if he was only a little bit involved," he proposes. "What do you think should happen to a guy like that?"

Lenford responds, "Unless I know the full situation, I'm not one to judge people ... but believe it or not, I'm telling the truth." Under further pressure, and sensing he has little option but to throw MacDonald a bone, he admits to contacting Daniel about drugs.

There is now some direction in the case. The tangled web of deceit has no longer just ensnared Jennifer and Daniel, but now his friend, Lenford. Police leave the meeting wondering: *Did we just speak to Homeboy?* But even if they have, what comes next throws them for a loop. After the interview, MacDonald discovers that on November 8 Lenford signed into work using a thumb scanner and remained there until midnight when his shift ended. Daniel also has an unassailable alibi: he was at work until late, as well.

On the other side of town, Detective Courtice is getting nowhere with his interview. Demetrius Mables has told him he had nothing to do with any murder, has no idea about a phone call from his phone and, besides, that night (November 8) he was working at a construction site.

That isn't enough to exclude Demetrius or Lenford from the investigation. Courtice and Cooke keep searching, thumbing through the series of phone numbers until they come across one that is also contained in Jennifer's Rogers Samsung phone. On November 29, Cooke sits down with Andrew Montemayor, a young-looking Filipino lad. When police first contacted Andrew's girlfriend, he grew faint-headed, felt sick, and wanted to throw up. As Detective Goetz later puts it, he was "terrified."

"I didn't talk to Jennifer November 8," Andrew begins in his police interview. But his denials won't do him any good.

Slapping a stack of documents on the table in front of the frightened man, Cooke tells him, "These are all the text messages. This is for November 8, all these pages," he says, leafing through the data. "How do you explain that if you didn't talk to her that day ... you texted her almost one hundred times — seven pages of texts. This is the day her mother was shot and killed, and you're texting her at that time. That concerns me, Andrew. You knew sooner or later [Jennifer was] going to get arrested, and she's sitting in that chair. She's going to tell us everything that happened: who she was talking to and how this thing came about."

The records show that on the day of the murder, between 4:30 p.m. and 10:26 p.m., Andrew and Jennifer texted each other a lot, so much so that the total — eighty-seven texts and four calls over six hours — was about half the texts the pair shared between August and November. Andrew, who isn't experienced in dealing with the police, can see things as clearly as the investigators. It isn't looking good for him. He can only play dumb for so long, and he eventually spills the beans. Andrew tells police that Jennifer called him that day, advising him how fed up she was with her parents, annoyed and suffering under what she called their brutal rules, which felt to her like house arrest. He says Jennifer said she was really "pissed" at them and wanted to get away from them. Andrew adds that she told him she'd planned a home invasion at her home that night but was going to make it look like a robbery. She told him the men would demand money and shoot her parents. Jennifer was to be tied up but not hurt. She said it was going to involve two people busting through the door and would begin when she got a text. Although Andrew claims at first that he thought she was mad, speaking out of anger or even joking, he also says Jennifer wasn't laughing and even states she sounded serious. He told her it was up to her what she wanted to do. As for the texts, he says they were about his enduring crush on Jennifer and the stress he was suffering at his job.

But this isn't all he shares. Andrew also tells the police that Jennifer approached him in the spring of 2010 about having her parents killed. He says Jennifer was angry about her issues with her parents — how they didn't trust her, how she felt "house-arrested." She said she wanted them killed, offed, taken care of, and asked him to help her find a way to do it.

From Jennifer's jailhouse letters around the time of this interview, we can see that she not only knew when police were interviewing her friends, but was afraid of what information they might reveal. In December, Jennifer wrote to Daniel, stating: "Talked to Ed [Pacificador] and he said he is talking to the cops again. I am nervous about that. He now doubts me as well. Adrian [Tymkewycz] is talking to them now, so he will probably be leaving my side as well. Why do they want to take all that I have left in this world? I am not sure I am going to be OK. I am one voice, muffled in a crowd of screams."

Andrew's comments definitely help strengthen the case against Jennifer, but they bring police no closer to the men who committed the violence. In the following months, police conduct hundreds of interviews, a process that consumes countless officers' lives for a time. Detective MacDonald, a young father, works straight through from November 8 to December 21. Detective Courtice says he survived on coffee and cigarettes more than a few nights. "Bill [Courtice] and I were always yelling at each other," says Detective Cooke with a chuckle about the late nights and long days they spent together in the office. "It could be about anything — the speed and flow of the investigation, its direction. Other times we'd just be bouncing ideas off one another."

Eventually, all the work, coupled with a bit of luck, pays off. Detective Courtice discovers that of the three major telecom companies in Canada, only one, Telus Mobility, stores all incoming and outgoing text messages for thirty days (to the chagrin of police nationwide, this has now ceased to be the case). It turns out the "Peter Robinson" phone is a Telus phone, so the police are able to request the records in time, receiving them on December 17. "I remember that day clearly. It was like an early Christmas present," Courtice quips.

And just as the officers hope for, the data is a treasure trove of information for an investigation starved of it. Within days, police contact two women whose numbers appear on that phone as contacts: Georgia McQuaid and Francine Johnson. When they speak to McQuaid, she types the number into her phone and comes up with the name of a man she knows called Indian, but that's the only information she can provide. It is Francine Johnson who gives up the goods, however. Despite having called her lawyer to sit in on the police interview, investigators get lucky when he lets McQuaid speak to Detective MacDonald privately — once the detective promises that his inquiries don't involve Francine directly. Francine admits that the number belongs to a man she knows by the name of David Mylvaganam. After running his name through the system, police discover he has no criminal record but that at one point was arrested on fraud charges in Montreal. And just like that, police have their first suspect who might very well have been inside the house.

After he receives a communication from Francine about what just occurred with the police, David panics. He doesn't want to contact Francine directly now that the police know his name, so he begins texting another person, an unknown male, to communicate with Francine for him. Police eventually garner this information, once again using the Telus storage system. The texts are deciphered with the assistance of Detective Gawain [the Welsh spelling of *Gavin*] Jansz, a Toronto police officer and an expert in street and codified language.

> **D:** *Dem bwoy de a di yard an a talk to Francy.* [Police talked to Francine.]
> **UM:** *What she do.*
> **D:** *Text her and tell her two link u on a different link u overstand.* [Get her to call you on a different phone number. Do you really understand me?]
> **UM:** *Y ct u tell me.* [Why can't you tell me?]
> **D:** *Dem a tak bout a m an a numba linkage bout rea.* [Police talked about an M (murder) and about a phone connection.]
> **D:** *Dem a sa a pure fakery a gawan over de.* [Police said bullshit went on over there.]

The conversation ends bluntly. The male on the other end, clearly worried about David's overuse of text communication to relay sensitive information, demands he stop and ring him immediately: *Call me nw.*

Later the two men and Francine share a three-way conversation, police say. And the next time police attempt to speak with Francine, she spends forty-five minutes yelling at them over the phone. Needless to say, she no longer co-operates with the investigation. But police are already hot on David's trail. The man on the other end of David's texts remains unidentified for the moment. A picture of David is immediately sought from Quebec police.

On January 6, Hann Pan walks into York Regional Police's Markham detachment to take part in a photo lineup police have prepared. Taking his seat, he quickly dismisses the first four of the twelve pictures out of hand. It is on the fifth picture that Hann hesitates for the first and only time during the lineup. He frames the picture with his fingers as if the man is wearing a hat. "I think maybe. I think maybe this guy," he says in broken English. "Maybe. Because long time, right. I can see him only ten minutes without glasses. I'm not 100 percent. I did not confirm 100 percent, but it very much like the person who held me."

It is the picture of David Mylvaganam.

One last stroke of good fortune for police strengthens the case against David. The owner of the "Peter Robinson" phone had texted social services his name, age, address, and social insurance number (SIN). The burner phone definitely belongs to David Mylvaganam.

"[Now] that's luck," says Detective Cooke, who indicates David had been attempting to secure welfare with the text.

Two days before that, Ricardo Duncan, a.k.a. "Ric," the man Jennifer had implicated as being the one who had given her Homeboy's number, breezed into a police interview room. After a lengthy interview, police realized they weren't dealing with the man Jennifer had painted as a possible suspect. "He's a security guard, not a murderer," says Cooke, implying he used his experience to decipher what sort of man police were dealing with. Nonetheless, Ric told the interviewers a fascinating tale.

Ric said he had met Jennifer in the spring of 2010, six months before the murder. His connection to Jennifer was through his roommate at the time, Andrew (Montemayor), who was a friend of hers. Ric said that when he met up with Jennifer at the coffee shop in Scarborough, she was highly emotional. She told him that she resented her parents, adding that she was angry about her situation and was feeling trapped. During one of the pair's two meetings, Ric said Jennifer asked him to kill her parents. But he said once he realized she was serious, he refused to speak with her again. The police soon discover that Ric was the black male Jennifer's uncle had seen her with at a coffee shop. The pair had shared eighty-nine texts between May and July of 2010.

On January 6, 2011, police receive the forensic report from the bullets recovered from Hann, Bich, and the couch in the Pan's basement. Experts have found that bullet fibres recovered from the couch match fibres on Hann's T-shirt and that the bullet fired through Hann's shoulder is from the same gun that fired the two bullets found in Bich's body. This means it is highly likely there was one triggerman. However, due to the fact that no foreign DNA was found at the house, this remains a case reliant on the cellphone information being uncovered. The "Peter Robinson" phone is still the catalyst of the investigation. The police are focused on one thing — arresting the three men who were in the house that night. They essentially eliminate Daniel and Lenford from their list of possible assailants, since they both have alibis. So who *was* there?

When the cell tower records are finally secured, police discover a clue that blows the case wide open: In the hour leading up to Bich's murder, the "Peter Robinson" phone can be seen travelling across Highway 401, which cuts across the northern part of Toronto, at 9:30 p.m. before heading northbound up Highway 404 toward Richmond Hill and Markham. While en route, the person using that phone contacted Lenford Crawford (9:45 p.m.) just after calling Jennifer Pan's Bell iPhone at 9:34 p.m.

While reviewing surveillance footage taken from a camera located across the street from the Pan home, a sharp-eyed detective notices that just prior to the Acura passing by, a light in Hann's study was turned on. The time was 10:02 p.m. The light remained on for exactly one minute and twenty-one seconds and was then switched off. Was this a signal from inside the house?

The grainy footage then shows the Acura driving up the road, turning at the street that runs kitty-corner to the Pan home, and (presumably) parking out of view. In the moments prior to gunmen bursting into the Pan home at 10:13 p.m., another call came in to Jennifer's iPhone from the "Peter Robinson" phone. During this call, both phones were pinging off the tower closest to 238 Helen Avenue. After the three-minute-and-twenty-three-second call, the "Peter Robinson" phone was turned off. The time was 10:09. The men, three figures, are seen running up to the house at 10:13. The upstairs lights come on at 10:15. The men were in the house for fourteen minutes before one man runs out at 10:30 and then two others exit at 10:32, returning to the car and speeding off at 10:33. Video then shows police arriving, sirens blaring, at 10:38.

Other than the fifteen minutes following the murder, the "Peter Robinson" phone is in almost constant use inside the car as it makes its way to Markham and back. The phone calls and texts numbers in Rexdale and one number in Montreal. Thirty minutes earlier, at 9:42 p.m. during one set of texts to Montreal, someone, likely David, makes a colossal mistake while in a conversation with an unknown female.

DM: *In a meeting with Kimble I will text you to call k love.*
UF: *OK, was that who I heard cussing, tell him I say whatup.*
DM: *Ya ya u now go to sleep for now.*

The stored texts once again prove indispensable. Police now know the name of at least one other person in that car — Kimble. Finding out Kimble's identity, however, proves to be a monumental task. In the coming weeks, police exhaust every avenue and investigate every shred of information they come across to try to identify him. Whoever he is, he is very diligent about keeping his identity hidden. "It was like finding a needle in a stack of needles," Detective Cooke says about the challenges they faced. "It was driving us crazy." Sure, "Kimble" is identified by his nickname, but police have no name or picture to go on. Cooke spends weeks and countless hours cross-referencing phones, interviewing people, and gaining bits of information, but it is never enough. However, this technique does provide some clues. Cellular data indicate to Cooke which phones logically belong to Kimble — constantly changing numbers, he texted the same contacts the following message multiple times: *Yo bro, this is my new number.* However, when those contacts responded "Who is this?" he always replied with one of his nicknames, usually Snypa. Alternatively, he used the name of one of his kids' mothers, Cooke says.

When Cooke runs the nickname "Kimble" through the national police database — the Canadian Police Information Centre (CPIC) — nothing comes up. But when he runs "Snypa," he discovers the name is linked to a number of people across the country. Listed in the details about one of these men is a request to call Toronto Police Sergeant Sheila Ogg, who has been searching for a suspect for more than a year. Can this be Kimble? After speaking to Sergeant Ogg, Cooke has a much better understanding of what may have happened on November 8. Just two weeks before Cooke's inquiries, a man by the name of Eric Carty was identified by a traffic cop after the car he was a passenger in was pulled over. Beside Carty was his good friend, Lenford Crawford, who was issued a traffic ticket. The two men were then sent on their way. "That was the first link we had between the two," Cooke says.

The collection by the police of personal information from members of the community who are not suspected of criminal activity is what's called "carding." This police technique is used to gather intelligence on those who might later have run-ins with the police. It is now all but outlawed in Ontario after months of campaigning by those who consider the practice to be a form of racial profiling. In the Pan case, though, the information proves indispensable.

Not long after Cooke and Ogg's chat, Eric's name makes the RCMP's most-wanted list when his picture is released in a Canada-wide warrant in connection with another murder case. Police receive information almost immediately about Eric's whereabouts. He is apparently hiding out in Brampton, a suburban city in the Greater Toronto Area. But when the police show up, he makes a mad dash and escapes. Police are closing in on him, though, and in his hasty departure, Eric leaves his asthma inhaler behind, complete with his full name and prescription information. Three days later, on January 28, police receive a call from an informant who tells them that Eric is in the food court at the local mall — Bramalea City Centre. Subsequently, members of the Peel Police street crime and gang unit make the arrest without incident that same day.

Police eventually discover that one of the twelve phones Eric Carty was using at the time — a collection that included burners and those belonging to various girlfriends — is registered to "Larry Davis," a name with an interesting story attached to it. Larry Davis was a New Yorker who shot six police officers in 1986 after the cops allegedly opened fire despite Davis warning them his children were inside the apartment that was under raid. Police said the purpose of the bust was to question him about the killing of four suspected drug dealers. However, at trial, Davis's defence attorney said the incident was the result of Davis having information about police corruption. After the shooting, there was a massive manhunt, and Davis survived on the run for seventeen days. He later became a folk hero, a symbol of resistance, considering the frustration black communities were facing with regard to their treatment by white police officers in the Bronx in the 1980s.

On February 24, Jennifer writes Daniel a letter from prison warning him about the police investigation. "I really wish I could see you, at least … talk to you. I worry about you in here.… How are you doing. Where you go. If you are being VERY careful. As you know, they are still looking into things."

After discovering Eric's whereabouts, police set up wiretaps on Lenford's and Daniel's phones and assign surveillance teams to Lenford Crawford, David Mylvaganam, and Daniel Wong.

Once the taps are in place, Daniel is summoned to one last interview. Detective Courtice wants to stir some chatter over the wires, and he gets his wish. The night before the interview Daniel and Lenford have a tête-à-tête in Ajax. An unwitting Daniel almost makes a costly blunder during the conversation, but a street-savvy Lenford stops him cold, reminding him the phones aren't safe.

> **L:** *I don't even mind making the mission as long as you say you gonna gas me up.*
> **D:** *Maybe we can just talk about it like, right now, you know what I mean?*
> **L:** *Huh?*
> **D:** *I can just talk to you over the — this phone.*
> **D:** *My phone, yeah. My phone's cool, your phone cool?*
> **L:** *No.*
> **D:** *No, eh?*
> **D:** *All right. I — well, I got 20 bucks. That should be good enough for you, right?*
> **L:** *Yeah. That's as good as a smidge.*
> **L:** *You have any trees?* [Marijuana.]
> **D:** *Ah, I wish, bro. Nothing, man.*

Daniel walks into the Markham police station at 9:30 a.m. on March 23 for what will be a gruelling six-and-a-half-hour interview. It becomes a wide-ranging talk in which he ends up contradicting himself a number of times and does plenty of backpedalling.

During his sit-down with Detective Cooke, he initially says he doesn't know Eric or David. When he's shown pictures of the two men, Daniel, seeming relaxed and chuckling, says David looks like "one of those Tamil guys" and that Eric "looks like Kimbo Slice," a well-known, and now deceased, mixed martial arts fighter. But then he tells Cooke that the pictures on the table are indeed Lenford's friends. "I've seen these guys

March 23, 2011, four months after Jennifer's arrest, Daniel Wong is back for a follow-up interview with police. During questioning, he admits that Jennifer Pan did ask him to kill her parents, but insists that he told her he wanted nothing to do with it.

before," he says. "I'm not sure if I saw them at the mechanic shop some time." But to find out more, Daniel tells Cooke he'll have to ask Lenford, who Daniel refers to as Roy. Daniel eventually comes around and admits during this interview that Jennifer Pan did ask him to kill her parents, but he told her he wanted nothing to do with it. He ventures a guess that she must have gotten Lenford's number from him, adding that maybe he even told her to give him a call.

After the interview is finished at 4:00 p.m., the pair link back up by cell two hours later at 6:02 p.m., with Daniel sharing just how dire the situation has become for them both, especially, he says, for Lenford.

> **D:** *I finished at like, five.*
> **L:** *Whoa, wow, wow, it seems like you — you been there all day?*
> **D:** *They got pictures of like, everyone, eh?*
> **L:** *Wow!*
> **D:** *Yeah, and I think the heat's on you, bro.*

L: *There's no reason to be on — any one of your friends, that's ridiculous though.*

D: *They were showing me how like, the messages and stuff like that.*

L: *What kind of message?*

D: *Like, "Oh, we — I gotta link up with this person."*

L: *...if they wanna know how much weed I, ah — I get rid of ... that's different. But, anything else like, come on like, am I really supposed to like — you know what I mean?*

D: *Don't believe a word they say.*

L: *When they came to my house and my parents already mad at me ...*

L: *They brought up my girlfriend's name which ... they put me in this situation.*

D: *You're gonna be hot bro, that's it.*

D: *I think they might have got something with me and like, stuff like that, but I'm asking you for car parts, right? So, there's nothing wrong ... they even brought up like, that time you messaged me through like, other people's phones, how I gotta meet some o' your brethren's too, make some paper* [money] *and shit like that?*

L: *They're just ... they're just jumping overboard.*

D: *They're even gonna say that the kid said something, you know what I mean?*

D: *They got like, a lot o' records. Like, they got a file on me, man.*

D: *People like callin,' who I talk to and messages, exact text words for word messages, yo.*

D: *Have you ... have you seen a lawyer yet?*

L: *No.*

D: *If it comes down to it and you don't wanna answer just dip* [leave]*...cause, like, it ... it's gonna get ... it's gone be hectic.*

D: *They're like, "I know this." I'm like, "Oh, man, it's just car parts guy," you know what I mean?... Car parts and weed, man, that's it.*

L: *But you know I'm all about modification. You give me something to modify and I'll do it for you.*
D: *You're my guy for like, souping up my ride. That's what I told 'em.*

The chat reveals many insights into Daniel and Lenford's conversation from the night before in Ajax. Daniel repeatedly reminds Lenford to stay on script, speaking to police only about their dealings in marijuana, or "car parts." At one point Daniel mentions the police might even suggest "the kid" said something. He appears to be telling Lenford that the police might try to catch him out by alleging Daniel himself ("the kid") rolled over and ratted him out. When he describes police having "pictures of everyone," he might be talking about the photos of at least seven suspects that were strewn across the table in the interview room, including Eric Carty, David Mylvaganam, and another man, Tim Conte, who comes into the picture later.

EARLIER, BEFORE DANIEL left the interview, Cooke gave him one last pep talk, imploring him to come clean. "Go home, think hard, talk to your family," he told him. "If you're not telling us everything, you hold something back and you want to tell us, you can always call me. You might say, 'Listen, I don't want to ruin the rest of my life getting dragged down by these guys and Jen, Al. I'm sorry, but here's what I didn't tell ya' … I think you need to do some soul-searching."

When the marathon interview ended, Cooke told Daniel that he "could have left anytime."

But Daniel explained that he wanted to make sure there was no doubt about his innocence: "I don't want it to seem like I'm hiding anything."

11
THE NOOSE TIGHTENS

Lenford's interview doesn't go much better than Daniel's when he sits down with Detective Goetz three days later. Police will note some significant inconsistencies in his statements. Although he's always admitted to knowing Eric, Lenford says he doesn't know Mylvaganam. However, police later locate two of David Mylvaganam's phone numbers stored in Lenford's cellphone — one under the heading "Rexfam" (Rexdale Family) and the other under a well-known nickname for David — "Rambo" — which he created as a contact in his phone about a month before on February 11, 2011. This number is for David's new cellphone, registered under the name of another Canadian politician, "Andrew Thompson." David purchased that phone the day after Detective MacDonald texted the "Peter Robinson" phone, asking the owner to call police.

When asked if he knows the name "Rambo," Lenford only admits that he has "heard that name before." Although police try to suggest to Lenford that Daniel threw him "under the bus" by suggesting Jennifer might have gotten Lenford's number from him because he refused to be involved in any scheme himself, Lenford once again refuses to take the bait. "All this is ridiculous to me," he replies. "I'm not involved in this ... I've never pulled a trigger in my life ... I would never do something like that," he protests when presented with the police accusations.

Police also discover that Lenford has Eric Carty's phone numbers in his contact list under "S-fam" and "Bro." Another phone that Eric started using just before the murder is under the name "Gully Team." Lenford's phone is "Gully G," and "Gully GS" is the phone Eric Carty began using after the murder, registered under the name of well-known comedian Mike Epps, who plays Day-Day Jones in the film *Next Friday*. "Gully Side" is registered to someone associated with a woman by the name of Silvia Powell — it remains unknown if this is a reference to her relationship status with Eric (i.e., his "Side Chick"). The term *gully* is described on the Urban Dictionary website as something from the street or gutter that is "rough, rugged, unpolished and hardcore" or a "gangster," used along with terms like *hood* and *street*.

Although Lenford isn't sure about many details during this interview, he is adamant about one thing: he doesn't know anyone by the name of "Ric," bolstering the story Ricardo Duncan told the police and discrediting Jennifer's.

Two days before Lenford's interview, on March 24, police called Demetrius Mables and (in his words) threatened him with arrest if he didn't come in for an interview that day. By this point, police had disproved his alibi, venturing out to the construction site where Mables had said he was working on the night of the murder. When Mables came in for the interview, he told a fantastical story of his actions on November 8 to his new interrogator, Detective Goetz, giving the police what would amount to the metaphorical finger.

"Originally, you said you were sanding floors at some house at nighttime," Goetz said to Mables. "We looked into that. You weren't there. You were [there on] a different night, on a previous week. So right now, you don't have an alibi for that night."

"I know, like, still trying to do my homework on that," Mables replied.

"Which is now more concerning than ever," Goetz said.

"Ya, I know, I understand that. I must have made a walk somewhere.... I didn't go into a vehicle still, you know. That day I didn't see nobody. You know what I think? That day there. I think me and my wife had an argument. And I left. I was on the road walking up Weston [Road]. I was just trying to vent — this is bullshit, the same bullshit, women and all that buck [arguments]. I think I lent somebody my phone then. But to say who I lent it to? I wasn't really paying attention to the person I lent my phone to." He would eventually clarify that the person was a tall white man, presumably much like the Caucasian assailant described by Hann as being in the house. But Mables couldn't hear what he said as he'd had his earphones in. "[I was being] a good Samaritan, not knowin' that being a good Samaritan was going to get me in this crap," he added, getting very animated. "Something like that [the murder] I could never do. There's things I could do and there's things I would not do. Everybody has mothers, fathers. Hell, no, that's a no, no, no. That's evil. That's crazy. That's something I could never do. I don't have the heart to do something like that."

Mables is never charged or prosecuted in this crime.

ON MARCH 28, Detectives Courtice and Cooke get another bright idea and, although it may seem like a long shot, it ends up working. Cooke visits the Central East Correctional Centre (a.k.a. Lindsay Jail), located about an hour and a half east of Toronto, to see Jennifer Pan who is being held in remand, languishing until trial four years after the murder. He brings with him a photo lineup, including a picture of Eric Carty. A belligerent Jennifer doesn't want to be interviewed, but Cooke coaxes her into a room, advising her she can leave any time. She is shown several pictures before Eric's is displayed. When she sees it, Jennifer responds by turning away and requesting that Cooke take the photo from her sight. She says he resembles Number One, but that she can't be 100 percent sure.

IT TAKES POLICE a while, but they eventually manage to get hold of a person by the name of Tim Conte, a Caucasian man and the owner of the first phone the "Peter Robinson" mobile contacted after it was switched back on at 10:46 p.m. while speeding away from the Pan home on November 8. Cell tower records show that when it was contacted, Tim's phone was close to Lenford's work, Kik Custom in Rexdale. Police believe this is the case's second bridge call after Demetrius Mables's phone called Jennifer's earlier that day — the idea being that the conspirators wouldn't want to be seen to be calling one another's phones; therefore, a third party was used to pick up a call from the hit man and to relay the message that the job was done to Lenford face to face.

When Conte speaks to police on March 31, he denies this theory. Instead he tells police that at the time he was in the back of his truck watching a movie on a television he had just purchased. He says he was with his then-mistress after going to his gym, which is near Lenford's workplace. Conte claims that's why his phone was near that particular tower. He later produces a receipt from Best Buy, explaining that he bought the television at 8:02 p.m. Tim is never charged with any crime nor prosecuted in this case.

One of the investigation's most significant interviews occurs two weeks later, on April 12, when police finally get in touch with Denise Brown, the woman who was texting with David Mylvaganam on the night of the murder. She also, it seems, knows "Kimble" and identifies both his and David's pictures for police. Soon after this interview, Denise recounts how she received a call from David. During that conversation, she got the feeling he was trying to discourage her from saying anything to the courts. "[He was saying] like, if I know anything, don't say anything type of vibe," she tells police, adding that he kept denying he was the one who committed the crime. "Nothing happened," he told her. "I don't know what's going on. Are you for me or against me? That's not my phone." David later admits it was, indeed, his phone, something Denise knew all along: the police have reams of their text conversations to prove she did. For Eric Carty, who has been ever so careful in the lead-up to and following the murder to avoid detection, it is this tiny detail — the "Kimble" text from David Mylvaganam to Denise Brown — that sinks him. It will remain one of the only shreds of hard evidence against him.

Data detection also uncovers the following texts from Denise's phone. Weeks before Christmas and a mere month and a half after the murder, David travelled to Montreal for the birthday of one of his children. In a bind for cash, he repeatedly texts the same unknown male seeking money.

> **DM:** *Low on funds.*
> **DM:** *Need some bread.*
> **UM:** *Wat r u doin wit ur doe?*
> **DM:** *Paying bills, taking care of my sons, put money on a car.*

Denise Brown, who later recants many of her initial statements to police, adds that none of David's above protestations about where his money was going are true. And when police discover that the unknown male in this conversation is the same male in the conversation with David when he spoke about Francine — one Eric Carty — it leaves them wondering: *Why is David asking Eric Carty for money? Was he still owed payment for the contract killing of Bich?* It doesn't appear that David ever got his cash.

Two days after speaking with Denise Brown, Detective Courtice gives the order to take David down. As he is already under surveillance, police wait until he is in a confined area — the notorious Jane Finch Mall. David is arrested without incident and charged with first-degree murder, conspiracy to commit, and attempted murder. The following day, police descend on Maplehurst Correctional Complex just west of Toronto, where Eric Carty is being held, and charge him with the same.

"It's the belief of the investigation that … two of these individuals did enter the residence and commit these horrendous crimes," Detective Larry Wilson is quoted as saying in a CBC news story that runs alongside a bail-hearing sketch of Eric sporting a trimmed beard and with his hair in cornrows. "The investigation is continuing, and we are looking for some more individuals involved in this. So I'm not going to get into too much detail. But we do have a connection between all the individuals that we are investigating."

It is Wilson's last comment that most frightens Daniel Wong and Lenford Crawford. These latest arrests, as they often do, spark more conversation over the wires between the two. On April 17 at 1:44 p.m. an unknown male calls Lenford on behalf of Daniel, who is no longer calling Lenford himself.

UM: *Yo, what's good.*
L: *Just here, what are you saying?*
UM: *Everything good?*
L: *Everything is good.*
UM: *Ya? I heard a couple of mans got in trouble down there … the kid told me.*
L: *That's what I'm hearing still but …*
UM: *You're good though eh?*
L: *Ya.*
UM: *Wicked, wicked.*

The "couple of mans" refers to Eric and David; the "trouble," their murder-one charges.

Their fears aren't unfounded; the heat is now so firmly on them, it's searing their ankles. But it isn't just their daily movements and phone calls that police are looking into. After getting the cell tower records for Lenford's and Daniel's phones on April 26, Detective Courtice has his curiosity piqued by the two men's movements in the hours following the press conference announcing Jennifer Pan's arrest. Surveillance teams that have been watching Lenford for weeks, report his movements as routine-oriented — largely involving travel to and from his family home, his girlfriend's place, Tim Hortons coffee shops, and work. However, phone data show that after Jennifer's arrest, Lenford drove east.

A mere six hours after the press conference, just after midnight on November 23, Eric called Lenford. This call sparked action. Records reveal that when Lenford finished his shift at midnight, hours after word of Jennifer's arrest hit the street, he ventured to Mississauga before heading to Daniel's house in Ajax, a city forty-five minutes east of Toronto. When he arrived, around 2:00 a.m., his phone and Daniel's phone were in the same location for about forty minutes. About twelve hours later, phone records show Lenford went back to Ajax at 2:23 p.m. Daniel's phone was using the same tower. Then, just before 11:00 p.m., Lenford's phone was in London, Ontario. Lawyers later wonder openly whether Lenford drove to Ajax after the press conference for an emergency meeting to discuss a "wrinkle" in the plans, namely, Jennifer's arrest: *Would Jennifer give them up? Who was next? Who would pay them now that there would be no insurance money?*

DANIEL WONG IS arrested at work in front of his colleagues at Boston Pizza on April 26, 2011. He is charged with first-degree murder, conspiracy to commit murder, and attempted murder. This call between the same unknown male and Lenford Crawford occurs immediately after Daniel's arrest.

> UM: *Yo.*
> L: *Yo what's going on?*
> UM: *Chillin man chillin. How's everything on your end right now?*

L: *Everything's good, hows everything on your end?*
UM: *Shit, OK so the, you know the kid right? The boys came for him today at work.*
L: *And took him?*
UM: *Yea, they're placing him under the same thing they got her under, conspiracy.*
L: *Wow, that's ridiculous.*
UM: *I don't know how that came into play but I just heard word the boys just came in didn't tell nobody where they were taking him.*
L: *Wow, you gotta be kidding me.*
UM: *But you're clear right?*
L: *Yea, that's just messed up though.*
UM: *Fuck I don't know what's going man, on the real on the real.*

The unknown male in the call soon becomes central to the police investigation after Courtice notices that Lenford also called him two hours after Bich's murder. It is soon discovered that this man also acted as a bridge between Lenford and Daniel. When police eventually call this number, they speak to a man by the name of Jeffrey Fu.

Fu walks into the police station on May 1, 2011. During a five-hour interview with Detective MacDonald, there is plenty of back and forth, but Jeffrey eventually comes clean. He is a close friend of Daniel's from his paintballing days, and a drug associate of both Daniel and Lenford. He says although he can't remember the exact day, at one point (around November 8) he got a call from Lenford saying, "Tell the kid everything's okay." He later relayed that message to "the kid" — Daniel. Neither man ever asked him to relay messages before that night and never after.

It is at this point police know that anything more out of Jeffrey's mouth can implicate him in a first-degree murder investigation. Before that can occur, police have to caution him as a suspect. Detective Courtice calls the Crown immediately, wondering whether a caution is necessary. "No," is the response, "we'll use him as a witness." And so, just as with Andrew and Ric, Crown attorneys decide Jeffrey will be just right to strengthen their case against Daniel and Lenford.

When Jeffrey is finally told the messages he was passing back and forth between the men is in relation to the murder of Bich Pan — the mother of his good friend Daniel's ex-girlfriend that's all over the news — his face loses all expression and goes "completely white," one investigator later says. The story Jeffrey tells police matches Lenford's phone records. Jeffrey admits to police that at some point after the murder, some men came to Ajax to collect a debt from Daniel that was still owed by Jennifer Pan. Daniel told Jeffrey at the time that one of the men had a gun and had threatened him. Jeffrey says he was paid a visit by Lenford soon after Daniel was threatened, at which point Daniel asked him to front Lenford some weed in order to take care of "Roy's Boys."

Investigators later discover that one of Eric's phones was also in Ajax on November 23, and that he had a girlfriend in London. When Daniel's and Eric's phones are cross-referenced, police find evidence that the pair were working together in the drug trade at certain points, but might not have always gotten along. Months prior to the murder, in July 2010, Eric scolds Daniel in a series of texts for not delivering the product fast enough: *I fucking told you that if he don't have it, I'm not going*, he texted. *You're slowing me down and never ready when I am*, read the next one. Eric finishes the string of communications by expressing his displeasure with the price and quality of the marijuana: *I'm not paying sixteen no more and make sure it's good.*

Prosecutors later surmise that the man with the gun doing the threatening — one of Roy's Boys — is likely Eric demanding money for the hit, considering Jennifer was arrested and was in no position to pony up. When Lenford drove to London, prosecutors later charge, he was likely delivering the fronted weed to Eric, who was resting with his girlfriend.

Lenford is arrested on May 4 as he smokes a joint in his girlfriend's Brampton driveway. He is charged with first-degree murder and attempted murder. Although police end the final press release with the phrase "Police expect to make more arrests," no further charges are laid in the case.

NOW THAT THE arrests have been made and charges laid, the Crown and police have to start building their case against the accused. This process will involve countless hours of work in the months leading up to the

Detective Bill Courtice (seated), Police Constable Bernadette Cwenar, and another officer discuss the case.

trial, which won't begin until 2013. Although there is plenty of talk about the potential to charge others in the crime or even to present the evidence against them in court (much of which surrounds one man in particular), prosecutors decide against it. This will mean that at least one man in the house that night, possibly the triggerman, remains unidentified in this case. Nonetheless, one veteran criminal lawyer involved in the case later says the detectives produced by far the most sophisticated telephone analysis evidence he's ever witnessed, scanning more than a million pieces of mobile phone data. He further questions whether other police forces might have finalized their investigation after charging Jennifer and Daniel and not worked so diligently to identify "the other players."

PART TWO
THE TRIAL

12

ALL EYES ON NEWMARKET

By the time the trial begins, two Crown attorneys, Jennifer Halajian and Michelle Rumble, have worked on the Jennifer Pan case off and on for three gruelling years. Poring over the raw telephone transcripts and data from 640,000 bits of phone communications to try to string together a narrative that spans more than a year — from around June 2010, when the Crown claimed Jennifer started plotting, until May 4, 2011, when the last of the five men, Lenford Crawford, was arrested by police.

Just one peek at the compiled phone records, including reams of digits populating endless spreadsheets, is a daunting venture, let alone studying raw records in order to engineer a successful murder case. Using the legitimate cellphones and burner phones of the accused men, along with their girlfriends' cellphones, the Crown attorneys string together a storyline from beginning to end, often from minute to minute. But it isn't just cellphones that lawyers are forced to study; there are also hundreds of hours of videotaped police interviews and wiretaps that require analysis.

Although the attorneys and police are burdened with so many anonymous phone and text messages, luck is certainly on their side at times. The police, more specifically York police cellular phone forensic expert Detective Bruce Downey, pulls off a significant feat by capturing hundreds of explicit texts that were sent or received on Jennifer's iPhone in the days leading up to the murder. It remains an open question whether the alleged mastermind, Jennifer Pan, figured that by disposing of her SIM card the messages would be lost forever. The texts become some of the most pivotal pieces of evidence in the trial, especially with respect to Jennifer, Daniel, and Lenford. Had Jennifer deleted those texts, they would have been gone forever. For example, one message from Jennifer to Daniel says: *Call it off with Homeboy.* To which Daniel responds: *You said you wanted this.*

The iPhone, which the Crown refers to as the "secret murder phone," contains the trial's most damning phone numbers, many of which aren't found on Jennifer's Rogers phone — those belonging to David Mylvaganam, Daniel Wong, Lenford Crawford, Demetrius Mables, and Andrew Montemayor (Andrew also spoke with Jennifer on the Rogers phone, but not with the same damning context). Cell towers garner other vital bits of data, especially in relation to the movements of David. The information also lands Eric Carty in trouble, irrespective of his knowledge of cellphones and how they are used during investigations, and despite the fact that he stopped using his phone hours before the murder, instead using devices owned by his girlfriends and by David.

This evidence proves pivotal in the Crown's case against the five suspects on trial.

THE NEWMARKET COURTHOUSE, located forty-five minutes north of Toronto, is selected as the site for the trial, despite some obvious drawbacks — the antiquated audio/video technology and poor acoustics will cause major delays in the proceedings and are often the subject of scorn by the sitting judge, Justice Cary Boswell. The trial is expected to last five months.

But before it begins, some 2,100 potential jurors have to be interviewed. Most claim they can't sit on a trial for the length of time it is projected to take, while others are too well acquainted with the facts of the case to be considered. With six lawyers involved, many of those interviewed are challenged and/or excused, and the process takes weeks. Paul Cooper, Jennifer's lawyer, requests that the court raise the amount of money paid out to ensure a more diverse group of people are able to sit on the jury, especially because none of the defendants in the case are white. Currently, rules state that jurors aren't paid if they sit for fewer than ten days. From days eleven to forty-nine, they receive $40 a day, and from day fifty onward they receive $100 per day. With Ontario's minimum wage set at about $11 an hour at the time, many potential jurors would earn more money at an entry-level job. Cooper fails in his attempt to raise the payout, and in the end only two jurors are from visible minority groups.

On the first day of the trial, there is a distinct buzz among the reporters. It has been three-and-a-half years since the murder of Jennifer's mother and the attempted murder of her father, and the media has been anticipating the day when this case finally comes to trial. It doesn't take long for the public — accustomed to waiting years for fascinating cases to reach the courts — to become re-immersed in the drama that is about to unfold.

The Newmarket Courthouse, though quite a large building, gives off the distinct feel of a small-town court, so when trial day arrives, the police at the front door running everyone through metal detectors and checking bags, knowingly converse with reporters about the case, understanding exactly why the court is such a popular destination that particular morning. It remains that way for the next three hundred days.

But it isn't just mainstream media outlets that are interested in the trial; there are more than a handful of reporters from the local Chinese, Filipino, and Vietnamese publications and television stations who show up each day. Not to mention interested members of the public who faithfully attend, including one young woman who appears to have a crush on at least one of the defendants. The court gallery also contains staff from the big dailies, local reporters, and even the odd courtroom sketch artist. Something else that is rarely seen, especially this far north of Toronto, is a pair of American reporters from a couple of the largest networks in the United States, who have made the trip up from New York City to sit in on the proceedings. Unlike the United States, under Canadian law, cameras and videos are forbidden inside the court's precinct, meaning the only images coming out of the courtroom are the odd sketch portrait of Jennifer or Hann, and the only time the lawyers will speak on camera is during the post-trial press conference outside the front doors of the building.

As a reporter, you know it's a big criminal trial when two particular journalists make an appearance: the *Toronto Star*'s Rosie DiManno and the *National Post*'s Christie Blatchford. Both women write in a unique style at odds with standard court reporters, injecting flowery adjectives and cutting opinions about the proceedings and testimony into their articles — something "ordinary journalists" are forbidden from doing. "All this horror — a mother shot in the head, her final words a plea that her daughter be spared; a father shot through the eye who miraculously survived his grievous wounds — for the obsessive love of a man who did not love her back," writes DiManno in one day's copy. "What was Jennifer Pan envisioning? That maybe murder wound bind them together forever, be their troth of romantic reconciliation? In their wake lies ruin … After emerging from a coma, it was his hospital bed account to police of that violent night at the family's Markham home that turned the tide of the investigation, transforming his daughter from a deeply pitied survivor — how tearfully she'd mourned at her mother's funeral, ravaged face captured by media cameras — to unimaginably wicked murderer."

It isn't just the gallery that is packed; beyond the bar is also crowded, with eight lawyers in all, including three for the Crown, who are accompanied by Assistant Crown Attorney Rob Scott and a number of interns and assistants, all of whom spend countless hours working diligently on their clients' files. The defence team includes Paul Cooper (representing Jennifer Pan), Edward Sapiano (Eric Carty), Peter Bawden (David Mylvaganam), Darren Sederoff (Lenford Crawford), and Laurence Cohen (Daniel Wong).

After the lawyers take their seats, the ragtag bunch of inmates shuffles into the courtroom — hands cuffed in the front, ankles shackled — and is led to the five-seat prisoner box located at the back just in front of the bar, which sections off the proceedings from the audience. Each seat in the box is separated by a wood-and-glass divider. At the beginning of the trial the lawyers ask for the defendants' ankle and wrist shackles to be removed prior to the jury entering so as to avoid the negative bias this might evoke.

Justice Boswell, a soft-spoken, innately patient and relaxed-looking man with a certain "average guy" appeal, takes his seat at the head of the court, where he will be flanked by the twelve jurors who will enter on his direction — four men and eight women — as the trial of the year finally gets under way.

Tall and lanky Lenford Crawford sits on the end, shoulders hunched, and as always, appearing calm. Next to him is a bespectacled Daniel Wong, hair cut short and still with a visible paunch. Eric Carty is next, now heavier-set than he appeared in his teenage mug shot. He has shed his cornrows and beard and his face is lightly stubbled, his head shaved. Next to him is David Mylvaganam, who has tamed the wild mane of hair he had in

(Top row) David Mylvaganam. Eric Carty.
(Bottom row) Lenford Crawford. Daniel Wong.

the first picture released to the media. His flowing locks are now contained in a ponytail at the back of his head. And finally, Jennifer Pan. She is now twenty-seven and looks much older than the childlike young woman who spoke with investigators during those initial days following the murder. Her rounded features have faded and her bone structure has become more visible. She is as tall and slender as ever, and her hair is longer (she keeps it in braids or neatly positioned ponytails throughout the trial). Unlike the others, who seem relaxed and casually chat to one another and smile, the prospects that lie before her appear to weigh heavily on Jennifer's mind.

The accused, other than those who have family members in the room, disregard the packed courtroom. Although this will change as the trial wears on, they seem blithely unaware of the severity of the situation, blind to the strength of the Crown's case. Presumably, they are optimistic about their chances for acquittal.

Daniel's mother, father, and brother are there that first day, Lenford's parents attend on occasion, but the fact that they have full-time jobs understandably limits their availability. The only people to show up for Jennifer, much later in the trial, are a few former colleagues from East Side Mario's, frankly still amazed that the quiet Jennifer can be involved in such a monstrous plot.

When the case finally begins, it does so in dramatic fashion. The crackle of the speakers signifies the start of the proceedings, the Crown having chosen to open with the audiotape of Jennifer's panicked 911 call. The courtroom grows perfectly still, everyone straining to hear as the importance of what they are listening to quickly dawns on them simultaneously. Suddenly, Hann's horrific groaning projects from the speakers. "I don't know what's happening. I'm tied upstairs. I think my dad went outside. He's screaming," comes a harried-sounding female voice. "My hands are tied, but I had my cellphone in my pocket. Please, can you hurry up! I can hear my father screaming. I don't know what's going on. He made an *ahhhhh* sound and he ran outside. Can you stay with me?" The young woman then starts to weep.

"Take a deep breath, okay?" comes the soothing voice of the operator. "We have lots of help on the way."

"I'm wiggling loose, but I'm scared to go anywhere.... They didn't hurt me. They had a gun to my back, but they took my parents downstairs and I heard pops. All they said was: 'You are not co-operating.'"

"Did they sound like gunshots?" the operator asks.

"I don't know," Jennifer replies. "I just heard pops."

The recording ends with an ominous introduction to the woman who will take centre stage for the next ten months in the lives of many present in the courtroom that morning.

"What's your name?" the operator asks.

"My name is Jennifer."

13

STRANGER THAN FICTION

For many in the courtroom, the 911 recording evokes a lot of emotion. Later, one witness tells me there were plenty of tears after the playing of the "soul-gripping" tape. "We weren't expecting it to start when it did. It was very emotional, so some people, they weren't mentally prepared. It was a great opening from the Crown's perspective, but some people had issues [with it]. It hit them really hard. There were tears and shock, hearing [Hann] screaming in the background. That affected people quite profoundly."

The Crown then proceeds in earnest: "On Monday, November 8, 2010, just after ten o'clock at night," begins Assistant Crown Attorney Jennifer Halajian, her raspy voice projecting confidently throughout the room, "Three men entered the Pan home in Unionville, a quiet neighbourhood in Markham. They were in the house for less than twenty minutes. Bich and Hann Pan were left for dead. Bich Pan died. Hann Pan miraculously did not. I am going to talk to you this morning about our theory of what happened that night, and why. Yes, this case is about murder, the planned and deliberate murder of an innocent middle-aged woman and the attempted murder of her husband in their own home on a quiet Monday night in a quiet neighbourhood. Murder that was arranged and paid for by their daughter, Jennifer Pan, that woman there [pointing at Jennifer], the woman [you heard] on the 911 call.

"But this case is also about love — love that a girl has for a boy, an obsessive, relentless love, and what she will do to keep him. Love that a father has for his daughter, and what he will do to protect her. Love that a mother has for her child, and what she will do to keep her safe. Love that led to what happened in the basement of an ordinary middle-class house."

With those simple words, what will be for some one of the most sensational trials in recent Canadian history, kicks off.

"In order to understand what happened on November 8, 2010, you have to understand the history, what happened before that, the chronology of what led to that night," Halajian continues. "Think of it like a map. Jennifer Pan's father, Hann Pan, will testify using a Vietnamese interpreter. He'll describe for you what he knew about their [Jennifer and Daniel's] relationship and how he discovered it. He will tell you about the ultimatum he gave Jennifer Pan to either choose the family or Daniel Wong, and why he gave it. You'll hear what steps he took to keep his daughter from Daniel Wong to protect her, imposing a strict curfew, wanting to know where she was if she left the house. He'll tell you why he was so opposed to the relationship, and he will tell you that in the spring of 2010, Jennifer Pan's lies started to unravel, lies that Hann Pan blamed on Daniel Wong. And so Hann Pan told his daughter that she will never be with Daniel Wong so long as he and his wife were alive. Jennifer Pan told police that this made her feel trapped. She deeply, bitterly resented it. It made her feel like a part of herself was dead."

The Crown's version of events becomes clear to everyone. This is a story of resentment, love, betrayal, money and, of course, a daughter's deadly deception. When the opening day comes to a close, photographers still have no photos to use for the next morning's front page, since all the accused are in custody and are shuttled in and out of the courthouse under high security and in blacked-out cube vans. Unfortunately, the only option is to hassle Daniel's family as they exits the courtroom, forcing Darwin, Daniel's father, to throw his coat over his head, his mother to hide her face under her hood, and his brother to grimace at the unwanted attention. This is the last day that Daniel's beloved mother, Evelyn, and one of his best friend, his brother, Richard, will attend, presumably because of the harassment. Darwin Wong, though, remains, attending each and every day until the bitter end, quietly taking in every last word said against and in defence of his son.

JENNIFER ARRIVES IN court each day appearing neat and clean despite her somewhat tired-looking wardrobe — she presumably has little or no access to new clothes, let alone any relatives who are willing to do her any favours. She walks gracefully into the courtroom each morning, posture as straight as an arrow, and sits down slowly. It is the way one might enter a room if wearing a gown, or as though an invisible, well-dressed man stands behind her, ready to push in her chair. Those mannerisms seem utterly incongruous with her shackled limbs. After her cuffs are removed, she rubs her tiny wrists.

By the end of the trial, she appears to be on quite friendly terms with some of the guards, often exchanging small talk, Jennifer smiling, always pleasant and courteous. This behaviour bothers some people, but others perhaps respect the guards for treating the prisoners with a modicum of human decency.

Each morning, from the comfortable wood-lined courtroom, the faint sound of slamming iron bars signals the impending arrival of the prisoners. A glimpse of the yellow institutional-style cinder-block walls can be seen in the brief moments when the guards open the door to usher them in. When Justice Boswell's presence is announced, all rise. Jennifer takes it a step further, shooting up, alert like a soldier at arms upon his arrival and exodus, each time performing a deep and respectful bow from the waist.

As the trial progresses, it becomes clear to the media just how few details about this girl's life have made their way into the public realm before the trial. In other high-profile cases, information tends to leak out — photos and details about the suspect's background might find their way into newspapers either through the victim's or suspect's families, or those with sources inside the police force. But not in this case. At the beginning of the trial, the public has seen only two indistinct pictures of Jennifer: one with her head bowed, the other a blurry image with her face partially obscured by a winter coat. Other than the names of the grade school and high school she attended, and the fact that she lived at home with few "marketable skills," there has been little to report.

To this day there are only a handful of pictures, and few of the people close to Jennifer or the others involved have spoken to the media. Jennifer herself, along with the other accused, repeatedly turns down the opportunity to be interviewed. The members of Jennifer's family — most notably

Hann and her brother Felix — and many other friends and relatives, similarly decline the chance to tell their sides of the story or to refute Jennifer's statements, likely just wanting to put the trial behind them.

As the Crown begins to reveal the shocking details about Jennifer's lies, deceit, and wild imagination, it becomes clear that this mastermind's alleged plot, organized with her boyfriend and his buddies, is only a fraction of the story. Behind this lies a shocking, bitingly ironic, and sometimes downright macabre story, one that truly is stranger than any Hollywood fiction.

In its opening, the Crown lays bare the task before it: five people stand charged with first-degree murder and attempted murder, but one key detail is missing — there is no forensic evidence (often seen as an essential element in any police investigation). No DNA was found at the house; there are no recovered weapons and no bloody clothes. There is one witness, but he was shot in the head. And neither the lawyers nor the police have any true image of who actually pulled the trigger. Despite these shortcomings, the Crown forges ahead, hoping its organizational skills, cellphone evidence, and a meticulously devised plot line will be enough to land multiple convictions. As such, the Crown goes in with the theory that it doesn't really matter who pulled the trigger — just planning the murders in tandem is enough to lock them all away for life.

"I told you that three men entered the Pan home that night," Halajian states tenaciously. "We know we don't have all three of them here together today, but that doesn't matter ... and for the rest of this trial we will focus on these five only, and we will prove that each one of these people — Jennifer, Daniel, Lenford, Eric, and David — knowingly participated. That doesn't mean they all pulled the trigger. They didn't. But everyone here had a role. All of them took part in the planning. All of them participated. At least two of them — Jennifer and David — were inside the house when Hann and Bich Pan were shot. David had a gun. Eric Carty was at the house, but whether he was inside or not, we can't say for sure. We know Daniel and Lenford were not there that night, but that doesn't matter. They were all instrumental in putting the plan into motion and they helped Jennifer carry it out, knowing full well what they were doing."

14

A FATHER BETRAYED

When it is finally time to call the Crown's star witness, the courtroom becomes silent. This is the one person everyone has been waiting to see. Hann Pan quietly walks into the courtroom, guided by a court-appointed victim services member. All eyes are squarely focused on him: the man who survived the savage attack, only to believe that it is his own daughter who betrayed him — allegedly responsible for the death of his wife and the destruction of his family. It is this treachery that becomes central to the trial, resulting in lawyers dubbing the murder the "ultimate betrayal," the cardinal "sin," an act so awful it is a direct repudiation of one of the founding tenants of modern Western civilization — "honour thy father and thy mother."

For the innately private Hann, it is not only the drama in the courtroom, which is packed with reporters, but the speculation and intense public interest in him and his family's life that remains so foreign to him. His discomfort during those first few moments as he ventures to the stand to face the destiny he believes his daughter chose for him is palpable. In the days that follow, he wears an open-collared black shirt and black ill-fitting dress pants that hang tenuously on his small hips. The small, bespectacled man — shorter than his eldest daughter by at least an inch, maybe two — lowers his gaze and excuses himself as he passes in front of the benches full of people, many wondering what is going through his mind at that very moment. Perhaps in response to all the prying eyes, some full of pity, others judgment, Hann raises his head and meets their gaze. Those in attendance, many expecting a man racked with pain from his injuries, don't see him wince even once in discomfort. Rather, most are thrown off by his unscarred face and healthy appearance. He seems physically unhindered by the two bullets that left him in a coma for several days. Hann, who is sixty years old at the start of the trial, doesn't have one grey hair on his head, his bangs covering much of his forehead. Although his face is unblemished, he later admits that his mind, heart, body, and soul remain anguished from the attack and the emotional scars he suffered after his family was torn apart.

But his composure in the courtroom betrays little of this. When Hann finally takes the stand, he does so with his head held high. His steely gaze only momentarily meets that of his daughter, who breaks into tears occasionally when the details of that night are discussed.

Hann shows an utter lack of outward emotion during what one can only assume are some of the most emotionally taxing moments of his life. The only noticeable sign of grief is perhaps his constant blinking, which grows pronounced during the particularly tough testimony. At his side on the stand is a Vietnamese interpreter — this despite the fact that he conducted many of his police interviews without the assistance of one. The use of the interpreter causes some confusion at times: Hann understands much of what is asked of him and often answers in broken English; other times he waits and uses the interpreter's services. Eventually, Justice Boswell advises him to answer only in Vietnamese.

Testimony through an interpreter is bad news for any reporter. By their very nature, translators tend to drain all the implied meaning from the speaker's voice, obliterating a person's individuality, tone, and choice of vocabulary. Instead of emotionally heightened testimony full of disdain, shame, anger, and pride, translators sap all of the substance from an individual's words, making even the most fascinating testimony seem almost mundane. There's no reading between the lines with interpreters.

Hann's answers are short and to the point. Despite the fervour that courses through the spectators in the courtroom, his words deliver a sort of resigned reality, the details of which he has grappled with for years since his wife was killed.

Hann recounts how, just months before the murder, he all but fulfilled his life's work. He and his wife, who immigrated to Canada decades before, finally paid off their $600,000 home and accrued a substantial amount of money in the bank, coming a long way since buying their first home in Scarborough. In what becomes a central detail in the trial, he explains how he and his wife took out $170,000 life insurance policies on their lives. Should they die, the money and their estate would be split fifty/fifty between their children, Jennifer and Felix. That would not only include their home, but the cars and other valuables — in total, about $500,000 each. He explains that when the policies were taken out, he and his wife sat down with their children and detailed how the money would be divvied up. A policy was also taken out on Jennifer, with Felix as the beneficiary.

Crown attorney Michelle Rumble quickly moves Hann on to Jennifer's educational career. He describes how, although he never attended his daughter's high school or university graduations, she spent a significant amount of time describing to him how her education was playing out. "She told the family she was admitted to Ryerson [University], and a few months after that she left the home and came back in the evening," he says. "My wife said if she kept on like that it would be hard for her, so Jennifer said she shared a room with a friend in downtown Toronto. My daughter said that to become a pharmacist, she needed to be admitted to [the University of Toronto] and she told me she was admitted. So many times I wanted to ask about my daughter's studying, but my wife said, 'Don't interfere.'" Hann then recounts how he once drove his daughter to her best friend Topaz's apartment where she claimed to have been staying for years. "It was very dark and there was no parking spot, so she showed me the house [where they lived] on the third floor," he says, noting he didn't see where his daughter went after she exited the car. "There was no parking spot, so I had to leave."

The implication is clear. Jennifer never went in; instead, she travelled to Daniel's home in Ajax.

Hann says that, just prior to Jennifer being caught in her lies, she would stay home Thursday and Friday nights before leaving again on Saturday afternoon for what she told him was volunteer work experience helping ill children, and how his wife would transfer money into her account when she needed it. Hann felt the wool was being pulled over his eyes with regard to Jennifer's life outside his home for years. But he remained mum about his suspicions until one day when he had enough. "I was frustrated and concerned something was not right," he tells the court before explaining how he felt after he found out she deceived him. "Because our efforts had been focused on her attending school, and she did not, and [she] lived with another person. My wife cried…. I told [Jennifer] to sever that relationship and return to school. She accepted and said she would return to school."

Some of her movements were curtailed at this point. However, before long, Jennifer was caught in further lies and Hann exploded with rage, drawing a red line at the front door of his home. "I said from now on you have no right to use the car and [you must] stay home," he says. "There was no trust in me and I wanted my daughter to go back to school. I wanted her to have a certain level of education and a future. There are two options," he told her. "You stay home and go to school. The second choice is you go with Daniel and never come back."

Jennifer made her decision and was finally accepted into Scarborough's Centennial College where she was to start attending classes in January 2011. About eighteen months after the argument, Hann says, he believed the challenges had ended. He believed the relationship with Daniel was over. "At that moment I saw that my family was very happy," he later tells the court. Oh, how blind he was.

Jennifer Pan in happier times.

From the very beginning, the proceedings don't look very promising for Jennifer's case and, as time goes by, they only get worse. The Crown consists of a pair of acutely prepared and clinical attorneys. Assistant Crown attorneys Michelle Rumble and Jennifer Halajian have constructed a sturdy case, erecting it like a wall, brick by brick, over the first few months of the trial. To ensure its impenetrability, they rarely deviate from the script they've worked so long to develop. Halajian, the brusquer of the two, seems more comfortable asking technical questions of cellphone experts, unconcerned with endearing herself to the jury. Her laser-sharp focus, especially when it comes to the massive data dumps, proves useful in compiling the information, but also in questioning those providing technical testimony. She means business, rarely relinquishing her determination to succeed, whether in the courtroom or in the hallway afterward. Rumble is the gentler of the two, with a softer, though equally scientific and determined touch. As such, it is Halajian who commandeers the dramatic opening; it is Rumble who tries to ingratiate the jury to the Crown's side, casting few aspersions during her three-day closing, setting herself apart from the rest of the male-dominated courtroom.

The only deviation from their premeditated style comes during cross-examination when Rob Scott takes the reins. Although he does little of the heavy lifting beforehand, it is he who Rumble and Halajian trust to manipulate the cross, meaning neither will have to deal with the negativity of brash confrontation or the improvisational attacks a cross-examinations can so often descend into. It is Scott who is quick on his toes, relishing his saucy role of the snide courtroom accuser who gets to face down Jennifer. But before Jennifer can even make it up to the stand, each witness heaps the weight of ever more evidence on her and the other defendants. The presumption (or interpretation) that quickly develops becomes crystal clear to the jury — Jennifer is not to be trusted, perhaps the central tenet for any accused hoping to avoid a conviction.

This is bad news for her co-accused. In this trial the fates of Daniel, David, Eric, and Lenford are inextricably linked to Jennifer's. Sure, Peter Bawden, and by extension David Mylvaganam, will later try to fight the impending tidal wave of negative sentiment against Jennifer, but it is of little use — it becomes clear: as goes Jennifer, so will go the others.

The only aspect of Hann's Crown testimony that might work in Jennifer's favour is how much time Jennifer had on her hands in the lead-up to the murder. After all, this young woman spent the seven months prior to the home invasion largely shut behind closed doors — hearkening back to Slade's questioning of Jennifer during her second interview: "What did you do all day?"

Hann responds to questions about the isolation Jennifer might have been feeling and the apparent lack of interest he showed in his daughter during that time: "I was working, so I did not know much, but I always reminded her to do the review of all her lessons to prepare for school," he says, explaining that during this time she was expected to go over her school notes, of which, of course, there were none, and practise piano in anticipation of some upcoming tests.

But truthfully, any sympathy garnered by these revelations only goes so far: isolation, after all, is no excuse for murder. Jennifer's lawyer, Paul Cooper, also spends time going over Jennifer's strict upbringing and "scheduled" lifestyle growing up. Later, when one person in the courtroom that day is asked how the testimony about Jennifer's rigid upbringing affected him, he says that it was nothing he didn't face as a boy. "It's no more strict than anything I was raised with," he says. He is not alone in this sentiment. Numerous female journalists of Asian and South Asian background leave the courtroom audibly singing from the same songbook, remarking how much stricter their upbringings were. "That's nothing! My dad used to ..." is heard more than once.

Always referring to Jennifer as "my daughter" and rarely, if ever, by her name, Hann does say that prior to the murder, he requested that Bich bring Jennifer "closer" to the family to help her forget about her past. "She started to think about the future again," he tells the court "I told my wife during this time ... there's time to take her out so that mother and daughter would have time to spend together which would help ... her sadness subside, bring the family back to Jennifer and Jennifer back to the family. That was my hope. When there were mistakes ... made, I showed my frustration, but she's my daughter ... Because with your daughter you always forgive and forget." Like other fathers who have tried to keep their daughters away from "bad apples," Hann likely figured that, once Jennifer immersed herself back in education, surrounded by young people striving for success, regained some of her self-confidence, and began looking forward to a new and exciting career, she would get over Daniel and be able to move on with her life.

As part of Hann's plan, in mid-October 2010, the family ventured off on a road trip together to Boston to attend a wedding. The following weekend Jennifer went to Ottawa and Montreal with her mother and an aunt.

Despite Hann's assurances, though, Jennifer's defence will reveal the significant resentment she felt toward her father during this time. Simultaneously, her defence will likely obscure her true feelings toward her mother, suggesting that she only planned to kill her father, making all interactions with Bich positive ones.

When the questioning turns to the behaviour of his daughter on the night of the home invasion, Hann says he saw his daughter speaking with one of the intruders "like a friend, softly."

Jennifer's lawyer, Paul Cooper, eventually stands up in preparation for one of the most difficult cross-examinations of his life. In any cross, a lawyer has two main goals: to elicit favourable testimony, and to impeach a witness's credibility. Any lawyer who aggressively pursues the latter with a witness like Hann would be a fool. One must always be aware of a phenomenon police call "victim blaming," which, in this case, would likely alienate most, if not all of the jurors. Cooper is left with only one option: to gain favourable facts by gently nudging Hann into admitting that a number of uncontrollable factors left not only his judgment and memory, but also his eyesight severely impaired on the night in question. To do this, Cooper has to walk a tightrope, attempting to throw a number of Hann's assertions into doubt without appearing to pressure, badger, or speak to him in a condescending manner. After all, from the entire courtroom's perspective, Hann is the ultimate sympathetic character — a widower through no fault of his own and a victim of the most cold-blooded alleged murder plot any juror can fathom. Furthermore, his age and difficulty with the English language make him appear all the more vulnerable to the lawyer's questions.

Cooper speaks in a respectful tone and spends considerable time gaining trust and showing sympathy while simultaneously attempting to create the narrative that Hann's testimony can't be relied on. This proves to be a monumental task. In a soft and calming voice, Cooper seeks to demonstrate that the murder was the result of a robbery gone wrong. "You came as a political refugee from Vietnam, immigrated to Canada, you are Canadian," Cooper says. "Like other Canadians who come and create our fabric from all over the world, you come with dreams. We talked about freedom, but you also had a dream about your family: that they would do better than you. They will never have to risk going through what you and your wife went through when you came to Canada."

After responding "correct" to each assertion made by Cooper, Hann finally speaks: "I hoped that the future of the following generation would be better than mine."

"Would you agree with me that this is sometimes called the 'immigrant's dream'?" Cooper asks. "You and your wife had worked hard. You and your wife worked in different jobs to get to the career you both had in order to own your own home. You and your wife were working hard to provide opportunities to fulfill the dream you had for both your son and daughter. You had hoped your daughter was pursuing the hopes and dreams you had for her."

Hann's response is tinged with disdain: "That's correct, and I also hoped that my daughter was a good person."

When Cooper comes to the discovery of the lies and the eventual ultimatum, with Hann pronouncing those fateful words, Hann says: "Any father put in that situation would have been very upset. It was in my anger that I made that statement. But it does not mean that I would not have cared about my children. I wanted solely for my daughter … to have a successful future. My daughter always maintained that she wanted to be a pharmacist."

Hann then explains the ominous moment when he delivered the statement that will mark the dividing line between what the Crown will allege are two Jennifers — the deceptive one and the murderous one: "When I die, you can do whatever you want."

"Human nature at a time when a person is angry, it's not easy to control the anger," Hann further explains. "Yes, in my anger I did state that. I was very upset, because all of our efforts had been focused on her and given to her to attend school, and she did not, and she lived with another person. I told her to sever that relationship and return to school. I told Jennifer that she had to cease the relationship with Daniel Wong."

When the conversation returns to the night in question, Cooper is able to establish doubt concerning Hann's version of events, but to what avail is unclear. He spends a considerable amount of time trying to discredit Hann's statements about Jennifer and her captor speaking in a "friendly" manner. He continually suggests that Hann didn't have ample time or viewpoint, especially without his glasses, to make this observation.

His eyesight was too poor, the glimpse too brief. He suggests there wasn't sufficient light for nearsighted Hann to see Jennifer, who he proposes was too far away from him. Furthermore, the event was traumatic, and given the time span in between the event and the trial, it was hard to remember.

Hann accepts some points and rejects others. During this line of questioning, Cooper scores some significant points. He catches Hann out on the description of what Jennifer was wearing that night, which he told police was white pajamas with blue flowers as opposed to the black yoga pants she was actually wearing. Cooper suggests the men might have entered the home through the garage, sneaking in after Bich came home, with Hann admitting the door to the house from the garage was never locked. Otherwise, the thieves, Cooper contends, could have climbed up the back of the house and entered into the home via windows on the second floor, another assertion Hann says was technically possible. He also admits that the last thing he heard before the ambulance sped off were Jennifer's tearful cries asking if he was okay.

Cooper plays an audio recording of Hann telling police that his daughter was "being held hostage" alongside him and his wife. In the recording, Hann also admits Jennifer appeared "sad" on the night of the murder and that one of the assailants was trying to calm her. Hann acknowledges that all this is true, but referring back to what he told police about Jennifer's demeanour on that night, he tells Cooper: "My daughter, I love her. How can I say bad things about her?"

However, one thing Cooper can't seem to escape is that if this was indeed a robbery gone horribly wrong, why was so little money — let alone anything else, including the two high-end cars — actually missing from the house? Hann testifies that when police finally forced him to go back home after six months of avoiding the residence at all costs, he found only three things missing: two rings from his original workplace, Magna, to commemorate fifteen and twenty years at the company, and a camera worth $100.

Cooper does his best to defend his client without upsetting the jurors; however, with six lawyers questioning Hann, more than one juror later expresses displeasure: "I felt bad for him and the situation he was in. They seemed to be twisting what he had said just days after he was shot in the head. But that's their job: to get the jury to see it their way."

15

A BROTHER'S AGONY

While Hann's story is clearly the most heartbreaking, Felix Pan's journey might be the most harrowing. Up to this point, his twenty-four years can largely be split into two parts — his life prior to the murder, as part of a loving and largely normal family, with a mother, father, and sister, all of whom he cared for deeply; and then his life after the murder, the day he lost his emotional rock, his mother, and his only sibling, Jennifer. His relationship with his father would never be the same either after that day.

After coming home to be with his critically injured father and to bury his mother and grandfather, Felix would have viewed his sister as a victim, showing tenderness, comforting her, and mourning alongside her. So many words of sadness would have been uttered between the two, emotions intertwined. But as the days and weeks went by, he watched as she progressed from victim to suspect and finally, accused murderer, at which point she was removed from his life forever. The next time he sees her, she is sitting in the prisoner's box in the Newmarket courtroom years later.

The tall, bookish young man appears awkward as he walks into the courtroom, much thinner than he was during his early university days. Throughout the Crown's questioning he maintains his meek and mild demeanour. Like his sister, he seems childlike yet mature beyond his years. He is reserved and well mannered. Whereas his father did his utmost not to appear weak, Felix appears openly vulnerable, wearing the weight of this traumatic event on his sleeve. His nervousness shines through, and he often peppers his testimony with *likes* and *ums* as he attempts to gather his thoughts. When he becomes emotional or frazzled — as questioning turns to his life's more sensitive moments surrounding his mother, father, and sister — his senses betray him with small coughs and sneezes and a constant need to clear his throat. His proper upbringing and politeness are displayed when, at one point, he apologizes to the court for having to describe how markings from a paintball gun resembled "bird poo."

It is in regard to his parents' life insurance policy that Felix draws a clear distinction between himself and his sister. When questioned whether he knew about the money he was in line for if his parents ever met harm, he says he didn't — that is, until his sister advised him. "After November 8, I asked my sister [about the insurance policies], just because we were dealing with funeral arrangements and things like that," he says, his voice cracking. "She told me that they did." When asked if she told him who the beneficiaries were or the amount of money that was involved, he curtly says, "I wasn't interested in anything more than that."

Particularly troubling are hearing Felix's utterances regarding his sister's graduation from university and how he not only saw the copies of her U of T degree shown in court, but the "original." He explains to the court how his parents weren't able to attend the graduation ceremony because there were no tickets and that neither was able to view pictures of the event because Jennifer's friend flew back to Hong Kong with the photos still in her camera. It's unclear whether he knows at this point that everything was a grand old charade perpetrated by his sister. Although he doesn't know many key details about Jennifer's personal life, when questioned, he is able to recall countless facts about her extensive lies about her educational career, showing just how intricately Jennifer weaved her web of deceit for all those years and how she made sure she explained even the tiniest details to those closest to her. "That's a photocopy of my sister's diploma," Felix tells the court when a copy of her fake degree is shown on a monitor. "I've seen it in the house. I've also seen the original. My sister [showed it to me] after she graduated. She picked it up from the school. She wanted to frame it. She needed to bring [the photocopy] around for jobs because she didn't want to bring the original."

He tells the court about his relationship with Daniel Wong, how Jennifer told him Daniel had an engineering degree, how the pair played paintball together on more than one occasion, hearkening back to Jennifer's attempts to bring Daniel closer to her family. Again, all this shows the court how the remnants of her lies lived on long after they were uttered. There is clear discomfort in Felix's voice when he discusses the interaction he had with his sister regarding her relationship with Daniel as it began to disrupt the family peace. "I was angry at my sister because my parents never knew where she was and she [had] to sneak around all the time," he says, referring to the argument that occurred in the summer of 2010. "They kind of wanted my sister to stop lying about everything. They wanted her to make a decision about whether she wanted to stay with him or stay with the family because of the way she was kind of breaking up the family. There was an argument all the time, and I feel like my parents thought it was a bad influence on her … when everything started, it was kind of like when she started to hide things from my family and go away for long periods of time."

Felix's description of his relationship with his mother and father might ring true for many. He explains that his father was his practical support and his mother his emotional. "[In high school and in university my relationship with my dad] was normal. He always wanted me to do well in school. I used to tell him when I had problems in school, sort of thing, and he'd always tell me to 'keep at it' and offer to find me a tutor and things like that. [W]ith my mother, I guess I was a little more emotional … so, to him I'd say, 'I'm not doing that well in this class,' and to my mother I'd say, 'I don't know what I'm doing in this class. I am really stressed out.' [My mother] was always around. She's always comforting," he adds, noting that she treated Jennifer in the same way.

While the Crown questions him, Felix is obliging and co-operative; however, when the defence takes over, his attitude becomes pricklier. And because Jennifer's lawyer has been informed by his client about Felix and Jennifer's upbringing, the cross-examination almost develops into a bitter pseudo-sibling rivalry, with neither side wanting to admit they are wrong. Felix can see what Jennifer is trying to do — deflect blame onto their father — in a bid to win back her freedom. But he isn't going to sit idly by while that happens. Given Jennifer's defence — which involves her admitting to a plot to kill her father only, due to his treatment of her — it is clear that Cooper is trying to draw a distinction between Hann and Bich's parenting styles. When Cooper suggests that

Hann was harder on Jennifer than he was on her brother, Felix takes issue with that — even though the testimony seemed to show that Hann was indeed harder on Jennifer than Felix.

Cooper raises the prospect that Bich was the ideal parent — comforting, loving, non-judgmental, and protective. When it comes to Felix's father, the defence attorney suggests Hann was often "uncompromising and controlling." But Felix battles back, explaining that his mother was also very demanding and did her share of yelling at Jennifer when she misbehaved. "What happens is when there's a family drama and my dad and my sister are really at it," Felix says, "my mom's angry with my dad for the way he's yelling at my sister, but my mom would still be angry at my sister."

When asked by Cooper if he confided in his mother because he could do so without fear of reprisal — unlike with his father — Felix says this wasn't the case; rather, he was just more comfortable opening up emotionally to women. "It's more like I didn't have that connection with my dad. I've always been good at talking about my feelings with girls more than guys in general," he admits. He further rejects the assertion that his mother would "accept him" as he was, unlike his father: "[My mother] also often pushed me to do well, but in a different kind of way." He also denies Cooper's suggestion that it was his mother who protected Jennifer from her dad, stating that often the roles were reversed. "They would both yell at her depending on the situation."

When Cooper suggests Hann was overly conscious of what those around him thought and was intent on his children growing up around the family's traditional culture, Felix corrects him and says it was actually Bich who was more concerned with keeping the children steeped in their Asian background.

Although Felix appears to be the more broken of the two Pan men, Cooper certainly has more leeway when questioning him than he had with Hann. After all, he is a young man, born and raised in Canada, who wasn't physically injured or even present for the attack. He can handle himself.

When speaking about the ultimatum offered to Jennifer, Felix rejects Cooper's suggestion that it was her father rather than his mother who wanted Jennifer to be home. He also dismisses the prevailing wisdom that it was Hann who was the hardest on Jennifer during the fight and says that it was his mother who offered her the ultimatum. "They actually both wanted her to be home," he tells Cooper. "They gave her the choice of either stay home or don't come home. This is when my mother was really upset and screaming at her. This was a bad time in the family. Everyone kind of kept to themselves after this. Whenever we would talk we'd be arguing about something. [We kept it] in the family."

Two of the only assertions Felix agrees with wholeheartedly are that his father used isolation as a tool to gain acquiescence from his children and that, in the lead-up to the murder, Jennifer was isolated beyond just within the family. After a statement Felix made to the police is played, in which he says his parents "locked her in the house" because they didn't like her boyfriend, he still maintains calling it *house arrest* is going too far.

Although Felix starts to break down during a number of discussions surrounding his mother, he always regains his composure quickly, fighting the instinct to surrender to his emotions. It is this inner battle that eventually bubbles to the surface. Despite the hatred that courses through his body for what he thinks his sister has done, he appears to have at least some pity for her. For breaks and legal discussions that need to be held without the witness present, Felix is often excused from the stand. It is during these times, when he passes through Jennifer's direct sightline, that Felix keeps his eyes on the floor as he walks by. Upon his final exit, clearly against his own desire never to see or interact with his sister again, he glances up at her. When he realizes Jennifer is gazing elsewhere, he averts his eyes, almost as fast as he took the peek, obviously embarrassed for sneaking it in the first place.

Despite the lengthy trial, many of the questions people ask in the aftermath of the Crown's theory go unanswered: *How could such a seemingly good girl do this? Why didn't she just move out? Was she pressured into it? Did she really murder them to be with her boyfriend? Was it really all about the money? How could she be so cold-blooded? Is she evil? Was she mentally unstable?*

16

"ASTONISHING TESTIMONY"

After Jennifer's admissions to Detective Goetz back on November 22, 2010, her defence was always going to be a struggle. It was during that interview that she admitted to a twisted sort of conspiracy in which she hired a man named Homeboy to commit, as she put it, "an assassination of myself." The version she chooses to tell in court resembles this sequence of events, but with some very major differences. First, instead of Ric giving her Homeboy's number, a detail she told police, she explains to the court that she accessed his number herself. Second, that up until the moment the men broke into her house, she was doing her best to cancel the plan. Third, Jennifer admits to a murder plot against her father, but insists the plan fizzled after Ricardo Duncan and Andrew Montemayor duped her.

An intrepid Jennifer takes the stand on August 19, 2014, proceeding to weave what the *Toronto Star* later refers to as her "astonishing testimony." During her gruelling seven days before the court, her lawyer, Paul Cooper, fights doggedly to prove her innocence. But will it be enough to change the minds of the country, or the court, for that matter? While on the stand, Jennifer bemoans the fact that everyone seems to have already made up their minds about her before she even opens her mouth.

Nevertheless, her defence proceeds as she and her lawyer lay bare her demented version of events. After revealing all her lies and deceptions to the world via her intricate testimony throughout the first two days on the stand, Jennifer maintains she grew "furious" at her father when he began

Courtesy of Marianne Boucher, CityNews.

neglecting and isolating her in the lead-up to the summer of 2010. It was after they discovered all her dishonesty that Jennifer felt the full force of Hann's and Felix's cold shoulders. But it was her father for whom she held the most hatred, she says. Seeking out her friends' advice, Jennifer eventually stumbled upon Andrew Montemayor, her old elementary school classmate. He'd long had a crush on Jennifer, and she spent hours on the phone with him, seeking a way to get rid of the "stresses" in her life. But soon after she allegedly hatched a plan with Andrew's roommate, Ricardo "Ric" Duncan, in which he would shoot her father outside his work, it became clear that Ric ripped her off for the $1,500 she paid him. Despite trying to call him countless times, he was no longer answering his phone. "I spoke with him over the phone to see if he'd ever gotten his hands on a gun a few times," she says, "and he then stopped answering my phone calls. I tried calling Andrew … he said he had moved out of Ric's home … he kept making excuses for Ric. I knew it was a sham." Both Andrew and Ric deny under oath that the scheme ever took place.

Jennifer claims it was this plot that resulted in her withholding the truth from police during her interviews, scared that if investigators discovered proof of it, they'd suspect her in her mother's murder, too. Eventually, Jennifer says she began to consider suicide and admitted she tried to take her own life. However, when that failed, her focus began to shift to another, less shameful way to achieve death. "I felt that I couldn't even take my own life," she says, "I felt that I had failed in every possible way in life." On top of the shame associated with suicide, Jennifer says taking her own life would have made the insurance policy on herself, for which Felix was the beneficiary, null and void.

Her new plan began after Daniel gave her his iPhone under the agreement that Jennifer would pass along any messages intended for him. During this time, she started to notice one particular individual named Homeboy was repeatedly texting the phone. At the outset she says she passed on messages mentioning the term *Bollywood*, leading her to believe the messages were in reference to burnt DVDs. However, she eventually noticed the term *Orange*, which she knew as the code word for an "ounce" of marijuana. When she realized she was passing drug messages to Daniel, she says an idea dawned on her. "Here I was with a source … someone who could potentially know the street ways and potentially help me in finding a way to commit suicide," she tells the court. "I inquired about it. I inquired how much it was to kill a person. The person on the line, Homeboy, said … for a friend it would be $10,000 to $15,000. In one conversation, I said … I wanted it for myself, and the person on the other end was quite shocked. They're like 'Really? You want to kill yourself?' And I said, 'Yes, I do want to kill myself.' They kept inquiring 'Are you sure you want to kill yourself?' And I said, 'Yes, I'm sure.' It took some convincing."

After dropping that bombshell on the court, Jennifer says the pair then came to an agreement for a $10,000 hit to occur sometime in the following months. She did have further stipulations for Homeboy, though: "I didn't want it to be at any sort of family event or where my family members would be the first ones to find me," she says, explaining that it was agreed that prior to the shooting she would "have the money, ready to pass it over." But for Jennifer — who Cooper continually paints as "immature" and infantile throughout the trial — it didn't take long before she changed her mind.

Throughout September and October, Jennifer says her circumstances began to improve after her family travelled to the United States for a wedding and she, her mother, and her aunt went to Montreal for a weekend jaunt. Her spirits were also buoyed by an early acceptance into college and the positive attention it brought with it. "My dad, in my view, was quite ecstatic," she says, regarding the moment she and her father accepted an offer for her to attend a Centennial College lab technician course. "He finally got to see the proof he'd been waiting for. That was a glimmer of hope that maybe I could reconcile with my father. So we talked about maybe getting a locker there, how I would travel to Centennial College. So we actually had a conversation ... in my heart it was very warming. I did feel my father had been different than he had been over the past year and a half, two years ... he actually told me that I was finally getting my priorities straight and I thanked him for it because if it wasn't for him I don't think I would have applied. He started to communicate with me more. Things at home were less tense. He was almost boasting about *my daughter going back to school again*."

She says it was at this point that she "ceased to want" the "murder-suicide" plan she had devised to go forward. However, it would not be that easy, she tells the court. Although Jennifer communicated her change of heart to Homeboy, she says he refused to allow her out of the contract without paying an $8,500 "cancellation fee." Despite her furiously trying to get the money together, Homeboy refused to let her be, repeatedly badgering her for cash. On Halloween 2010, Homeboy, his cellphone pinging off the towers closest to her house, threatened to come to her home while she handed "out candy to trick-or-treaters" with her mother. "He said he was going to do it tonight," she tells Cooper. "I was shocked. I was saying to him, kids are in the area, I'm handing out candy, I can't step out, and where do you want to meet? I don't have the money. I started to freak out because I thought they were coming ... to shoot me and kill me."

Jennifer and Cooper then spend hours methodically going through hundreds of texts recovered from her Bell iPhone. Instead of messages seemingly referencing the murder of her parents as the Crown alleges, Jennifer tells the court that many of the communications were attempts to recover enough money to pay Homeboy. She has a more difficult time explaining her multiple text conversations with Daniel. One text from Daniel to Jennifer that says *I did everything and lined it all up for you* is passed off as one big misunderstanding. But her response to what it exactly meant shows just how convoluted her version of events has become. "I understand that [text] to be that he had talked to Homeboy on my behalf ... for the plan that I wanted to abandon," she explains, remaining unbowed throughout these irrational contradictions.

It was on the morning of November 8, she says, that she received the Homeboy text: *2 after work OK will be game time.* This was not a text between plotters about the murder of her parents, she says. Instead, Jennifer insists that she replied with a phone call, pleading with Homeboy to wait until she had the full cancellation fee. "If you don't want partial payment, please wait until I can meet you," she tells the court she begged him. After spending the rest of that day rounding up money from outstanding debts among her friends, Jennifer says she received a phone call, including a three-minute-and-twenty-three-second call with a stranger from David Mylvaganam's "Peter Robinson" phone. During these phone calls, she says, the following was repeated by the nameless voices: "Where's the money? We need the money."

Jennifer also recants her admission to police that she unlocked her home's door after receiving a text requesting "VIP" entry. When questions turn to what happened to her iPhone's SIM card, Jennifer explains how Number One stole the SIM card out of her phone. "He was fidgeting with the phone with one glove off. I don't know what he was doing," she says. "The iPhone company gives you a little pick to open the SIM card slot. I had that available nearby … I know he opened the cartridge. I don't know how … when he was slipping on his glove and coming around I could still see the gun was still pointed at me … [before] quickly slipping the SIM card into his pocket." When asked why she didn't tell police this throughout her almost ten hours worth of interviews, she insists that she was afraid no one would believe her.

"I admit I'm a liar. I admitted I was a liar. I admitted I lied to the police in the police station, but I was scared," she says. "I was scared of being caught in a concoction, but on November 8 there was nothing, nothing that was supposed to be happening. Yes I lied because I didn't want to get in trouble for making these plans and plots that I eventually abandoned weeks after because I knew I had blown a lot of my thoughts out of proportion. I am being truthful here." When her parents were being led to the basement, Jennifer says she felt helpless as her mother cried out for her: "I want to be with my daughter, please bring me my daughter."

Jennifer weeps in court as she recalls her response. "'I'm upstairs. Mom. I'm upstairs.' I begged my [captor] to untie me so I [could] go with them. All I could hear is my mom's fading voice going down the stairs, yelling for me. In response, I kept yelling back and telling [the] intruder 'Please just let me go with my mom.' I don't know why they were separating us." A distraught Jennifer describes how she managed to hear her mother's last gasp for breath. "I heard two gunshots and my mom scream," she testifies, whimpering. "I heard another gunshot. I heard my mom. It was almost like an exhale. It was like her last breath. But I had a feeling in my heart that that was the last breath I heard."

When she is asked why anyone would believe a woman so entrenched in deceit, Jennifer reiterates that this time she is telling the truth. "I know a lot of people have already judged me. The whole world has judged me," she tells the jury. "[I'm facing] twenty-five years to life here, I understand that. My point being is I have nothing to lie about today. Even if I get sentenced and this jury finds me guilty, at least I can rest knowing that I know that my mother was never a target in my life, never, and I know that November 8 was just a shock to everyone else as it was to me."

Although Cooper delves deep into Jennifer's upbringing, her scheduled youth, and her belief that her parents favoured her brother over her, there is nothing close to the tortured existence growing up that some expect to hear from her defence. One lawyer later says: "I was waiting to hear how she'd been locked in a closet, hit with a ruler, berated by her father, but there was none of that."

When it is Rob Scott's turn, it is an open question just how catastrophic his cross-examination is going to be. After all, Jennifer is an admitted liar and the evidence and her testimony leave her vulnerable on so many fronts. Scott's sarcastic style can sometimes land him in trouble with judges; but he's wily enough to use it only when he has a jury firmly on his side. By this juncture, he feels secure that most people in the room want him to confront Jennifer's past, her lies, and her conflicting statements head-on. And she certainly appears confident enough on the stand to be able to handle it.

Much of Scott's questioning centres on the simple yet supremely effective point that, despite being given hours of opportunity to tell the police exactly what happened in her house that night, she waited until the trial to unveil this version of events. Is the court to believe that Jennifer waited three-and-a-half years to reveal the actual events of that night, wasting the opportunity for the police to catch those actually responsible? If so, it is clear, Scott argues, that these aren't the actions of a loving daughter.

Courtesy of Marianne Boucher, CityNews.

Jennifer can do little to refute this line of inquiry, largely because it is true. So instead, Jennifer blames the police, insisting she was too tired, frightened, and frazzled to tell the "real story" during the police interviews: "I had told them my descriptions, the events that happened in the house, besides the SIM card, which I had not thought of at that point, but it had been such a long interview. I had just buried my mother. I was not in the mood to be there ... I was exhausted at that time."

But even without this stirring line of questioning, it wouldn't have taken much time for Scott to punch holes in Jennifer's new version of events. The prosecution questions her statement that she discovered Homeboy's name when he texted the iPhone. Scott insists that the entire premise of her story is faulty, considering there were no texts from Lenford's phone to the iPhone prior to Jennifer's first text to him in mid-August. "There are no phone calls, there are no text messages from Homeboy to that Bell phone before August 18," Scott states. "Therefore, when you told this jury that you learned about Homeboy [from] all the messages and texts he sent about *Bollywood* and *Orange*, that was a complete lie. There weren't any."

Jennifer says she can't remember "what happened during what phone call four years ago."

Scott doesn't relent. "The reason that you lied and said you got his name from messages he had left or texts that he had sent is because ... you feel the need to protect the love of your life, Daniel Wong. [He] gave you [Homeboy's] name." Scott then gets to the heart of the matter. "What you did early on in the police investigation is really try to save Daniel Wong and keep him out of all this by saying, 'Oh, I got the name, number for Homeboy from Ric Duncan, scary murder guy,'" he says. "You tried to frame an innocent man in some kind of home-invasion murder in order to save Daniel Wong."

Faced with this accusation, Jennifer doesn't wilt; unlike during her police interviews, she remains upright, trying to provide plausible answers to each question. Some who were present that day say they had the impression she was very well coached for her testimony. However, as the day wears on, she comes under increased pressure.

"Your mother is brutally murdered in your basement twenty metres below you," Scott continues, "and what you do is go into the police station twice in the following week and lie to them. And there's only one reason you lie to the police the day after your mother is shot in the head — to keep Jennifer Pan from getting into trouble."

"I was scared to get in trouble, yes," Jennifer responds without blinking.

"Right, because it's more important to you in your world that you stay out of trouble than the police find your mother's killers," Scott snaps. "That's your thought process. Jennifer Pan is about Jennifer Pan."

"Disagree," she retorts.

"Then why don't you sacrifice yourself as the good daughter so that they can find the real killers of your mother?" he asks.

"That's why I am here."

"Why weren't you there in November 2010?" he shoots back.

"Because I was very scared."

"You're not scared. You're selfish and you're greedy."

"I don't agree with that."

Scott carries on in this vein, painting Jennifer as the "attention-seeking" daughter in a fascinating courtroom diatribe. "You love to be the centre of attention," he suggests. "You love getting awards [for skating and piano] … it gets you attention and it gets you recognition and people pay attention to you. You're not invisible. And you loved playing the victim with Daniel Wong because it got you attention. And you like telling the jury that you're a self-harmer and you cut yourself because it makes people look at you and say, 'Wow, we should be concerned about you.' It gets you more attention, doesn't it? And when you planned this murder of your parents, I'm going to suggest to you, you loved being the centre of attention. You loved that Andrew Montemayor was in contact with you constantly to talk about it on the night of this murder. That someone was interested in you and interested in this drama, right? I'm going to suggest to you, you were excited at the prospect that, the day after this murder, you're going to be a victim yet again on the front page of every Toronto newspaper and people will pay attention to you and say, 'Poor Jennifer Pan.' And you were in a good mood on the evening of November 8, right? And when you're in a good mood with your boyfriend, Daniel Wong, you guys do the baby talk and 'Hey, monkey, monkey, and *oooo*, what do monkeys say [referring to the couple's baby talk that night].' That's when you're in a good silly mood and you're having fun with Daniel Wong. You do that when you're in a good mood, because we've seen you in a bad mood. The evening of November 8 you were in a good mood. Things were coming together for you. That was going to be the night of the start of your new life. Your new life with Daniel." He adds one more shot across the bow. "It is coincidental that on that day and in the evening [of the murder] you were in contact with each and every one of these co-accused that are in court today, right? Just a coincidence?" he tellingly asks her.

When Laurence Cohen approaches his cross-examination, his association to Daniel Wong, as his legal representative, seems to win him some favour with Jennifer. At the outset Jennifer begins to agree with much of what Cohen puts to her, presumably in part because they happen to be her true feelings. However, this turns out to be a huge miscalculation on Jennifer's part. Cohen's approach mirrors that of the police, acting as though he understands Jennifer's feelings to gain trust and information before turning the tables on her. The problem for Jennifer is that, in agreeing with his assertions, she reveals the type of person she is to the court — the eternal victim. The exchange that takes place between the two largely consists of Cohen weaving scenarios Jennifer is comfortable enough with to accept, then using that very testimony against her, eventually making her out to be the manipulative ex-girlfriend who essentially got Daniel caught up in a murder investigation. "You bore the brunt of the [house] cleaning and your brother was elevated to be this prince that goes wherever he wants and comes home and does what he pleases," he says.

She admits she felt "unappreciated."

"You, Jennifer Pan, are a good person and you're unappreciated for your endeavours. 'I do good acts and I get abandoned. I get abandoned by the people who love me. I give and I give and I get nothing back.' People have judged you harshly." Jennifer agrees to all of these statements during Cohen's masterful cross.

> LC: You appreciate the horrific nature of this crime, right?
> JP: I cannot tell you how many nights I have not slept.
> LC: The allegation that someone could kill their parents, who provided and sacrificed their lives, is the ultimate in betrayal, right?
> JP: You nailed it.
> LC: You've lived under that shadow, that horrible suspicion, for many, many years now.
> JP: Correct.
> LC: You've been put under the microscope of being this horrible person, a murderer, they're suggesting.
> JP: A cold-hearted one, yes.

Over time Cohen begins to alienate Jennifer, suggesting she isn't a victim but rather a "pathological liar" — someone who is habitually untruthful and essentially believes her own lies, an individual who repeatedly used mind games and deceit to control and manipulate Daniel along with everyone else in her life. It is no doubt an effective line of defence for Daniel, but in the end it is nowhere near enough to sway the jury from its final decision, which is likely based primarily on its opinion of Jennifer, who takes a beating during these days.

Part of the problem, of course, is that, besides acting as her defence, Jennifer's version of events provides all the lawyers a treasure trove of information they can use in their own crosses to bring her down a notch. However, one must wonder how this will affect the fates of their clients, all of whom sit directly beside Jennifer and her sinking ship.

Out of one side of her mouth, Jennifer tells the jury members that she did mastermind a plot to shoot and kill her own father, but then out of the other she tells them that November 8 was all one big mistake. Jennifer enthusiastically admits to creating a world of deceit for much of her adult life, but then wants everyone to believe that in this one instance, after all these years, she is being honest. Finally, to believe her version of events, Jennifer is asking the court to engage in a quantum leap of rationality, which no one is willing to do. So much so, that it's like shooting fish in a barrel to impugn her character and point out inaccuracies.

17

A SPANNER IN THE WORKS

It is during an almost month-long break in the middle of Jennifer's testimony that one defence lawyer suffers a health crisis — Edward Sapiano, counsel for Eric Carty, the man the Crown has described (along with Jennifer herself) as being the plot's linchpin. Unable to seek a new lawyer seven months into a very complicated trial, it is decided that Eric's case will be severed from the rest and will be heard separately in an entirely new trial. This turn of events, which almost claims Sapiano's life, has a profound impact on the trial. After all, Eric is the accused with the most dubious past; in fact, he is the only defendant with any significant criminal record at all. It isn't until November that the jury and the public discover the truth about Eric's police record involving gun-related crimes.

Although Peter Bawden (lawyer for David Mylvaganam) has been granted the right to bring Eric's past out in court from the get-go, he refuses to do so, possibly fearful of reprisal attacks on his own client by Sapiano (representing Eric Carty). So, in the end, it is Jennifer's lawyer, Paul Cooper, who brings into evidence the fact that at the time of his arrest for the Pan murder, Eric was already being held in prison on charges that he killed a man named Kirk Matthews — a first-degree murder charge (of which he is later convicted).

Although the police say Eric is a suspect in at least one other shooting, it is the murder of Matthews that lands him in significant trouble.

It was 3:25 a.m. on a wintry night, and Eric was skulking near the projects on Rexdale's San Pietro Way. As he approached the target vehicle, he is alleged to have seen twenty-four-year-old Kirk sitting with his girl in his SUV outside his mother's house. Kirk's girlfriend said Eric asked for either a cigarette or a light. When Kirk exited the vehicle to oblige, Eric shot him in the chest. Kirk's girlfriend ran to the house of her boyfriend's mother screaming, while Eric is said to have run in the opposite direction, jumping in a getaway car waiting in a nearby parking lot, and made good his escape. Kirk's mother quickly called 911 as she ran to her son's side. When she asked her dying boy what had happened, he responded "Snypa shot me" — a statement recorded by 911 operators. As he lay dying on the road, he told his mother not to worry: "I'm going to be okay, I'm going to beat this thing." Those were his final words.

Although the police identified Eric as a suspect within days, putting out a warrant for his arrest, it was a long while before they finally caught up to him. Eric was on the run for more than a year before he was caught.

The Matthews case raised some uncomfortable questions for the Toronto Police Service, considering Eric remained in "hiding" for such a long period of time. Although he was certainly keeping a low profile, he was also out and about, at one point appearing in a very public hip-hop video. He was also living with known girlfriends and even attending his children's birthday parties. The bottom line is that the Pan murder was committed while Eric was a wanted man. One wonders if he might have been caught sooner if the murder he was implicated in had taken place outside the violent confines of Rexdale.

Eric's removal from the courtroom alters more than a few game plans as the trial continues. Up until that point, all the defendants remained united. But that doesn't last long after Eric's seat is vacated, leaving neither he nor his lawyer in the courtroom to contest any evidence brought forward. Jennifer's lawyer, Paul Cooper, attempts to further solidify her defence that the murder was a robbery gone wrong by a gang of thugs led by Eric, a man he can now refer to as a "psychopathic killer with a bad shot." Cooper suggests that Eric — hungry for money and unwilling to wait for Jennifer's "cancellation fee" — took it upon himself to rob the Markham home where he expected to find a huge cache. Enraged when he didn't find the loot he was looking for, he and the group killed Hann and Bich.

Peter Bawden, David Mylvaganam's lawyer, also takes the opportunity to paint Eric as the chief bad guy, a "street rat" who, unwilling to use his own cellphone for fear of police detection, chose to use the phone of his young cohort, David — little more than a pawn in his game. Despite this strategy, it must be said that neither Jennifer nor any of her co-defendants ever turn on one another during the trial. As a matter of fact, Jennifer even assures the jury that none of the men in the prisoners' boxes were involved in the home invasion. "I know the descriptions I gave to police. I know their faces in my head, and sitting here alongside them … indications, whether voice or certain distinctions, don't match the intruders," she says, making more than a few people question exactly who was using these men's phones on the night of the murder to call her.

In the end, it is only Bawden who changes course, selecting a different path in defence of his client. After Jennifer, it is David who faces the most problematic defence. After all, he was the primary user of the "Peter Robinson" phone. It was this phone that was tracked travelling from Rexdale to Markham and then used to call Jennifer before the murder. It was also used after the attack to allegedly bridge calls to the others allegedly involved. Furthermore, Hann, a man who was clearly never supposed to survive, picked him out of a lineup two months after his wife was gunned down. It is also suggested by the Crown attorneys, who show the court plenty of phone communication directly and indirectly mentioning the sale of firearms — *Get me ur cheapest book* [gun] *u have. Even if its* [sic] *worn out just plan 2 do a quick ting and dump it* — that David was a gunrunner. He also happened to be the unlucky user of a Telus phone that received the following text: *5 each ting* and *Bt u all da way and all ten 4u. Easy ting* was the response. Later this will be translated to mean that each life he took was worth $5,000 and that if David killed both, he'd get all $10,000.

Instead of accepting a jury verdict against his client — which is growing increasingly likely — Bawden decides to fight against the impending doom with what's known as an "alternative suspect defence." Bawden's approach to this is simple: now that Eric's trial has been severed, he will increasingly paint Eric as the violent manipulator who took advantage of all those around him, including David, his younger, less-experienced understudy.

"Why did [David] let Carty use his phone if he knew Carty was planning murder?" Bawden asks the jury. "Carty ... would never use his own phone. Carty was the organizer of so many of these events. Mr. Carty has a propensity for violence. As much as we know now about Eric Carty ... did anyone in the car know that night what Eric Carty would do when he was in the home? I would submit the answer is no."

Despite his suggestions, to this day there remains no evidence — disregarding the original assertions of Jennifer that Eric was Number One — that Eric was ever in the Pan house that night. The reason for this strategy is simple: Hann's descriptions involved two dark-skinned males in the house and one lighter-skinned male. Bawden is essentially saying those two men with darker skin were Eric and another man who was not on trial, a Black male by the name of Maurice Green.

Rather than conducting the murders himself, Bawden argues that David remained in the car as a getaway driver. He didn't know the robbery would escalate to murder, and if anything, he should be convicted of manslaughter. "I'm going to start by being blunt. [David Mylvaganam] is in a car on his way to Markham and there are some ... guys that are in that car in dark clothing, baseball caps, and carrying guns, " he says. "Clearly, there's a plan of some kind, and he's involved in that plan. Those are facts that you just can't dispute. Did the defendant know that another participant would probably murder Mrs. Pan and attempt to murder Mr. Pan in the commission of a home-invasion robbery? The answer I would urge you to find is no."

Things must have been growing increasingly desperate by this point for David to allow his lawyer to further implicate Eric, a friend and mentor with a penchant for violence. But Bawden's legal strategy also implicates Maurice Green, who has plenty to lose, including his freedom — considering until that juncture, he is free of prosecution, notoriety, and charges. This betrayal won't be looked upon kindly in either man's neighbourhood. Luckily for Maurice, although he has been a person of interest in the police investigation, he is never charged. This means he is in a unique position of essentially being his own witness, meaning there are allegations against him but no firm evidence or people waiting in the wings to discredit his testimony.

For the Crown, which is well on its way to securing four convictions, minus Eric, this is an unwanted development that can possibly lay waste to all the work they have so meticulously put in so far. If Bawden is effective in his questioning, Maurice's testimony could derail the entire trial, putting doubt and confusion into the minds of the twelve jurors, who are only meant to focus on four people in the prisoners' box. As such, it is left to Rob Scott to essentially act as Maurice's defence attorney, objecting to lines of questioning, discrediting witnesses, before repeatedly attempting to divert the eyes of the jury during Bawden's questioning of Maurice, as well as those attempting to implicate him — "Move along folks, nothing to see here."

Among the eight witnesses called as part of the defence's alternative shooter theory is one of Eric's good friends, Silvia Powell. Silvia is the woman whose phone number was stored in Lenford Crawford's phone as "Gully Side." But this isn't the only link Silvia has to the case: besides being Eric's close friend and often putting him up for the night, she is also close friends with two of his girlfriends, Katherine "Kat" Chum and Leesha Pompei. Furthermore, in the lead-up to the murder, her phone number shows up repeatedly in many of Eric's associates' call logs, with police suspecting Eric repeatedly used her cell to conduct business so to create distance between him and his activities.

As she approaches the stand, Silvia, who many suspect of being Eric Carty's girlfriend at one time, strikes a very lonely figure, seemingly torn between the two men in her life. On one side, of course, is Eric: "He'd give me advice [about] what to do [about my children's] fathers, because they're not helping in any sort of way. With my son's father, he did try to talk to him and be in the picture with him. He was funny and nice and very outgoing. He cared a lot about kids, and he was just always supportive." On the other side is Maurice Green, the former boyfriend she says was initially so great with her and her three children that she thought she was living in a "fairy tale." It was a relationship she thought "was going to last." But the fairy tale soon turned sour, she says, admitting to the court that Maurice lied to her, telling her he was twenty-six, that he had his own place, and implying his name was "Darius." In reality, he was thirty-five years old, sparsely employed, and living with his mother. Despite these revelations, the couple remained together for several months (August 2010 to spring 2011).

Silvia recounts for the court the events of one evening in and around November 8, 2010, that stands out in her mind. (She doesn't recall the exact day, but knows it was around this time.) Before nightfall she and Maurice became embroiled in an argument about his belief that she was having an affair with Eric, something she denied. Silvia then tells the court how Maurice told her he was leaving to go "on a move with 'S'" (meaning Eric, a.k.a. Snypa). After she saw him leave in a dark car with black-tinted windows, she says she became involved in a discussion with her roommate, Kat Chum, over Kat's concerns that her boyfriend, Eric Carty, was cheating on her. Silvia tells the court how Kat felt Eric was "playing her for a fool" by two-timing her. "She thought a lot of times that he had somebody else," Silvia says. "But she never knew for sure."

The pair decided to text the girl Kat thought was Eric's mistress, Silvia says. To their surprise, the girl texted back, and after they described Eric's appearance and body shape to her, she told them that she was, in fact, dating this man. They then used Silvia's phone to try to call Eric, but got no answer. Although Silvia can't remember doing so, phone records then show that her phone called Maurice's phone six times in a three-minute period around the same time. The implication is obvious: when she and Kat couldn't reach Eric directly, they called Maurice, knowing the two men were together.

When Maurice and Eric returned to the apartment later that night, Silvia says she noticed that Maurice was dressed in different clothing. After she and Maurice went to her room, he handed her a bag of clothing, the same clothing he had left in, but now they were covered in blood. When she asked Maurice what had happened, she says she was told: "Don't worry about it. Just get rid of them." It was on Valentine's Day in 2011 when she confronted Maurice anew about that night, during which she says an upset Maurice told her he "went on a move with S and it was like S wasn't even there." In a police interview, she said Maurice told her: "Don't ask me about that. I don't want to talk about it."

It sounds like convincing testimony, but when the Crown gets hold of Silvia, all bets are off. Right from the start, Rob Scott implicates her in all sorts of inconsistent behaviour, suggesting that, in a bid to protect Eric, she simply inserted Maurice's name into the mix. After all, the closer one looks at her relationship with Eric, the more one might question her testimony against Maurice. Scott digs up comments from her police interview when she told investigators she had, in fact, been romantically interested in Eric. "I liked him. I did have interest in him, but it didn't go any further," she told investigators. "Like, we never got any closer, because I had my kids." Scott then raises the number of times the pair communicated in the lead-up to November 6 — 350 calls and texts over four weeks. Were they just close friends or lovers? Another troubling aspect of her testimony is her apparent refusal to implicate Eric in even the slightest manner.

When Scott begins questioning her about whether she knew Lenford Crawford, she says she knew "of him," but insists she had no idea why Lenford would have her phone number in his phone under the listing "Gully Side" and refuses to admit that she let Eric borrow her phone to call him on November 8. Scott shows that on the morning of the murder, at 10:00 a.m., Lenford's phone contacted her phone and then her phone contacted Lenford forty-six minutes later. But once more, Silvia refuses to admit it might have been Eric — instead, she says she didn't know who used her phone. When asked whose friend Lenford is, she initially says: "I don't know." This leaves her vulnerable to attack, and Scott doesn't hold back. "Well, you know whose friend he is," Scott says, raising his voice. "He's Eric Carty's friend. So don't tell us you don't know whose friend he is, you know whose friend he is, he's Eric Carty's friend."

"Yes," she responds.

"Don't tell the jury if you know it's the truth, something that's not true, okay?" he presses. "We'll agree on that?"

"Okay," she replies.

"Does it not make sense that your close friend Eric Carty was using your phone to talk to his friend?"

"No."

"It wasn't certainly you?"

"No."

Scott eventually cuts to the chase, asking Silvia why she goes from not mentioning anything about Maurice in the first police interview to all of a sudden telling police about the bloody clothes in the second interview. "Did you substitute Maurice for Eric Carty?"

"No."

"Would have been an easy thing to do right because he was at your house that night, right?"

"No, I did not."

"Because you don't rat out your friends. You're not a snitch, right? Right? That's a code you live by, isn't it? Right?"

"I'm sitting here, so what does that label me?"

"Well, you're not here because you want to be here, right? You're not here ratting out your friend because you're not saying anything that's hurting Eric Carty, right? That you're aware of?"

Although Silvia initially says she doesn't remember talking to one of Eric's girlfriends between the first police interview and the second one, while she is on the witness stand, Scott reminds her of what she told police. "She did ask me like, what I know," she told Detective Cooke during her interview, "but I told her I don't know nothing because I never told anybody, really, what happened with Maurice."

"Did that discussion ... influence what you said to the police the second time you went to them?" Scott asks.

"No," is her response.

Before the end of their exchange, Silvia further admits that she also visited Eric in prison, throwing into question where her allegiances lie.

"Would you implicate your ex-boyfriend, Maurice, in order to get Mr. Carty out of trouble?" Scott asks. "Did you do that in this case?"

"No," replies Silvia. In a bid to try to repair some of the damage that has been done to Silvia's credibility after this injurious exchange with Scott, Bawden skillfully plays one of the most emotional videos seen during the trial, even more so than Jennifer's manic police interviews. The police interview involves an inconsolably sobbing and weeping Silvia who has been asked to identify the man who gave her the bloody clothes. When officers leave the room, she repeatedly makes a number of audible grunting noises before she is seen saying to a picture of Maurice: "Oh, God. Oh, I love you."

Bawden also asks a number of pointed questions concerning how she feels implicating Maurice in a murder. "I don't know the words to use," she says before describing Maurice as having been "very important" in her life.

Silvia isn't the only controversial witness to be called. Another one of Maurice's girlfriends, Ashley Williams is also the subject of much consternation and debate in the courthouse. Although she claims to be unavailable for a proper examination in court and under oath because she is still living in the United Kingdom, the video statement she gave to the police is played for the jury. During Ashley's interview in September 2013, she implicated Maurice in the murder of Bich and the attempted murder of Hann, telling investigators that he told her: "I shot this man in his head and I messed up. He didn't die."

When it comes time for the suave and stylish Maurice to take the stand, all eyes are fixed on him. Unlike many of the other witnesses — who respond in a variety of fashions to the glare of spectators, judges, court staff, the jury, and the accused, ranging from nervousness to belligerence — Maurice seems perfectly at ease. He is well dressed and polished and clearly accustomed to the spotlight.

Taken at face value, some of the evidence presented to the court paints a damning picture of Maurice, but there is plenty more to the story, as he soon describes. He maintains his cool under questioning, speaking in a calm and collected voice, responding to questions in his deep baritone. His reply to the accusations is simple — Ashley's comments are blatant lies to get back at him for cheating on her and then breaking up with her.

Maurice tells the court that Ashley visited him once or twice a year, making the trip across the pond from her home in London. And, although they talked about marriage, he explains that because she never ended up moving to Canada, the chatter about a family never grew overly intense. He says he ended the relationship after she hacked his emails one too many times. Although the subject of philandering comes up countless times in this trial— most notably involving Maurice, Eric, Daniel, and David — it is with only Maurice that it turns into an actual defence. He admits to having at least two other girlfriends during the time he was dating Ashley, including one woman with whom he had a child, and Silvia.

For many people testifying, these sorts of details might harm their reputations, especially with female jurors; however, for Maurice it raises significant doubt concerning the veracity of Silvia's and Ashley's statements. After all, he says, he broke both their hearts. Essentially, he testifies that their statements to police are those of two women scorned, and that neither can be trusted. Maurice and Ashley eventually broke up in 2013 after six years together. It is only afterward, when she hacked all his social media accounts — deleting information and changing settings — that she discovered his infidelities, he says. It was at this point that she began threatening not only his life with statements to Maurice like "my mom's going to be crying over a son" but his livelihood, personal relationships, and freedom — "I should hope for jail, rather than death." Furthermore, he says, Ashley began contacting his loved ones and slandering his name. It was her lust for revenge, he says, that prompted her to investigate the details of the murder online, call police, and then use media reports to lie about his behaviour. She made a number of statements to police, many of which are played for the court, that he takes issue with. It is in these accusations, Maurice says, that one can see the deception she is so well versed in.

He agrees that he might have told her that police were looking for him at some point and that he had to attend court. However, he denies her allegations of a Facebook video in which he can be heard bragging about conducting robberies and home invasions. Maurice also refutes the suggestion that he owned a gun that he nicknamed "Karma." After a lengthy clip of Ashley discussing Maurice's involvement with guns and hiding out from police, Bawden doesn't have the opportunity to speak before Maurice asks, "Can I tell you what's on my mind?"

Bawden agrees, and Maurice continues. "What's accurate with what she's saying is the part when I told her that I had court in May 2012, with the homicide detective coming to my mother's house. She's very powerful. For instance I told her why I went to court, she'll go searching on the Internet … and read the whole description of everything and try to implicate me. She's putting on this innocent woman act, but behind closed doors she is not who you think she is. She's very dangerous. She's a hacker … I lost my Instagram. She deleted everybody. She went in my Twitter, tweeted stuff, made up fake profiles. She went on my Facebook, changed my settings. She went crazy from there. She 'so-called' put a hit out on me."

Maurice's phone records are next on tap, showing that he was in heavy contact with both Eric and Demetrius Mables in the lead-up to the murder. The data revealed there were four calls from Eric on November 6, two days before the murder, leading eventually to a twelve-minute conversation at 7:25 p.m. that night. There are also two calls to the phone of a girl by the name of Ayan Mohamed, another of Eric's girlfriends, on October 29; three phone calls to Demetrius's phone on the day of the murder; and eleven text messages with Eric on November 16. When asked on each occasion if he told Ashley Williams about these calls and texts, Maurice replies no. So the question becomes: Did he tell her he was so heavily involved with so many of the alleged conspirators in the days leading up to and immediately following the murder?

Maurice is eventually faced with a disquieting question. "If I understand your evidence correctly," Bawden says, "Ashley has essentially fabricated an allegation against you of murder. Are you aware of any means by which Ashley could have possibly known that your phone records would demonstrate links with so many of the characters who appear in this murder trial?"

In response, Maurice returns to his faithful line, essentially "hackers are going to hack."

It is later put to Maurice that, while it is his testimony that Ashley is vindictive, he's never said that about Silvia. "Well, I thought she wasn't, to be honest with you. These are angry people here. After our relationship, it seems that she did [go crazy]. Silvia got a tattoo on her chest with my name a month after I met her. For me that's too soon for someone to do such a thing like that, and it's big, right across her chest. She put *M* and spelled out my last name with a heart. Maybe I have a bad choice in women. She's very angry that I cut it off … maybe she's angry and went off."

Maurice will eventually do his best to put an end to the rising tide of vexing coincidences. Courtroom drama rarely gets better than what happens next. A frustrated Maurice — continuing to insist that the Ashley the jury sees on the screen is not the same one he witnessed after the breakup — finally plays his ace card, whipping a USB drive out of his pocket. "This is the angel [Ashley] you guys are going off of," he says. "This is the angel that you're taking information from. She's out to get me and I have proof of that."

On the drive are saved conversations and photos and screen grabs that Judge Boswell suggests make Ashley "appear to be a little unbalanced." The images not only prove that Ashley made harassing phone calls, but repeatedly contacted Maurice's girlfriend, sending between thirty and forty texts a day before threatening to blow up her house, forcing her to move three times. But she didn't stop there, also posting "racist and deplorable" photographs to social media, juxtaposing one of the girlfriend's children beside a picture of a baboon, and calling another a "devil child." In other screen grabs, Ashley threatens Maurice's life, alleging her father is in the Mafia and she is going to put a hit out on him.

In its closing, the Crown sums up its reluctance to put its faith in either woman. "I am not going to review the long list of problems and inconsistencies with the evidence of Ashley Williams and Silvia Powell," Assistant Crown Attorney Michelle Rumble says. "Our position is you can't rely on their evidence. It wouldn't be safe to do so."

Maurice Green is never charged as part of the proceedings and remains an innocent man.

18

JUDGMENT DAY

After the ten-month trial ends, the jury is sequestered to a hotel room, where they will review all the relevant facts in the case — and there is a lot of information and testimony to discuss. The twelve jurors debate for four days before reaching a decision on the fates of each of the accused. Judgment day finally arrives for the four defendants on December 13, 2014.

The packed courtroom buzzes with fervour as the four men and eight women file in and take their seats. Lenford, Daniel, and David reveal almost no emotion, choosing instead to look only bewildered, perhaps knowing deep down that their worst fears will soon to be realized. Jennifer, on the other hand, tries to hide her fear with an outward display of playfulness. Dressed in black with a frilly white silk blouse and her long black hair tied in a ponytail, the twenty-eight-year-old does her best to appear as if her spirits are high. At one point, with her lawyer Paul Cooper alongside her to show support, she smiles nervously and picks lint off Cooper's robe, brushing her hand across the fabric to make sure any trace of it is gone. It doesn't take long for her expression to change, though. She stands and gazes straight ahead as the ruling is uttered.

The foreman makes a point to look each of the defendants in the face as he reads out the verdict he and his co-jurors have come to. The accused don't return his stare. Instead they glare into the abyss of their futures. None show any emotion as the word *guilty* is repeated over and again for each of them for first-degree murder and attempted murder.

When it is David's turn, one of his relatives takes the news particularly hard, screaming at the top of her lungs before running from the courtroom and hollering as she races through the hallway, heightening the tension hanging heavily in the courtroom. Upon her return, she stands with her arms spread, mouthing "Why?" to which David, from behind a thick panel of glass, mouths to her the words "It's okay."

When Jennifer's news is delivered, she simply bows her head. One lawyer later says that Jennifer waited until the press left before shedding her fair share of tears, "shaking and crying uncontrollably." In the aftermath of the verdict, another lawyer says the words she repeated included "They didn't even give me a chance," a reference to the jury's four short days of deliberation.

After the trial, Jennifer's lawyer stands with his legal team in front of the courthouse, a huge crowd of reporters hanging on his every word, snapping pictures and shouting out questions as he speaks into the microphone. "[Jennifer] has no relationship with her father," Paul Cooper says. "She has reached out to him. For her, this has been exhausting. For everyone involved it's been a very long time. She's absolutely devastated by the verdict."

A post-trial press conference outside the front doors of the court building.

Detective Courtice, sneaking a smoke away from the cameras and spotlight after attending the entire trial, admits he doesn't know what to think. "I have mixed emotions," he says. "Reflecting back on the night it happened, Mrs. Pan was murdered and her husband badly wounded. In that sense there's some closure, but it was a tragedy."

When she is sentenced about a month later, on January 23, 2015, Jennifer is given the maximum penalty the Canadian law allows: twenty-five years without the chance for parole. She will be in jail until 2036. Jennifer listens to the sentence in her usual seat in courtroom 401, but this time with her head between her knees.

Justice Boswell is succinct in his judgment, stating that Hann and Bich did not deserve "the death penalty [Jennifer] imposed on them. This was a business transaction ... the commodity, death."

The following morning, a large photo is published on the front page of the *Toronto Sun*, Canada's largest tabloid, next to the headline "Daughter from Hell."

The headline from December 14, 2014, after Jennifer Pan was given a life sentence for plotting the murder of her mother and the attempted murder of her father more than four years earlier.

Edward Sapiano, Eric Carty's original lawyer, later remarks on the "brilliant" performance by Michelle Rumble and Jennifer Halajian. "I told the Crown at some point in the trial that the two of them had raised the bar on significant prosecutorial performance. It was an exceptionally complicated case, the most complicated case I have worked on. They did a massive amount of work and analysis in which the smallest detail was not overlooked. They worked harder and better than any Crown I had ever seen. They locked themselves in their office day after day sifting through line after line. It was a maze. I think they will get a judgeship and I think they should get it after this."

19

EPITOME OF EVIL

Away from the sensational stage of the first trial, Eric Carty stands alone in the five-seat prisoner box in a grey vest, suit pants, and burgundy collared shirt on December 7, 2015, to meet his own fate. It is in the same Newmarket courtroom where his mistrial was declared more than a year earlier. There is just a handful of people present and only two reporters left from the fifteen-odd from before. Eric's shackles are removed before he takes his seat. His trial was originally slated for February 2016 and was scheduled to last six months. But, intent on sparing the Pan family another gruelling trial, it was the Crown's opinion that it was best to move on. Faced with fifty consecutive years in prison for two murders, if found guilty for the Pan homicide, Eric put his belligerence toward authority aside and cut a deal with the state. It remains unclear how much his decision was influenced by the actions of his co-accused, whose defence team firmly placed the blame on him for the crime in the initial trial. As a result of his admissions, during the proceeding, he is held in protective custody.

Eric and his new lawyer, Craig Bottomly, worked out a compromise with Crown attorneys Michelle Rumble and Jennifer Halajian. In return for Eric's admissions, he will be sentenced to eighteen years in prison to be served alongside the twenty-five years he is already serving for the murder of Kirk Matthews. In return for the significantly reduced prison sentence, Eric agrees to admit to certain aspects of the murder of Jennifer's mother. Although the charge he admits to is conspiracy to commit murder, one investigator says his admissions are so substantial that he could have just as easily confessed to first-degree murder.

In the first trial, the Crown repeatedly reminded the court that the threshold for first-degree murder is not as high as one might suspect. Rumble highlighted this in the first trial as she addressed the jury in her closing: "If someone knowingly does something to help plan a murder, he is guilty of first-degree murder. You don't have to decide whether David [or] Eric pulled the trigger. They, along with Jennifer, Lenford, and Daniel, all helped carry out the plan." On this day those words ring hollow.

In the agreed statement of facts, Eric concedes that he was first contacted by Lenford in the early hours of October 27 when Lenford explained Jennifer's plan to him. It was at this point he agreed to help. His role was to recruit the people to enter the home, provide a vehicle, and show up at the Pan home in Markham on the night of the murder. Later that same day he started making inquiries about a rental car. The murder might have gone ahead two days later, on October 29, but one of the associates Eric planned to bring on board was busy that evening. Eric also failed to score the rental car. Lenford and Eric continued to plan on Halloween. Eric says that Lenford drove to Markham (as the tower records indicate) with Daniel, while he continued to try to find an accomplice. While Lenford and Daniel chatted on the phone outside the Pan residence that night, Eric managed to contract David for the murder, admitting that the "10 stacks" and "5 each ting" text was a discussion about payment. David would get $5,000 for each body and agreed to the spoken contract.

The new date set for the murders was November 3. Eric demanded that $2,000 in cash be handed over at the Pan house upon arrival. The fact that Eric couldn't find enough gas money to attend became a non-issue when Jennifer cancelled the plan. Two days later the tools to carry out the crime were still up in the air because David told Eric he was still searching for what Eric agreed was a "cheap, new firearm." Eric and Lenford continued to discuss the plan on November 8 and eventually came to an agreement — the murder would take place that night. Eric also admits to bringing their mutual friend, Demetrius Mables, on board to call Jennifer on their behalf that evening. Loading David "and at least" one other man into a car, Eric drove from Rexdale to Markham. At 9:34 p.m., as they made their way to Markham, Eric says he called Jennifer and asked her to make sure the door was unlocked. A half-hour later, Eric parked the car. Less than ten minutes later, three men, each armed with a gun, entered the Pan home. Fifteen minutes after that, they left. This is all Eric will admit to. There is no confession about being inside Jennifer's home on November 8.

Compared to the packed house that heard the verdict against Jennifer and the others, the court this time seems barren, with only a few people to witness Eric's conviction and sentencing. The young man appears calm as he stands beside his lawyer. His mother, several of his six siblings, and a slew of young women are also in attendance. Justice Michelle Fuerst asks Eric to stand, and then reads out his sentence for his part in the murder of Bich-Ha Pan and the attempted murder of Hann Pan. Eric is sentenced to eighteen years and won't be eligible to apply for parole until he has served half that time.

Justice Fuerst grants Eric a transfer to a prison in Nova Scotia or British Columbia to serve out the rest of his sentence after he requests to be separated from the numerous "negative influences" in his life that he has built up over his thirty-four years. One seasoned investigator says this can be a common request in Canadian courts, explaining that it's "easier time" in those provinces. Eric's mother is distraught, and seeks consolation from family and friends.

In her decision, Justice Fuerst calls the crime the "epitome of evil."

PART THREE

HOW COULD THIS HAPPEN?

20

A NEW COUNTRY, A NEW LIFE

Huei Hann Pan was born, and grew up, in Vietnam during a time of great turmoil. When he was a young man, at the end of the 1970s, the vicious decade-long war with the United States had left his nation devastated and millions of his countrymen's dreams in tatters. He had attended college for tool and die and diesel mechanics, and four years after the fall of Saigon, at a time when chaos and panic still ruled the streets, Huei Hann Pan left for Canada where he was admitted as a political refugee along with some fifty thousand other Vietnamese and Asian asylum-seekers who arrived during 1979–80. Hann endured a harrowing journey as part of a group historically known as "Boat People." The ships were sometimes at sea for months, and the unfortunate passengers faced attacks from pirates, disease, and starvation. The boats held people from a wide variety of social classes, including both peasants from the countryside and more educated urban dwellers.

At the age of twenty-six, Hann arrived with virtually no knowledge of the English language and an equal amount of money in his pocket. He and his compatriots landed on Canadian shores just as the nation was experiencing an economic downturn of significant proportions. Oil was up in price, and the country was struggling with slow growth, while unemployment steadily rose. The influx of Vietnamese was noticeable in a nation of twenty-four million people, which up to that point contained fewer than four hundred thousand people of Asian descent. Many of Hann's fellow refugees chose to settle in the largely French-speaking city of Montreal, a good fit, many thought, considering Vietnam's history as a French colony. Hann, never one to back down from a challenge, instead ventured to Toronto. When he and many of his fellow refugees arrived in the city, many chose to settle in the former municipality of Scarborough where many who belonged to the city's small Asian population already hung their hats. In 1971, the population of Scarborough was about 354,000, of which 39,820 were immigrants (by 2011, 70 percent of residents here were immigrants — 80 percent from Asia).

After meeting only briefly back home, Bich-Ha Luong, who arrived in Canada with her father and other family members, became reacquainted with Hann. The pair courted, married, and moved in together. Their meagre salaries delivered them to the Malvern neighbourhood, one of the roughest parts of Toronto's most challenged communities. Starting out was difficult as the hard-working pair set about establishing themselves. Thankfully, they weren't alone, with thousands of their fellow countrymen also determined to start fresh, shed their war-torn country's strict class system, and build their families into something their parents hadn't dreamed possible. Like thousands of immigrants and refugees before them, they were in the new world, the land of opportunity, where social mobility depended on more than just your name or background.

In this new world, money is the common currency that acts as more than wealth, and buys more than material goods. It can also deliver the respectability and status many immigrants crave. Back home, that sort of social mobility was rarely attainable. Viewing their own futures as forgone by that point in their lives, Hann and Bich made their main goal the building of a future for their children. Armed with the tools acquired during their class-conscious upbringing, they were able to properly set about bettering the family's lot. For countless refugees, the goal was simple: to join the middle class. Canada, unguided by the constricting caste system from back home, was just the place to do that. Living within a foreign culture and a language they didn't know, surrounded by prejudices, Hann and Bich put their noses to the grindstone.

While other countries have traditionally divided social classes on the basis of money, power, authority, inheritance, and sometimes skin colour, the situation in Vietnam, a country bordered by China in the north and Cambodia and Laos in the west, was different. The centuries-old system that divvied up classes was one often based on education. If you weren't one of the chosen few, learning was the currency that could provide upward mobility to anyone with the right amount of ambition. As in China, where the Pans traced much of their lineage, a strict hierarchy ruled in Vietnam. Other than the emperor and royal family, classes tended to be based on knowledge and accreditation, which equalled power. Outside royalty, it was the intellectuals and the business class who resided atop the spectrum, with the farmers and manual workers in the middle and artisans and the labourers at the bottom. But wars and revolutions helped create a new and reinvented middle class, one where success could be achieved through sheer effort.

Vietnam was heavily influenced by Chinese culture and religion, and was ruled by Confucian norms. This was embedded in the very fabric of society. The ancient philosophy could be described through five essential and authoritative relationships: the subordination of subject to ruler, father to son, wife to husband, younger brother to elder brother, and mutual respect among friends. Authoritarianism remained the cornerstone of such hierarchies. As in many traditional societies, chauvinism was common, and families often preferred to have sons over daughters.

To reinforce just how important education was in the society, it is vital to understand how difficult it was to join the admired ruling classes of such countries. A civil service examination could be attempted in which the applicant was tested on his knowledge of Chinese classical literature and philosophy. If candidates succeeded in becoming accredited as scholars, they were then eligible for appointment to the imperial service, which was the most prestigious route to power, status, and wealth possible. In Confucian Asia, the dream of glorious academic achievement delivered untold influence and wealth for an entire family.

"Villages and towns pooled resources and sent their best and brightest to compete at the imperial court, hoping that one of their own would make it to the centre of power," writes Andrew Lam, a Vietnamese-American author, in *The Huffington Post*. "Mandarins were selected and ranked according to their performance in the rigorous examinations, which took place every four years. Vietnam was for a long time a tributary of China and it was governed by mandarins, a meritocracy open to even the lowest peasant if he had the determination and ability to prevail."

One of the most famous Chinese sayings about studying is a poem that goes like this: "In the book, there is a lot of food, a house made of gold, and a pretty girl." The message was clear: education could bring you all you desired in life. However, all this focus on study could have a polarizing affect on society. While it prompted many to work hard in order to achieve success, resulting in plenty of educational enrichment, it could also have damaging results on others. Because there were so few university places available, relentless competition began at school for those ten years old or younger, and could last until students were in the highest levels of their education, leaving very little time for play or social development, sometimes resulting in emotional disorders among young people.

Frugality ruled Hann's early life in Canada as he set about raising enough money to secure his family's future and to buy his first home. He and Bich ended up buying a three-bedroom house on a suburban street, which today is lined with drab homes spilling out goods, including broken bikes on the front yards, unkempt lawns, and numerous cars in the driveways, some long dead. The home still stands near the corner of Sheppard Avenue and Markham Road in the shadow of a 1980s building sometimes locally referred to as the Malvern Penitentiary because of its drab and institutional appearance. Many of the building's residents consider the term offensive, especially since a number of positive changes have occurred over the past few years. Even in the midst of Toronto's housing boom, in which detached houses go for more than $1 million, until a few years ago you could still buy a two-bedroom apartment in the building for $80,000.

An honourable man, with deeply held convictions surrounding dignity, Hann knew his family relied on him. And he was fortunate in his early years, landing work at local car-parts manufacturer Magna International. But it wasn't only Hann who exerted great effort; Bich worked alongside him for years on the line. They hoped their efforts weren't in vain; neither wanted their children to have to toil in car-part-manufacturing workshops to make a living. Hann held dreams of his offspring's success — one would be a doctor and the other would improve on his accreditation as a machinist to become a full-fledged mechanical engineer. Dreams of this sort aren't only the ideal in Asian countries — where there is a hierarchy of professions — with law, engineering, and medicine at the top — but across the globe. This pressure is particularly high in Asian countries because career choice does not only reflect on the child but also the parents.

When their daughter arrived on June 17, 1986, the couple agreed on the English name Jennifer. They thought it had a lovely ring to it, and it meant she wouldn't be encumbered with a full Vietnamese name at an English school. Although he slowly picked up the language through work, Hann never firmly grasped English. At home, the family spoke Vietnamese and Cantonese. Jennifer was raised in this sort of environment — a Chinese-Vietnamese home perched in multicultural Scarborough.

Bich was the glue that held the family together. Hann's punishing schedule often left him feeling as though he deserved a rest after work. Bich stepped in to cook meals, wash up, and later pack the children's lunches. She ensured the children had a family life they could revel in. However, she was no shrinking violet and, like her husband, she could also be strict and uncompromising. Although she didn't always agree with Hann's views, it was his opinion that most often won out, following the "father knows best" approach prevalent in so many traditional homes. After a blow-up, it was Bich who quietly knocked on her children's doors to smooth things out. Hann also used her as an intermediary, knowing his own temper sometimes landed him in emotionally heightened situations. Bich preferred to remain in the home taking care of her family, but she did have a social life, and especially enjoyed dancing.

Hann was very social and liked to fix things, always wanting to help others with odd jobs. Besides a few close friends, many of his dearest relationships were those within his immediate and extended family circle. His and Bich's large families, mostly Bich's, provided the Pans with more than enough company. The Pans spent weekends visiting Bich's brother's family, the Luongs, who had a daughter two years younger than Jennifer, named Michelle. When she was younger and still an only child, Jennifer became the closest thing Michelle had to a big sister.

Jennifer's father began teaching her from the moment she was conscious of his efforts, and the bright-eyed baby responded gleefully, enjoying her father's attention. It was from her mother that Jennifer learned emotional intelligence and tenderness. As Jennifer grew older, her father's attentive nature shifted from a doting daddy into the home's disciplinarian as he prepared to raise a respectful, obedient, and hard-working daughter.

He was strict and rarely let down his guard. In many homes of Asian heritage, the tender emotion the disciplinarian shows is often restrained. When children misbehave, a parent might show deep disappointment; when they achieve, praise can be muted.

Success was expected in the Pan home. Many first-generation immigrants, especially ones arriving from Asian countries, see praise as an inhibitor, sensing that, once children are complimented, they might feel as though they've completed a task and no longer need to put effort in to continue to improve. This, as many see it, can lead to mediocrity. These are but two aspects that make up a centuries-old form of child-rearing only recently dubbed "tiger parenting" by Yale law professor Amy Chua. The term became a buzzword after she released her bestselling and controversial memoir *Battle Hymn of the Tiger Mother* in 2011.

In her book, Chua describes a tough-love method of child-rearing, one widely practised by parents across the Asian world and beyond, including in many immigrant families in the West. She writes about techniques she used with her daughters involving harsh regimens, high expectations, and psychological control, including inducing guilt as punishment for misbehaviour. Some claim this can cause children to feel as though they won't be loved if they don't fall in line with their parents' wishes; however, Chua submits that if done right, these techniques can lead to monumental success. She argues that, parents who prioritize school work above all else and encourage their children to engage in activities — including athletics and cultural pursuits — to win awards, can mould children so that they're more likely to achieve.

Chua believes that the love and devotion of parents for their children should be used as a means to an end: a paved path to prosperity. In order to gain acquiescence, those who fail to meet their parents' expectations can be berated with name-calling and emotional threats such as removal of toys and gifts, and in extreme cases, even birthdays and Christmas. Because of children's lack of knowledge and experience, choice is removed, giving parents the task of making many, if not all, pivotal decisions for them, both in their daily lives and beyond. However, one must be careful taking Chua's words too literally, since she writes in an often lighthearted but correspondingly biting style, often mocking her own behaviour. Contending that tiger parenting is practised in different forms throughout the world, she lists a number of activities her two daughters were never allowed to engage in as children. Those include: attending sleepovers and play dates; participating in school plays; watching television or playing computer games; choosing their own extracurricular activities; and getting any grade lower than an A.

The principal rules, according to Chua's *Battle Hymn of the Tiger Mother*, go something like this: school work always comes first; children must always be two years ahead of their classmates in math; they should never be complimented in public; parents must always take the side of the teacher or coaches above their children; an A-minus is a bad grade; and children should only be permitted to engage in activities in which they can eventually win medals (always gold).

Chua is justified in her mind in part because of the Confucian virtue of filial piety, a vital aspect of Chinese culture that dictates that children have a lifelong duty of respect; and obedience, and care for their parents and elderly family members. This is legitimized by parents' intense sacrifice for their children. In return, children must hold up their end of that preordained bargain, spending their lives repaying their parents by obeying them and making them proud. A rudimentary guide to the Confucian social contract might go something like this: *I will spend all my time and money ensuring your safety and success as a child, but when I grow too old to take care of myself, I expect you to do that for me.* This viewpoint was in opposition to Chua's husband Jeb's philosophy. "Children don't choose their parents," he tells her in the book. "They don't even choose to be born. It's parents who foist life on their kids, so it's the parents' responsibility to provide for them. Kids don't owe parents anything. Their duty will be toward their own kids."

Part of her message is derived from what she sees as a major failing in modern Western society. She attempts to illustrate how Western parents spend an undo amount of time focusing on a child's self-esteem, but miss the point, falling short of the desired results. Chua argues that only accomplishments can lead to a child's true confidence. It's only through adversity, hard work, and subsequent achievement that abilities can be developed and genuine self-esteem accrued.

There is plenty of proof that Asian homes produce adults who possess academic, professional, and certain personal skills that are largely unrivalled, especially in the United States. According to evolutionary anthropologist Gwen Dewar, founder of Parenting Science, a child psychology website, decades of research suggest that Chinese kids have two big advantages in contrast to Western kids. First, Asian parents tend to emphasize effort rather than innate ability as the determiner for success. Second, their children's peer groups support one another when they work hard at school. The suggestion is that when adolescents in the United States perform well at school, they often get rejected or called names by their peers. Traditional forms of Asian parenting often result in children learning vital characteristics for success, including self-control, tolerance of frustration, and the ability to engage in hard work. "While in the dominant Western culture in the United States, the desired child-rearing goals are independence, individualism, social assertiveness, confidence, and competence," write researchers in one paper on Asian-American parenting, "traditional Asian families tend to be culturally collectivistic, emphasizing interdependence, conformity, emotional self-control, and humility. These cultural values produce deeply ingrained family values, such as a strong sense of obligation and orientation to the family and respect for and obedience to parents and elders."

A 2000 census in the United States shows the success that Asian Americans have achieved — 50 percent have a college or graduate degree (twice as many as Caucasians). Compared to other ethnicities, they have the highest rates of college degrees, advanced degrees, and highly skilled occupations, such as medicine, law, and engineering. The median income in Asian-American households is also the highest, and Asians are the most likely to be married and live with their spouses. Despite making up less than 5 percent of Americans, Asian Americans form 17 percent of incoming Harvard freshmen and almost 30 percent of Harvard medical school students. However, Dr. Helen Hsu, president of the Asian American Psychological Association, insists that, while tiger parenting can lead to plenty of good grades, it often also results in "extremely poor emotional indicators." Although it would be foolish to say that any book, including Chua's, can accurately illustrate the scenario inside another person's house, the similarities are so striking between her account and the parenting style described by Jennifer in the Pan household — sometimes down to minute details — that the role of tiger parenting in Jennifer's life should be examined.

21

GREAT EXPECTATIONS

For a naturally obliging and obedient girl like Jennifer, the parenting style in her home drove her to go over and above her parents' expectations. From the outside, it might have looked as if she was the ideal daughter, happily performing her tasks to the highest standards imaginable without resentment or contest. And, in part, that was true; however, this behaviour lasted only as long as her parents were able to shelter her from the outside world, the activity of others, romantic involvement, and her own insecurities. During her youth, achievement was marshalled via the never-ending schedule of activities and the practice regimen that followed. Jennifer spent her formative years attempting to make her parents proud. When she didn't succeed to their standards, she redoubled her efforts to prove her mettle. As a result, she developed an unrivalled ability to learn new skills. She was put through a tireless childhood, one in which she followed a well-trodden path for Asians across Canada and around the world, beginning piano at the tender age of four. Like careers, sports, education, and cultural pursuits, for many Asians, have their own hierarchies — violin and piano are at the top, percussion instruments — which at least one author says her parents implied might lead to drug use — are at the bottom. At the same time, art and culture are often used to distinguish the middle class from those beneath them. In her article "On Tiger Moms," Julie Park quotes political theorist Hannah Arendt: "In this fight for social position, culture began to play an enormous role as one of the weapons, if not the best-suited one, to advance oneself socially, and to 'educate oneself' out of the lower regions."

Two years after she began piano lessons, Jennifer started competing in the cutthroat world of youth figure skating. Both pursuits were solitary ones in which Jennifer could achieve awards, prizes, and trophies as proof of a job well done. Only in individual sports, as opposed to the team sports preferred by many Western families, can success or failure be accurately measured; physical ability aside, it's determined by the amount of effort you put in. Although they quickly fell by the wayside, Jennifer was also enrolled in swimming and *wushu* (an ancient Chinese martial art).

None of these expensive pastimes were Jennifer's choice, and although they were heavy strains on the family's pocketbook, they were a sure way to raise a high achiever. University professor and researcher Julie Park argues that, in many homes, the purpose of musical or sporting performance is not to express oneself or create something beautiful, but rather to demonstrate one's ability and technical proficiency to impress judges and win competitions. Jennifer was well and truly on her way down this path, a similar route taken by countless families who must start their lives again in a new country. It's their determination to ensure success for their children that drives them. But it can extend beyond class distinction and venture into ensuring children land a quality job with a good salary and health benefits, which in turn provides a comfortable and successful life. However, the problem with children following a parent's path is that it often begins and ends with someone else's decision, and can be based on a restrictive cultural outlook, often shunning children's instincts to distinguish themselves. When children deviate from this constrictive path, it can be construed as error or delinquency rather than individualism.

There were some major victories. Despite Jennifer never being involved in the decision to take up piano or skating, she developed a passion for both. Skating provided a release from what Jennifer called her "scheduled life," which had her on the move almost constantly as she grew up, travelling throughout Southern Ontario on countless winter weekends to attend regional competitions. It was during these contests that she continually fought her fear of falling or letting down her father, who was always by her side. "I was petrified of the competitions," she said while talking about winning trophies. "I wanted to be Daddy's girl."

When she was out on the ice, she felt free of the controls in her life. Despite natural inhibitors, including severe asthma and poor eyesight — which allowed her to see shapes but no definition — her innate abilities and unbridled will to succeed saw her improve at an astonishing rate. Ultimately, though, it was often her dedication to the task that brought her success and ever more pressure to reach greater levels of achievement. "I'd rather skate than walk," she later remarked, describing how she felt when the tension left her and she began to perform with ease. "It was just feeling the breeze on your cheek, having control of what I did, and the way I moved. There [were] no restraints."

Although her love of skating was intense, it was piano and the emotive world of music that really got her heart racing. Music provided a space where enjoyment and hard work met without fear of pain or punishment, allowing Jennifer to cultivate her life's one true passion. The piano was her therapy — a place where she could release pent-up emotion and shed the emotional ups and downs she claimed dotted her childhood. "I love music. Piano is almost second nature to me…. It brings out all your emotions. You can put all your feelings into it, pour it all out there," she said. Jennifer was equally ambitious in school. Raised Catholic, like her father, as opposed to Buddhist, like her mother, Jennifer attended St. Barnabas Catholic School. It was here that the intense pressure she was under to perform at the highest level was apparent, according to one teacher. Jennifer described herself as "not just the teacher's pet, but the school pet," which to this day, nearly two decades later, is still talked about by some of the staff. Often shunning schoolyard activities, Jennifer spent hours in the office helping administrators to complete tasks. She not only volunteered to check homework for grade ones and twos and help them with their reading, but she also watched over them during lunch-hour and recess. It was during this time that she fostered her adoration for small children.

Long-time school secretary Jeannine Brown remembers a virtuous and respectful young girl, always around the office wanting to help. "She was talented and very respectful," Brown says. "She was one of those students other teachers were always talking about."

Jennifer's grade eight teacher, Frank Wilcott, who's been teaching at the school for most of his thirty-five years in the profession, says she was not only one of his favourite students, but a "great role model" in the class who scored between 85 and 95 percent in almost everything she did. "She was a great student to have in your class," he says, explaining she was in the top ten best students he ever taught. "She was meticulous and neat. She handed in her work on time. She was someone the others could emulate. I didn't have very many negative experiences with her. I would have taught her from junior kindergarten to grade eight if I could have."

It was this dedication to pleasing her teachers that left an indelible mark on Wilcott's memory. He recounts how she whipped out her agenda before he even got that evening's assignments out of his mouth. "As we talk, I can picture her [in her] seat," he says. "She'd be done before I even wrote it on the board. She was first to hand her stuff in, and she'd compete to hand it in first." But it isn't only her scholarly pursuits at which he still marvels. He also remembers her keen athletic ability. Although she was never allowed to try out for school teams, Wilcott says he was once left awestruck at Jennifer's grace after witnessing the eleven-year-old figure-skating during one school trip. "I saw her performing single axels with ease in grade seven. That was very impressive," the long-time coach says, noting her dedication was astounding. "She was more than driven. She never settled. And she could be trained. That doesn't sound nice, but for a coach it's hard to find. I like that. I like a little fire in your belly."

However, Wilcott also saw the other side of Jennifer's commitment to success. He explains how she was the ultimate perfectionist, driven to the point of concern. On top of teaching many Asian students, he says, he was raised around Asian classmates who complained about 99 percent marks on their math tests. One, he notes, always remarked that mathematics was a "perfect science" in which it was possible to receive 100 percent. He faced similar issues in his classroom, often, he says, with Chinese and Vietnamese students whose parents didn't "smile or applaud efforts," sensing that might lead to "complacency." Wilcott recounts an instance in which the parents of one of his highest-performing students complained and threatened to move their daughter because he frequently praised what he called her "almost perfect work." And although he never witnessed this behaviour with Jennifer or her parents, he remembers worrying about the atmosphere at her home where he felt it might have been a situation where "nothing was good enough."

"[Jennifer] was a high achiever, to the point where you'd be worried she was trying to keep up to a standard at home," he says. "If she received a mark that she didn't like, she'd never complain, but sought out advice for the next time and then [she'd] do it. She would take it to heart. She never lost focus, maybe to the point where it's not healthy, like *Okay, Jennifer take a break, take a breath. It's okay, you didn't get perfect. It's okay.* She wouldn't say it out loud, but you could read it in her body language as she was walking away. And the look on her face. She never complained … but she would take it to heart." Wilcott says this was especially true if she knew what sort of marks her friends achieved. "Her friendship circle was very similar," he says. "They seemed to be friendly, but they always had a little competition going. I never saw Jennifer do this, but Tiffany would let Jennifer know if and when she achieved a higher mark. You could see fire in Jennifer, that she would want to do something better next time. She would not have wanted that to happen again."

Wilcott further remarks that he noticed Jennifer's joylessness in class several times, which at one point prompted him to organize creative-writing workshops and in-class group skits to provoke a show of unbridled emotion from her. While the exercises were moderately successful, he also observed that Jennifer was so intent on perfection that she'd memorize not only her own lines but everyone else's. "She wasn't disliked [among classmates], but she was kind of cold, especially with the way she moved around," he says. "I wouldn't call her dour, but maybe sour. I never saw her as jovial or excited … openly happy or smiling about something … everything was serious."

Jennifer later said it was around this time that depression made its first foray into her life. She said she felt unloved, unworthy, and over time developed a keen sense of self-hatred. "A lot of young teens have a deep internal emptiness and insecurity, and this can be amplified if the teen has acculturative or identity stress and also does not feel loved and supported by family," says psychologist Dr. Helen Hsu. "Asian-American families tend to show love by pushing their kids academically, providing good food, but tend to demonstrate far less verbal and physical affection than Western families. Teens often mistake that for lack of love."

According to Julie Park, in many overly strict Asian homes "fun, pleasure, and joy" are devalued and life begins to seem like "nothing but toil." Rather than the pursuit of happiness, life becomes more about hard work, meaning "happiness was, at best, the incidental by-product of success and respectability." Inside the home, a parent's goals can become solely driven toward having obedient, well-behaved, and above all, honourable children; while outside the home the focus is the achievement of academic credentials, competitive accolades, and career achievements. "Children who are taught to privilege academic success are more likely to suffer from stress and depression," writes Park. "Straight A's, gold medals, promotions, and Nobel Prizes are not simply rewards of one's hard work, but evidence of one's worth. Specific achievements are never enough ... [they simply] fuel the desire for success."

Jennifer explained how much of her youth became about a never-ending and punishing schedule of extracurricular activities, training, and school work. "Working hard and coming home from skating at ten o'clock sometimes," she said, "I would work hard for school until midnight in elementary school. I tried to stay up late nights and wake up early for morning practices." Although Jennifer had plenty of chances to interact with her immediate and extended family, social relationships outside the home weren't fostered. A by-product was that Jennifer was left emotionally stunted and, to quote her own lawyer, by age twenty-four she had the "social skills of a fifteen-year-old." Like Amy Chua's children, she was rarely allowed to go on play dates or sleepovers, and when she was, her parents controlled both the duration and parameters. "I only ever had two [sleepovers] — one was at my own house and one at my friend Cecilia's house," she said. "But I was picked up right away the next morning and dropped off late that night." She only occasionally attended birthday parties for her friends, that is, if she didn't have to practise piano or participate in one of her other extracurricular activities. "My father wanted me to focus on school or piano ... he wanted me to focus on something, something productive." Writer Amy Tan, in a jaunty retelling of her youth in the essay "Midlife Confidential," aptly describes Jennifer's situation when she says that the three "F-words" in her home were *fun*, *freedom*, and *friends*.

Instead of growing up around friends, Jennifer spent much of her alone time with a huge collection of stuffed animals in her room, babying them as if they were her children, sleeping with them, and naming them. Her favourite "stuffies" were monkeys, three in particular, including Mr. Chipmunk, Mr. Bubbles, and Munkey. These characters played a role in her life well into her twenties. Her childlike tendencies could not only be seen in her stuffed animals, but in her diary, which spanned from childhood right up to her mid-twenties. In her entries, according to those who read them, she laid out her grandest dreams and aspirations, supplemented with bubbly drawings in the margins, which one investigator describes as "all puppy dogs, rainbows and butterflies." He also uses those words to describe her childish style of writing.

In many ways, however, Jennifer might have grown up not realizing how much she missed the social interaction real friends could provide; after all, she had her cousins, who were always around. While she always sensed something was missing, she was also very busy, and simply didn't have time for much else. She also had her beloved little brother, who she could befriend, bond with, and baby. When Jennifer was three, the family's second child, Felix, was born. The happy-go-lucky boy's arrival was a boon for the family, providing Jennifer with a social and emotional attachment that turned the home into a happier place. Jennifer, meanwhile, became to Felix almost like a second mother. The pair's bond grew unshakable. He looked up to his sister for guidance while providing her with the eternal playmate she longed for, as well as a sympathetic ear and a window into the childhood she felt she missed out on.

Very early on, the pair's roles were cemented: Jennifer, the overachieving big sister, and Felix, the family baby, who felt comfortable in his role. "My parents did push my sister a lot … for me it was always okay to be worse," he admits, saying he never wished to be like his sister, never wanted to be under that sort of pressure. "My sister was always too perfect almost. Like when we used to do piano, my dad got mad at my sister for coming in second."

Along with strict gender roles, the first-born is often forced to carry the burden as the example for the rest of the children. This is, of course, true in many homes, but is particularly pronounced in Asian ones. If the first-born happens to be female, that burden grows ever stronger. Dr. Helen Hsu, who was raised in a similar environment and has worked in the field of psychology for more than a decade, says first-born children often feel the brunt of their parents' wishes. "It's a powerful feeling, one of 'You owe us. We sacrificed everything and we have a huge burden,'" she says, explaining the filial piety phenomenon. "Duty and loyalty are seen as paramount. Girls are supposed to take care of the family and act as a second mother. [Parents] truly believe that forcing them to go to Stanford will truly make them happy. [Parents] were raised to believe that all you have to do is push and [your children] will have a good life."

Like his sister, Felix was a precocious child, but he was softer and not nearly as tenacious as his big sister. Therefore, he was far less responsive to Hann's controlling tendencies. He excelled in mechanics as a boy, always tinkering, taking things apart, and trying to figure out how they worked before attempting to reassemble them. And, like Jennifer, he shared an emotional bond with his mother. "My mom would just watch over me. If I had a question, I would ask my mom," says Felix. "I was a lot closer with my mom than my dad." In many ways, the Pan household seemed to resemble an old Chinese adage: "strict father, kind mother."

In the essay "Parenting of Asians," Ruth Chao and Vivian Tseng write that, in Asian families, often "fathers exert high degrees of authoritarian control and mothers manifest high degrees of warmth. The traditional role of fathers as authority figures also implies that fathers do not typically display much closeness and affection toward children." However, this is not to say that mothers aren't difficult. Bich had high expectations of her children, and she would grow enraged, yell, scream, or cry when they were not met. Chao and Tseng write: "In studies of Chinese from the P.R.C. [China], Taiwan, and Hong Kong, mothers in all three countries were more warm and less restrictive than fathers, but they were also more demanding."

Felix says his mother was always "comforting," while his father was "controlling" but always trying to lead them in the "right direction." However, listening to Jennifer and Felix describe their upbringing, it is clear they had different experiences inside the Pan home. If Hann viewed his daughter as self-assured, with prodigious abilities, he appeared to see Felix as sensitive and, a late bloomer, someone who would achieve heights of success in school and otherwise with a little more time and guidance. Just by being himself and, on account of being the second child and a male, Felix got away with things that Jennifer never dreamed of doing in her youth, including coming home with poor grades. And while Felix always excelled in math, partly because of Hann's assistance, he earned poor grades in many other subjects. His overall marks would eventually grow so bad that in grade four he was moved to a private school after Hann grew unsatisfied with some of the teachers at St. Barnabas.

Similarly, in piano, Jennifer's teacher, Ewa Krajewska, who also taught Felix and her cousin, Michelle, says, although Michelle was much better than Felix, who left the conservatory only years after he first began, neither could hold a candle to Jennifer. "He was lazy and she was not," Ewa says matter-of-factly. "Parents didn't push him because he was second. [Jennifer] tried to help him, but he didn't listen. Michelle was good, but not as talented as Jennifer. Jennifer wanted to be first at everything. She was a perfectionist. When I was telling her there was a mistake or we had to change something, she'd listen. When I saw her next, she fixed it."

Whereas Jennifer took criticism to heart and worked even harder, the extra pressure never helped Felix. In academics, he seemed to retreat from conflict and often performed worse when pushed — much like in piano. However, it would be misleading to say that Hann was any gentler when it came to Felix. He was unafraid to show his anger with either child. Felix says his father was uncompromising and refused to demonstrate any sympathy toward his son after an accident, even when it caused intense physical pain. One time, Felix says, his father grew enraged after Felix fell off his bicycle during a family bike ride. "I fell off my bike and broke my arm. My dad comes by and yells at me. He walks his bike and my bike home and I walk home alone [crying]." In another instance, he explains Hann's reaction after Felix chopped off part of his finger using a kitchen knife. "I cut my finger, [and] he yells at me — 'How did this happen? Why did you do this?'" Felix says he eventually grew to understand the behaviour was "tough love," pointing out that his father yelled all the time and often sounded angry, but "that's just the way he speaks."

Felix makes a point of describing an instance when, expecting a tirade at his mistake, he was instead treated gently by his father. "That's kind of how my father is … like tough love in a sense, he always got mad at me if I did something wrong, if I was lazy or he thought I was lazy. I remember when we first moved in to [238 Helen Avenue]. I accidentally spilled a bucket of sand, and he was so angry at me just because he thought I was really lazy at the time. But then, a couple of weeks later, I had my scooter in a box and it dropped and broke a tile in the kitchen, and I thought he was going to be really mad at me. But he kind of was like 'I'm not going to get mad at you for this just because it was an accident and you were trying to help clean up the house.' That's all he wants from me. He wants me to be hard-working, I guess."

Julie Park, in her article "On Tiger Moms," insists that, depending on how the tough-love message is implemented and followed up on, it can be viewed as either proactive parenting or simple abuse that can backfire over time. "[Tough love] often leads to gridlocked conflict, unwillingness to empathize, festering resentment and long-lasting family strife," she writes. In some overtly strict Asian homes, the words "I love you" are never uttered. Hugs are just as rare. Instead, parental love is often shown through action.

Another American journalist, Candice Chung, in an article entitled "Why Chinese Parents Don't Say I Love You," writes about her experience growing up in an emotionally rigid household. "Like many Asian families, we'd become incredibly proficient at reading cryptic emotional signs," she writes. "There may not be big hugs and open praise, but once in a while, mum would put an unexpected fried egg in our noodles or dad would try and make conversation by asking us to pronounce, then spell every street name he's ever had trouble remembering. Those, as we'd try to explain to our friends, are their 'affectionate sides.'" She continues by saying that some Chinese parents display love through irony, screaming at you for spending too much money on them and fighting to the death in a restaurant for the right to pay the cheque. "Chinese families know how to love fiercely," writes a blogger quoted in the article. "They do it through immense generosity, unwavering loyalty, and a lot of food." The rationale is that Asian-American parents' affection is conveyed through instrumental support, devotion, close monitoring, and aid for education, rather than through physical, verbal, and emotional expressions such as hugging, kissing, and praising, which are typical indicators of Western parental warmth.

Dr. Helen Hsu says there are positives and negatives to both parenting styles, noting that while some of her Western friends received plenty of love, care, and affection growing up, they were also kicked out of their homes at the age of eighteen. "Asians are kept by their families in strength-based relationships in which they are kept in the family unit, almost no matter what they protect and shield you from harm," she says. "The other side is that no matter what you do, they always want to weigh in."

Hann, for example, might have shown his love for his family by never blinking when his alarm clock went off at 5:00 a.m. This unwavering loyalty saw him forgo all but a few years of his existence to provide a solid foundation for his family. Hann's devotion appeared so great that he would have sold the shirt off his back if it meant Jennifer could continue her piano lessons, the basis for her later successes. This seemed so valuable to him that, without it, his own well-being was meaningless. Often exhausted after a day's work, he jumped at the opportunity to work overtime to pay for her skates or expensive lessons. He spent almost nothing on himself or his wife, wearing the same tired clothing for years on end until the family was secure. Suppressing his own ego for the sake of his family was not only the way he was raised, but also how everyone around him had grown up. He didn't just spend his hard-earned money on Jennifer's extracurricular activities, but also used his free time to drive her across the region on his weekends, showing devotion to his baby girl in the best way he knew. Although Bich begged Hann to visit Vietnam on holiday, he utterly refused, insisting that he wanted his children's future guaranteed first.

Despite Hann's cold exterior, he was immensely proud of his daughter and her achievements. The first destination for any visitor to his home was the cabinet containing Jennifer's plaques, scholarships, awards, medals, and ribbons. One of the most prominent photo arrays showed Jennifer wearing a sequined figure-skating outfit performing a variety of graceful movements. But Jennifer's achievement exacted a high price. She felt pressure to succeed in not only one but in all her pursuits from an early age. Hann originally wanted her to be a doctor, but that would eventually shift because, as Jennifer put it, her father knew she "didn't have the stomach for it." She was expected to come in the top three at piano recitals and figure-skating competitions, preferably, as she often did, first. She was encouraged to shoot for the Vancouver Olympics in figure skating and the Beijing Olympics in martial arts. Goals she said were originally her father's soon became hers.

The valedictorian award at her school was another objective. Like Amy Chua's children, she was to learn math two years before the rest of her grade. She succeeded in this, as well, resulting in her scoring in the highest percentile for her age at a prestigious math contest in Waterloo, Canada's own version of Silicon Valley. If there were signs of belligerence, fatigue, or indifference, Jennifer would be measured versus her contemporaries.

In many strict homes, inadequacy is fostered inside children as a means of motivating them to prove otherwise. Often that's the surest way of ensuring children understand just how important success is. It is the competition with others that drives them to push ever harder. In Jennifer's case, she said this included comparisons to classmates, fellow piano players, skaters, swimmers, and perhaps most searing of all, her "kid sister" and cousin, Michelle Luong who, like Jennifer, was a perpetual overachiever in school. "My dad and my mom — well, mostly my dad — [would say] 'well, you know did you hear, Michelle, oh, she's looking like she's on her way to many awards this year,' hinting that I didn't get any awards the year before," she said. "[My parents would say] 'I wish you could have been that person.' It's what I have heard all my life. So … it's nothing." Chua explains it was normal for her to say to her children: "You're lazy. All your classmates are getting ahead of you."

One online commenter, posting below a Chua article promoting the book *Battle Hymn of the Tiger Mother*, resents this sort of parenting: "Growing up I hated it and thought it was very unfair (especially as I saw my younger siblings having more liberties than I did — like going out to play with friends on a weeknight and/or before finishing their homework). There was definitely no warm fuzzies from Mom. Never a 'great job' or 'I love you,' or even a hug, really. I always got the sense that no matter what I did, it was not good enough and was always compared to X person that was better, so I was constantly pushing myself. I dreaded the days that I got B's on my report card. I was ashamed to tell my mom and she never really actually scolded me but I felt so bad personally that I would lock myself in my room or the bathroom to cry over my "failure"…. My mom would also compare me to cousins to allude that they were better … my grades were never good enough."

Another commenter says her mother used to make her rank her classmates from "smartest to dumbest," asking her not to associate with anyone who ranked below her. One of the main criticisms of tiger parenting is that, while children raised this way may grow into responsible, hard-working, and successful adults, they often fail to become leaders, instead, becoming "hoop-jumpers," according to Hsu.

Jennifer said many of her issues first arose at the time of her grade eight graduation when she discovered she wouldn't claim the valedictorian or any other prize at her school. She felt spurned, as if all her hard work had amounted to nothing. Julie Park says this can often be the case when "children ... stake their sense of personal esteem on public affirmations of success" such as awards and prizes. Jennifer appears to have felt a deep sense of failure as a result of missing out on an award. "I was one of the top of my class in elementary school," she said. "I tried very hard to get the high marks, but during ... grade eight graduation, I didn't get any solid prizes for all my hard work. Because I had taken piano and skating from a young age, when I did well in those occasions I got medals, I got ribbons, I got badges, trophies.... All that [hard work] accumulated to nothing or no credibility at the end of grade eight. [They] just brushed me aside. I didn't even get one single good behaviour [award], so I just thought that in high school, what was the point in trying? It was important to me because I had felt growing up the recognition had come from my figure skating and my piano, and that was solid 100 percent recognition ... you can be boastful about ... [that] you can boast about ... to friends and family, 'Hey, I got first place: here's my gold medal or second place or third place,' so it was almost proof that I had done well. When I didn't get any awards ... I was shocked ... I felt I was almost invisible in that school for the ten years I attended and tried very hard. I even went back years later. [The] new principal said 'Oh, you're Jennifer Pan' and ... they had heard about me, so I just felt like even more of a disgrace because I was like, I had done so much work people are talking about me, but I didn't get any recognition for my hard work."

Although Frank Wilcott doesn't remember exactly how the winner of the valedictorian award was chosen that year, he figures it was handed out to the most well-rounded student, someone who was a stellar citizen, working in the community, popular with teachers and students, and says those who excelled in team sports at school always did well. "Maybe teachers misguided her, leading her to believe she would win," Wilcott adds. "I hope not." Regardless, Jennifer described this moment as the crushing blow from which her scholarly ambition never recovered.

22

A CHILD'S FIRST DECEPTION

When Jennifer first walked through the doors of Scarborough's Mary Ward Catholic Secondary School, she had little idea what to expect. She had no friends there and little experience making new ones. For the conservative and routine-orientated Jennifer, the change was unwelcome at first. She might have adored the buzz and vibrancy of the place, but she felt lonely and timid, the two vulnerabilities the fourteen-year-old dreaded showing the most. However, Jennifer, like her father, never made a habit of shrinking from challenges. And, while she might have been nervous, she battled her inner fears, determined to find her way. Although she spent years in a tight-knit circle of like-minded friends, she also regularly engaged with adults, especially coaches and teachers, and developed a confidence in conversation and a keen sense of how to speak to people, at least those who didn't intimidate her. Those who knew her during those nascent years described her as a run-of-the-mill grade nine student, one who didn't stand out in a crowd. She was humble, quiet, and soft-spoken.

"At five foot seven inches, she was taller than most of the other Asian girls at the school, and pretty but plain," friend Karen Ho later wrote. "She rarely wore makeup; she had small, round wire-frame glasses that were neither stylish nor expensive." She was not overly fashion-conscious along with many others in the late 1990s. Jennifer wore her long jet-black hair in a variety of braids and ponytails. In social situations she maintained her composure with constant eye contact, an unassuming and overtly friendly person, and what Karen called her trademark "high-pitched laugh." Ho further remarked on Jennifer's intensity, which shaped so many of her relationships, pursuits, and interactions throughout her life. "In conversation," Ho wrote, "she always seemed focused on the moment — if you had her attention, you had it completely."

Another friend, who simply identifies himself as J.B., tells me that while many girls at the school manipulated their Catholic uniforms in provocative ways, rolling up the skirts at the waist and unbuttoning their dress shirts, Jennifer preferred bulky sweaters and black pants. The former piano player, who first met Jennifer at age twelve, describes the school as very multicultural with a large contingent of Asians, who made up roughly 60 percent of the school, meshing with Italians, Indians, and African Canadians, who made up the other 40 percent. "There was no segregation; none whatsoever," J.B. says, explaining how that culture at the time stood in stark contrast with another nearby high school.

Like many grade nine students, Jennifer found it difficult to make close friends right away. But she was spared having to eat her lunch alone because of her constant companion — music. It was the band that provided her with the trusted inner social circle she had always longed for. And it was in this inclusive environment where she was immediately surrounded with students of similar upbringing, most of them from Asian backgrounds. She played the flute. The band room became her hangout, a place where she could be at ease and be the person she had always imagined herself as — someone who was happy and friendly. And while she was secretly tormented with feelings of self-doubt and insecurity, she tried to foster a breezier side with which everyone would enjoy interacting.

The school was a place where "geekiness was celebrated," as Karen put it, an environment where Jennifer found her niche and felt the acceptance she said she didn't experience at home. Jennifer's network of friends always remained limited, but it did expand outside band to a certain degree when she met two of her closest friends, Topaz Chiu and Adrian Tymkewycz, in French class. "We became a clique; a little group of friends," she later remarked, smiling as she reminisced. Topaz was one of her few female friends and eventually grew so close to Jennifer, that they called each other sisters. However, Jennifer always said she was more drawn to males, preferring their easygoing nature to what she saw as girls' "cattiness."

If even the most mundane high schools can be liberating experience for teenagers, then Mary Ward was a revelation for Jennifer. It wasn't just her new social circle that she found liberating, but also the school's novel approach to education. Dubbed the "self-directed learning" format, the program provided students with the opportunity to choose their own schedule. Each course had eighteen units and, once complete — whether in one or six months — the extra time could be used to focus on weaker subjects. However, on any given day, former students said staff found so many kids loafing around doing nothing that the school was forced to hire hall monitors to patrol the corridors. "It became a real problem because everyone was just hanging around," J.B. says, explaining that was why both he and Jennifer hung out in the band room where they always appeared to be focused on music. The problem many faced with all that autonomy, including Jennifer — raised under a strict regime — was that all the liberties came at a high price.

Hann, secure in Jennifer's foundation, had eased up on her somewhat. Now, he was spending much of his time focusing on Felix, who had switched schools due to his poor grades. However, Jennifer's piano and figure skating were still being pursued intently. She might have experienced unbridled freedom at school, but from the time Hann picked her up each day, sharply at 3:00 p.m., she was back on schedule. "My father picked me up right after school," she said. "I would be going to either piano classes, skating classes, going home quickly to pick up my gear ... or having a quick dinner before I commenced those other things. So I was pretty scheduled."

Jennifer said she wanted to try out for school sports like the track team but wasn't allowed to, and had no time. It was under this regimen that Jennifer reached a proficiency level in piano that Ewa Krajewska, her teacher of almost twenty years, says she has only seen a handful of times since she began working with students more than forty years ago. It wasn't only her teacher who saw her potential. Other students at the conservatory looked up to Jennifer and aspired to one day play like her, although few achieved that dizzying height of success. J.B. describes her as one of the top students at Scarborough's New Conservatory of Music; indeed a number of pictures of Jennifer clutching trophies, all dolled up in her Sunday best, still hang in the school. "She was very talented," says J.B., who was a few years younger than Jennifer. "She was always winning first prize. Music was my main focus back then. At fourteen she was the best student in her class, playing Chopin's *Fantaisie-Impromptu*. It was impressive that she could play that at that time. I still play [piano] and I can't even play it now. It's very hard on your fingers and you need a lot of stamina."

Ewa says Jennifer had rare talent and was willing to practise two hours a night to achieve her goals. "She had a good memory, and it was very easy for her to prepare," she says, explaining she taught Jennifer from age six to age twenty-four. "She really wanted it, she loved the piano. It was her passion. Her father or mother would always come with her and wait in the lobby. Her parents may have been pushing her. She wanted to play in all the festivals. Parents used to push their kids a lot; now, not so much. [Jennifer] also volunteered at the festivals and helped students. She was very bright, smart, and so nice. She could have been a concert pianist." Talking to me, Ewa points to a bust of Mozart sitting with pride of place on top of her piano. "She brought me this from Austria. We had a special bond."

Jennifer continued playing piano throughout her teen years and into her twenties, getting not only immense pleasure from it, but tangible results. The late nights spent slaving over her school work so she could score nineties, however, fell by the wayside. By this point, Jennifer had realized there were more important things in life than trying to be Little Miss Perfect. Instead, she began to spend more time on the phone with friends. Hann and Bich were happy to cut her slightly more slack — but where Hann gave an inch, Jennifer took a mile. Midway through grade nine, Jennifer found herself scoring a mid-seventy average, boosted by two exceptions: music and math, both of which she was handily acing. But this might have been because of an accrued proficiency rather than hard work. "In high school, I kind of gave up," she said. "I didn't try as hard anymore. [My marks were] average. There were some courses I excelled in, such as music — one of my passions — and math. Other ones, not so much. So I would just say [I was scoring] average. I had ninety marks for music, but for science and for some of my later math courses and history, I was [around] a seventy."

Faced with the dilemma of what to do next, Jennifer cowered at the prospect of showing her parents the level to which her marks had dropped. Telling the truth and handing over the real report card, which represented a drop of 20 percent in most of her subjects, she felt would have caused an explosion of anger. She might also see the life she'd been settling into reworked, filling any spare time she had with tutors and more expectations. The other alternative — deception — proved far more appealing. Jennifer implied that her decision could be traced back to her childhood and her traditional upbringing, which involved a strict code regarding which personal and family-related details she was allowed to share with the rest of the world: "What happens in the family stays in the family." Jennifer said that it was in this environment as a young girl that she developed a proficiency for recounting "white lies."

Felix also remarks on the phenomenon, explaining that his family never wanted people to view them as lesser than they really were, and when there was a family secret, everyone was expected to shelter it from the outside world. Projecting the right image was very important not only to Hann but also to Bich, and the children knew this. Despite any turmoil at home or any sadness Jennifer felt inside, she always hid those emotions, wearing what she referred to as her "happy mask" in public.

It was this first deception, though, that led Jennifer to forgo her last refuge, her family, and begin using that same "happy mask" in the presence of her parents and extended family. Instead of facing up to the consequences of her tumbling grades, she decided to show her parents the image they'd deem acceptable. This was in order to maintain the status quo, which was more manageable than the truth. Her rationalization was simple. At the time, Jennifer saw a forged report card not as a life-altering fraud, but rather as a chance to buy some time so that she could pick up her grades in the upcoming semester. Armed with the knowledge that many Canadian students learn soon after beginning high school — universities only consider your two final years when deciding on acceptance — she thought she would have plenty of time to pick up her marks. With some old report cards in one hand, and her arts and crafts set in the other, the fourteen-year-old forged her first report card with the help of a photocopier. "That was one of my first lies," she said. "I had faked it, because [on] my first report card, some of my marks were not what I would have had in elementary school. They were not A's they were not A+, they were in the seventies, low seventies, and some of them were high, but the part where it says whether you have been trying hard in school or whether you participate in class, it was satisfactory."

That evening, Jennifer walked into her father's study and handed him the manipulated document. Her palms were sweating and her stomach did flips as he scanned it up and down. When he finally looked up and smiled, she realized, to her surprise, that her shrewd but amateur manipulation had worked: her father had bought it. Not only was she in the clear, but she later remarked how, at that moment, the tactic of deceit in return for peace became reinforced in her mind. "He was still himself. He was still happy. He didn't notice anything different in my demeanour," she said. "He was actually trying to push me harder in skating because, at that point, skating was the weaker of school, piano, and other things he looked highly upon. So, I did feel really guilty, but at the same time I rationalized it with myself and felt that maybe one or two report cards wasn't so bad.... My friends had marks that were the same."

It wasn't only peace at home Jennifer was after. Bogus report cards also allowed her to shrug off her emerging sense of insecurity regarding her abilities, namely, that she was "not as smart as everyone thought." While her excellence in elementary school, piano, and skating might have proved her abilities to others, high school brought with it plenty of more competition, and achievement wasn't as easy to come by. She swept her self-doubt under the carpet, meaning she'd never have to try hard and fail at school again, leaving the tenuous confidence she clung to intact. And while she did feel shame, she said a greater worry was the rippling repercussions that would have resulted if she had shared the truth. "I didn't want to disappoint my family," she said. "I didn't want my parents to feel ashamed of me.... I hid most of my feelings from them so they didn't know how I felt about not being able to excel, so I forged my first report card."

However, Jennifer said this feeling came largely from Hann, as opposed to Bich, who she said was more sympathetic to her plight. "My mother was very different," she said. "All she wanted was for me to do the best that I could. She would take me aside sometimes, she could read me, she was almost like I was another her. So she knew something was up, and she knew I was putting pressure on myself ... because I was still skating and still had piano at this time. And she knew my passion for those two, and when I didn't win competitions, she saw how disappointed I was. And sometimes, when my father wasn't around, she'd console me, especially during the nighttimes, when I would let my emotions out by myself. And she'd say, 'You know all we want for you is just your best. Just do what you can.' Lying to my mom was heartbreaking, and I felt so disgusted with myself."

Deception is nothing new to Western youth, especially when it concerns lying to parents. However, engineering this sort of deception might be unthinkable to Western teenagers, possibly because the perceived consequences of failure aren't severe enough to drive them to perpetrate this depth of trickery. But for Jennifer, and many others in similar circumstances, fooling your parents into believing you're doing one thing while really doing another is not only considered but often acted upon. For many Western children, bringing home grades in the seventies is acceptable, although many parents might work with children or seek help for them in order to improve grades. For others, it might be considered a job well done. In the Pan family, anything under an A was unacceptable. After all, her parents knew she could do better — anything less than a top grade was construed as simple laziness. While someone in her predicament — falsifying report cards — might add in a few A- or even B+ grades to help make the document appear genuine, not Jennifer. Her report cards contained A and A+ grades almost exclusively. "I thought that's what was expected of me," she said.

"Tiger Mom" Amy Chua phrases it like this: "If a Chinese child gets a B — which would never happen — there would first be a screaming, hair-tearing explosion. The Chinese mother would then get dozens, maybe hundreds of practice tests and work through them with her child for as long as it takes to get the grade up to an A. Chinese parents demand perfection.... That's why the solution to substandard performance is always to excoriate, punish and shame the child."

There is a well-worn joke in Canadian high schools in which a North American grading system is juxtaposed next to an "Asian grading system." Normal system: A = Great, B = Good, C = Average, D = Bad, F = Fail. The Asian system: A = Average, B = Bad, C = Catastrophe, D = Disowned, F = Forgotten Forever. Whether real or imagined, this explanation by Amy might provide a window into Jennifer's mindset about the possible consequences of receiving poor grades.

It is this sort of pressure that prompts dishonesty, according to some researchers. For many children, especially girls, the easiest alternative is to pretend. Researcher and journalist Julie Park, who was raised in a strict Korean household, writes that this sort of behaviour enjoys a "long and cherished tradition within the [Asian] community. The most resourceful children know there are many shades of acceptable pretense. It is simple enough, for example, to put on a show of obedience in the presence of one's parents, and then turn around and do whatever the hell one pleases as soon as they are out of sight. Some families have a kind of 'don't ask, don't tell' policy. Or one can simply lie. What may appear as 'Asian' hypocrisy and sneakiness from the outside is often the only solution to a desperate situation: parents are appeased; children get some breathing room; harmony reigns; everyone wins. All it takes is a little creativity."

The reality was that Jennifer wasn't doing "whatever the hell" she wanted, though. She was, by all accounts, a well-behaved and well-mannered girl putting in an average effort at school. A friend of Jennifer's at the time told Karen Ho that for Jennifer, living under her parents' rules was like "tyranny." "They were absolutely controlling," Karen wrote. "They treated her like shit for such a long time."

Jennifer's story garnered widespread attention from Asians all around the world, many of whom empathized with her home life. And while many Westerners might have expressed shock at her forgeries, countless commentators declared understanding, writing about how lies had shaped their youth. "I forged my dad's signature when I got an unacceptably poor grade on a test in Chinese school: eighty percent. I was nine," one Web commentator wrote. "I got caught and it wasn't pretty. Also, I seriously considered some pretty morbid stuff because I was put on academic probation at [the] University of Toronto. I ended up dropping out in shame."

Similar stories were replicated in comments from a multitude of Asian countries. The reality is that young people learn how to lie in their own homes, directly from their parents, researchers say, but have a variety of reasons for exercising the ability to deceive. "Children are quick to learn that lying can be useful when trying to avoid punishment, create a better image, influence others' behaviour, or form their own identity," one website, Truthaboutdeception.com, dedicated to the phenomenon of deception, states. "Children with higher IQs who are more socially outgoing, or who are raised in a controlling family environment, are more likely to use deception. Unfortunately, deceptive behaviour tends to increase over time, especially during the teenage years, when children are trying to assert their independence. And to make matters more complicated, teenagers tend to put rewards ahead of risks, causing them to act more carelessly [and often more deceptively] than parents would like."

One might argue that, while Jennifer started lying to "avoid punishment," that wish morphed over time until it grew into a means to "form her own identity." Dr. Helen Hsu, who also works as clinical supervisor for youth and family services at the City of Freemont in San Francisco, says she hears countless stories in her line of work about this sort of behaviour, whether that be lying about report cards or switching majors in university and never telling parents. But, she adds, that it goes far beyond lying about academics, often extending into people's personal lives. Dating in many restrictive Asian households is strictly prohibited until children are out of university or get jobs. While some choose to obey, whether by choice or otherwise, others choose to lead double lives. "Until my husband and I started dating, he never told [his parents] about the girls in his life," she says. "He led a normal life, but didn't tell them. The thinking goes 'I am not making them worry, but I can still lead my life.'" She adds that the ironic part of this sort of behaviour is that later in life, many Asian families will remark to their offspring "Why aren't you married?"

Julie Park also recounts her friend's situation, who, long after she moved out of her home, decided to let her boyfriend move in without her Korean parents' consent or knowledge. "For two years her boyfriend could never answer the phone, for fear that it might be her parents calling," she says. "Whenever her parents visited, they had to evacuate his possessions and erase all trace of his presence from their apartment. She explained: 'It's better that way. They didn't need to know. They didn't want to know. Why stir up conflict? Later we got engaged and then married. So it all worked out.'"

In *The Opposite of Fate*, Amy Tan lightheartedly writes about the view her mother took on dating and describes her lesson on boys like this: "If I kissed a boy — a boy who probably never brushed his teeth or washed his hands — I would wind up diseased and pregnant, as bloated as a rotten melon."

Jennifer, too, was strictly forbidden from dating in high school or beyond. "I wasn't allowed to have a boyfriend," she said. "I was told it would be a distraction to have a boyfriend anywhere before university ended."

When asked if it's common for teenagers to date secretly at her school, Mary Ward principal Andrea Magee, says it often depends on whether the parents are first-generation immigrants or not. "I don't think it's an uncommon issue," she says. "We see secret relationships because the girls are not allowed to date. We hear that people are 'secretly dating,' holding hands at lunch. It's always been there. Some [parents] are more permissive; others are less. When they first come from another country, they are more cautious, keep [kids] at home more, and wield more control. When they have been [in Canada for a while], they might relax."

Family strife surrounding issues of young love is far from an "Asian thing." In fact, it might just be the largest source of family upset since the dawn of modern society. In this sense, Jennifer is far from alone. Countless other cultures around the world not only set limits on the class and ethnicity of partners, but also on the families from which they come, education, career aspirations, perceived behaviour, age, et cetera. "When you have a highly diversified school, you don't know what taboo cultural baggage or other standards are back at home," Andrea says. "It's the clash of the cultures." For immigrant communities, the problem can often be magnified not only because they are often surrounded by foreigners but because the rules of engagement when it comes to relationships in adopted countries often don't fit traditional views. While many first-generation immigrants don't involve themselves in Canadian culture, many of their children certainly do. "That's where my mind conflicts," Jennifer said. "I'm born in Canada. I see my friends dating and everything like that, and yet in my heart, I feel like I need to follow and be with family first."

Jennifer was not only banned from dating, but Hann also took steps to ensure she wasn't preening herself for the opposite sex. She was never allowed to wear makeup or cover-up to hide her acne. Her father forbade her from plucking her eyebrows or dying her hair, one friend says. Although she longed for the kind of edginess others in her school were able to display, Jennifer was prohibited from wearing mascara, according to friends. In contravention of the rules, one of her former colleagues says she sometimes sported a blue hair extension outside the house. When a friend questioned what Hann would do if he caught her, considering her age, Jennifer told her: "He would not like it. He would be upset and just cause problems."

One point that Jennifer and her parents disagreed on, was the significance of a teenage relationship. Hann and Bich, like countless other parents, were fearful that one mistake could ruin their daughter's chances at success, or that the wrong boy could lead her in a direction opposed to theirs. Choosing a partner required a mature mind to ensure the right set of circumstances was met, again with the focus on a successful future.

Jennifer, on the other hand, was being exposed to the world of teenage exuberance where girls and boys experienced crushes on each other from week to week. The inference garnered from this sort of emotional fluctuation is that relationships are learning experiences, and love can come and go like the wind.

But the reality was that Jennifer only ever wanted to find the one boy of her dreams. She was an old-fashioned romantic and dreamed of finding her one true love and being with him for good. Inevitably, young love would soon flourish. Over the next year-and-a-half, her relationship with one of her best friends, Adrian Tymkewycz, blossomed, and in grade ten the pair started dating. Their nervous, youthful relationship was a trial of sorts, and very innocent. It amounted to going over to each other's houses to watch television and holding hands. And, although Jennifer always maintained relationships weren't allowed in her home, Adrian appeared to be a quiet exception in her parents' eyes. The teenager, of Ukrainian decent, was clean-cut, studious, well mannered, respectful, and well-behaved to a fault. His mother was a piano teacher, and he always wanted to be an engineer. The pair spent hours on the phone, and when Adrian visited, he engaged with Hann and Bich. "In their eyes, he had a well-rounded life," Jennifer said. "He had a car of his own, he came over, and they were able to interact with him." If the relationship had worked, it might have been agreeable to the Pans. However, like so much teenage love, it fizzled almost as soon as it began. "We realized we were better friends than boyfriend-girlfriend material," she said.

It was during these six months that Jennifer met a new boy, a person who changed the course of not only her existence but her entire family's lives forever.

23

YOUNG LOVE

At first, Daniel Wong was just another one of the boys Jennifer hung out with in the hallway and in the Mary Ward band room. In this environment, students could do more than just fish instruments out of lockers to practise. It was also a hangout for those eating lunch or on a break with nowhere else to be. Most of all, it was a destination for those wanting a safe haven, a place to be around like-minded people.

Because of the school's philosophy surrounding self-directed learning, band members were regularly found hanging out, gossiping, fiddling with electronics, practising their instruments, coaching one another, or finishing school work. It was in this atmosphere that Jennifer and her bandmates formed a bond in which they pushed one another toward musical success. Their dedication to the band brought them achievement and reward. In grade ten, the stage band organized a trip to Salzburg, Austria, Mozart's birthplace. Hann and Bich said no at first, whether because of the cost or nervousness at the prospect of her travelling away from home for the first time with so many other young people, but Jennifer wasn't going to let this opportunity pass her by. With her trademark dedication, she managed to raise more than $3,000 to book her place. "I wasn't able to go at first, because my parents weren't going to give me the funds, because it was in the thousands," she said. "So I had to fundraise by selling Hershey chocolates. The proceeds went toward paying for our tickets."

When the plane finally touched down in Austria, the giddy teens were abuzz with excitement. However, it was this feeling of exuberance that eventually led to Jennifer's first major medical emergency. But, as is often the case, it's life's distress that brings out a saviour. On this day, it came in the form of a young man she always knew, but had never thought of romantically.

In Austria, unlike Canada at that time, smoking was still legal in most public spaces, including the music hall where the Mary Ward brass band played one of their first overseas concerts. After the show, during which Jennifer nailed her "white picket fence" xylophone solo, she began suffering from coughing fits as her childhood asthma flared up. Away from her parents for the first time, and anxious about what this might lead to, she started to suffer shortness of breath that led to a panic attack as she contemplated the worst. After being escorted off the bus to get fresh air, it was not her boyfriend, Adrian, but the spiky-haired, bespectacled Daniel Chi-Kwong Wong who came to her rescue.

Daniel, the band joker, was a year older than Jennifer. Always up for a laugh, he was never seen without a smile. The word most of the women in his life used to describe him was *goofy*. But on this occasion, as Jennifer began to black out, it was Daniel who took charge. This became the defining moment of her young life. In her youthful mind, unaccustomed to the emotional attention of a male, she elevated Daniel to the status of her white knight. "Daniel was there, taking care of me, teaching me how to breathe in, breathe out," she said. "He pretty much saved my life on that trip. If it wasn't for him, I don't know if anyone on that trip would have been able to calm me down and get my breathing proper without them taking me to the hospital. It meant everything to me."

The reality is that Daniel did little more than tell Jennifer to relax and breathe and show her some attention. But for Jennifer, it wasn't so much what he said to her, as the emotion with which he conveyed the message. For Jennifer, a girl who said she never felt loved, this was that epic instant, one in which a boy finally presented her with his unbridled devotion and compassion, raw emotion the likes of which she'd never experienced. Raised completely immersed in a fantastical world of Disney-style love stories and fairy tales, Jennifer, an ultimate fan of the 1990s movie *Shakespeare in Love*, believed this moment far surpassed any that occurred in a Hollywood script.

One woman who worked with Daniel and met Jennifer (I will call her Allison) understood her intense emotion, and says it's common with girls at that age, herself included. "Girls mature a lot faster, so they're thinking about their one true love and having a protector forever in life in the grand scheme of things very early. Girls end up obsessing and fixating. Guys are just like 'I like going to the movies with you, and holding your hand, and making out.' So they're not thinking at that stage at all yet. There's a disconnect between the male and the female. We start prepping for [love and devotion] very young. It's that instant that girls are herded toward. That's why so many girls liked Daniel, because he [was] sentimental and introspective. He was able to talk to these girls on that level and was interested in it. He wasn't doing it to get in her pants."

Jennifer and Adrian's relationship continued for the rest of that year (2003) as she became better acquainted with Daniel. But she knew very well who she'd end up with. There was no comparison, really. Daniel's influence was not only one of tenderness, but his characteristics also spoke to the little girl inside Jennifer who felt as though she'd missed out on her childhood. Daniel showed her that life was about far more than school work and awards. Sure, he might have cared about scholarly pursuits and his marks, but for him, there were more important things, like laughter and good times. These came easy to him with his relaxed and outgoing persona. Jennifer could see intimately that it was this approach that allowed Daniel to cultivate friends well beyond the confines of the band. He was a Cantonese speaker with a Chinese father and a Filipino mother. Daniel and Jennifer had much in common, too. They were both excellent musicians, well versed in the piano and like Jennifer, Daniel was steeped in his family life and had a younger brother (Richard).

Daniel had a thing for sweet, cute Jennifer, as well: a young woman, it seemed, who truly needed him. He was just coming off another relationship and was single at the time, having had a number of love interests by this point. After months of long conversations on the phone and lengthy lunches, timidly flirting between classes, Jennifer finally made a decision, and she and Adrian went their separate ways, but promised to remain close friends, something very important to both of them.

Over the summer, Daniel and Jennifer became closer. She wanted to scream the news about her newfound love from the rooftops, but knew what could happen if her parents found out. "It was hard because, once you fall in love, you want to share it with the world," she said. "It was especially hard not to share that part of my life with my mom, as I would have liked to." She kept the relationship secret from most people, with many friends later stating that they never even knew the pair was dating. "When school started," Jennifer said, "it was still, as they call it, the 'honeymoon phase.' We would hang out during school hours. My dad was still picking me up at 3:00 p.m. So that was another lie. I kept him a secret."

Since that day in Europe, Daniel was the sole person who could calm the storm of emotions that often brewed inside Jennifer as her active mind continually turned. She said he was like a kindred spirit, the only man to have ever "figured" her out. At school, she and Daniel grew ever closer, and he became her rock, her best friend, and the one person in the world with whom she could share her innermost thoughts. The pair was in almost constant contact. Because she almost never saw him outside school, she had to prevent herself from calling him every free moment she had — between classes, alone in her bedroom, and even in the middle of the night when she couldn't sleep. He never made her feel needy, meaning she could reveal her vulnerabilities to him and he to her. For Daniel, the pair's love developed into an addiction; for Jennifer it was a compulsion. J.B. suggests that Daniel became such a focus for Jennifer that he would never see him without her tagging along. "I saw them together a lot," J.B. says. "I never saw her talk to anyone else. It almost seemed like he was her only friend."

This was not the way Jennifer described herself and her social standing while at school. "In school I was almost what they would call a social butterfly," she said. "I had band friends, I had arts friends, I had communications and design friends. I had the friends that excelled in sciences — one of them is a doctor — and engineering friends, so I had friends I would say all over the map. From jocks to — sorry about the labels — geeks, to nerds."

Others take J.B.'s position on Jennifer's social status. One online commenter posts that the school was divided along race lines, and insists it was far from the "bohemian utopia" described by Jennifer's friend, Karen Ho. "I went to Mary Ward with Jennifer and Daniel," the online commenter writes. "They were not popular or well known. They were band geeks. Daniel smoked pot. Jennifer was invisible. Maybe they were known in the Asian circle. Mary Ward was a very race-divided school."

Meanwhile, at the Pan home, harmony reigned as long as Jennifer went to great lengths to keep the peace and to make her father proud.

MUCH AS IN high schools across the free world, teenagers at Mary Ward were ascribed labels for the type of people they were. These were based on a handful of activities they were involved in, how they looked, acted, the clothes they wore, and the people with whom they hung out. Jennifer might have been the quiet and awkward young girl who spent a considerable amount of time in band. Daniel Wong's persona, on the other hand, was much wider because of his many influences. Certainly, he was in the band — a trumpet player who played both inside school and outside in the Filipino community marching band — but he also ran with a much more varied group of friends. One significant difference between Daniel and his bandmates, all too often referred to as "band geeks," was that Daniel smoked pot. His best friend was black and he listened to hip hop. But at his core, Daniel was a geek — a moniker that is much more celebrated now than it was in those days. He loved nothing more than watching movies or playing video games — *Call of Duty* being his favourite.

When he was younger, Daniel also showed a dedication to a variety of hobbies, games, and pastimes. He was the best of his friends at the classic video game *Street Fighter*, but also learned how to complete the Rubik's cube, and was an excellent pool and foosball player. One of his long-time friends says Daniel was extremely generous and thoughtful, sometimes catching her completely off guard by randomly buying her birthday presents or small things that she might have mentioned in passing. Despite this, the pair never dated, and she states Daniel was never interested. She also says he was an excellent musician who played piano far better than she ever did, despite her weekly lessons. Daniel, on the other hand, mastered the instrument on his own. "He was a good guy and a good friend; very musically inclined," she adds. "He always listened and was good at giving advice, about boys or otherwise. He always tried to put me on the right path and said I should try and finish school 'so you don't end up like me.'"

Daniel, it seemed, was a true gentleman, in part because the most dominant figures in his life were women, and he enjoyed a loving relationship with both his mother and grandmother. He got along fabulously

with most women, with whom he could have the close, bonding relationship his sentimental nature relished. It was with men that Daniel
had far more complicated relationships. Around males, he was more
of a follower than a leader, which led to displays of toughness because
he was always concerned with his reputation, and tried to prove he was
"cool" by acting in a way he thought others expected him to. As such,
those around him often took advantage of his keenness to fit in. Allison
puts it like this: "Daniel had a street sense, but he wasn't very tough."

For Jennifer, who had felt unappreciated for much of her life, Daniel
made her feel as though she was being heard; he made her feel safe.
Perhaps, most of all, he accepted Jennifer unconditionally. In return,
she gushed openly in love letters that she wrote to him, declaring her
undying infatuation. In one, she wrote in silver pen and then outlined
a number of the letters in gold pen to form a second love letter from
within. Jennifer was a creative soul, and like many girls her age, she
loved pretty things. She only used the cutest stationery for her notes
— including Hello Kitty writing paper — and often doodled hearts in
the margins. In one letter, she employed a large piece of legal paper to
etch an elaborate flower made from the words "I Love You" written over
and over, hundreds of times, swirling and curving to create a real piece
of art. But there is also evidence in these letters of Jennifer's insecurity
within the relationship, which can be seen by her repeated statements
suggesting she loved Daniel more than he could ever love her. Very
quickly in their relationship, the letters show Jennifer's entire being was
consumed by her feelings for him.

While this relationship might as well have been Jennifer's first, it
appeared that a number of girls fell for Daniel. By grade ten, he had collected a memory box of letters, many folded intricately, passed between
teenagers in class, from at least four girls. It was this same memory box
in which police later discovered Jennifer's love letters from prison the day
they raided the home of Daniel's parents. In one, a girl writes hundreds of
times, but with far less artistic flair than Jennifer, "I Miss You" over and
over again. Another girl is seemingly overcome with emotion for Daniel.
"I don't know what I'm doing," she writes. "I don't feel worthy."

Daniel spent a lot of time with his tight-knit family. As far as his parents were aware, outside the home, Daniel was the same rambunctious

but innocent boy he was inside. And to a certain extent, he was. But eventually he started living a double life himself. Like Jennifer, he was so good at it that, when things went bad, his family was utterly astonished to find out what he was really up to. One online commenter, who describes himself as one of Daniel's closest friends in high school, gives some insight into the kind of person Daniel was to his buddies in those days: "I loved that guy like a brother in high school. We were very close friends and hung out every day. I truly respected him. He was honestly the nicest guy I knew in high school. Always smiling, laughing, cracking jokes, lighting joints ... I smoked a lot of pot in high school."

Schoolmate J.B. almost refuses to believe that Daniel was guilty of the crimes with which he was eventually charged. "Daniel was very much into trumpet," J.B. says. "Daniel was a very enthusiastic guy, always a smile on his face. He was very open and had lots of friends."

Eventually, as Daniel's focus on school began to dwindle and his marks fell, he and his parents agreed that he would change schools to focus more on his studies as he prepared to enter university. Since he wanted to pursue music, he attended Cardinal Carter Catholic Secondary — an arts-centred high school on the other side of Toronto — for grade thirteen. Although the move made it harder for him and Jennifer to spend time together, the pair was already used to keeping their relationship under the radar and conjuring up ways to meet up without arousing attention. Jennifer started skipping school on a regular basis, which revealed just how far removed she had become from the elementary school student who wouldn't have dreamed of ditching class, even in cases of illness.

This was the beginning of the slow drift away from the girl her father thought she was. By this point, what was meant to be her main focus — her education — had become a minor detail in the face of the head-over-heels emotion she felt for Daniel. She was gradually drifting away from her parents' sphere of influence into his. This isn't to say the couple was up to no good; Jennifer remained a good girl who was risk-averse. She didn't drink, engage in sex, or smoke pot.

"Once [Daniel] left for Cardinal Carter ... it was harder to see him, so that's when more hidden secrets and lies would come out," she said. "He transferred out, but he'd come ... see me. I would skip school sometimes and go see him and in the summertime when my parents weren't home, before or after. Or, if I didn't have skating that day, I'd call him up and ask him if he could come over and we'd just watch TV."

Daniel was eighteen at this time, but because of a somewhat sheltered childhood, he had never learned certain life skills or experienced the hard lessons some of his friends had by that point. It's those very lessons that can come in handy, especially when teenagers start to drift from their comfort zone into activities that are more dangerous. In this sense, Daniel's ambition outweighed his good sense. Wanting extra money (eventually spending it on a flashy new car), he began selling weed. Always one to have some sort of pastime, he started hanging out at a popular run-down pool hall and bowling alley called Club 300, just north of Scarborough, in a heavily populated Asian part of Markham. The hangout was open twenty-four hours and was large enough so that the owner never minded stragglers loitering around even though they weren't spending money.

Back in those days, Club 300 was on the police radar. It was frequented by all sorts of people, many with little else to do but hang around. In this environment, there was always someone looking for pot. It was Daniel who decided to fill this void. It didn't take long for him to gain enough customers to earn decent coin. However, he knew what was at risk and, although he could have grown his business exponentially, he used his street smarts to figure out a safer path to prosperity. He decided to keep it small and local, only dealing with those customers he was well acquainted with. "The people I dealt [with], I know who they got it from," he later said. "I know their families. It's not just buddies that I just meet." He revelled in the role of dealer, always in demand by someone, able to do his close friends favours, his cellphone always blowing up. He was doing well, and it wasn't long before he was able to score that high-end car he'd always wanted — an Audi.

Jennifer spent her fair share of time at Pacific Mall, near the pool hall, but she frequented Club 300 far less and denied ever taking part in the illegal trade, saying this was Daniel's business and his alone. "I wanted nothing to do with it," she said. "So I refused to know what he was doing. I don't go around him when he's doing that kind of stuff. I don't like it and I refuse to be a part of it." However, when she felt that someone else might tell the court about her activities, Jennifer admitted to delivering weed to at least one high school classmate and being present for a number of drug deals. Although she remained conflicted about the activity, there was a part of her that found Daniel's business exciting. If Daniel was playing the role of drug dealer, Jennifer herself didn't mind the increased influence, occasionally taking on the part of a drug dealer's girlfriend.

Despite Daniel's cautious approach to dealing, it didn't take long for the authorities to catch on to his business venture. He always figured dealing drugs was a calculated risk, assuming that if his customers stayed loyal to him and no one squealed to the police, he'd be safe. What he never figured into his plans was the possibility of being nabbed by the police with product on or around him. But that was exactly what happened one night when he was arrested by Toronto police. It was the worst time to get caught, since he was on his way from his weed connection to his friend's house to unload it. Investigators discovered a pound of marijuana in his car. Because of the sheer amount, he was convicted of possession and intent to traffic. Since he pleaded guilty right away and gave up his source, he was spared jail time and took great care to hide his new rap sheet from his parents, Darwin and Evelyn. Considering that his parents would have hit the roof if they ever found out what he was getting up to, Daniel was buoyed by his ability to keep things on the down-low. Unfortunately for him, he didn't take the hint. A short time later, he was awoken in the middle of the night when his friend got caught by police in his car with a quantity of the drug ketamine, also known as "Special K" — a horse tranquilizer and party drug. The incident occurred, Daniel later said, when his buddy promised to get his Audi detailed, but instead went "gallivanting off" trying to "pick up girls." During this escapade, Daniel said his friend was nabbed for possession of between a half ounce and an ounce. His friend's indiscretion led to yet another entry in Daniel's growing profile on the police database. That same friend eventually ended up in jail.

Daniel's car was impounded, and he had to fish it out of lockdown at the Markham police station — the same place he'd years later be interviewed as part of a murder investigation. This event cemented things in Jennifer's mind: Daniel had to get out of the game. With Jennifer worried, Daniel figured it was high time he reconsidered his involvement in the criminal world. "For Jen's sake, I stopped as soon as I got in trouble. I didn't really do anything else after that," he said. "When I got arrested, reality hit me in the face that I shouldn't be doing it ... it was just friends who asked. I would say, you can call this person." He also distanced himself from the negative influences in his life, including moving his hangout from Club 300. "I [didn't] go to the places, and I [didn't] talk to the same people that I used to hang around with," he added. "I got a new group of friends. When I got out, I got out completely." With Jennifer's support, he switched gears and settled into a more legitimate lifestyle with a brighter future. He started attending York University for music, with aspirations of becoming a performer or music teacher. Eventually, the transmission on the expensive Audi he'd worked so hard to buy blew, and he had to junk it. He bought a new, and more practical, Toyota Corolla, then landed a job at Boston Pizza where, after eight short months of hard work and dedication, he parlayed his dishwasher job into a kitchen manager role.

Jennifer, seeing her man succeed in such remarkable fashion, especially given what he was rebounding from, got a job herself at the East Side Mario's in nearby Markville Mall. Hann appears to have been skeptical of this employment at first, but Bich convinced him to encourage his daughter's pursuits rather than stymie them. Only wanting the best for his daughter, he not only agreed to the job, but also gave her access to the family car to get to and from work. The likely compromise was simple: if Jennifer's marks started falling or her piano playing suffered, she'd have to stop work and refocus. To make Hann happy, Jennifer also redoubled her efforts in figure skating. Because skating remained the weakest link, Hann encouraged her to sign up with a new coach he had heard about at the York Region Skating Academy, Katerina Papafotiou, who was considered a top coach in Southern Ontario.

"They were looking for something more serious," Katerina says. "They … wanted her to improve. Ninety-nine percent of my students come from that background [Asian]." She says, while this sort of upbringing can lead to dizzying success on the ice, it can also lead to parents meddling with students training inside the rink. "I have seen parents be very, very strict in different manners. I do hear stories of high-performance skating where parents are aggressive with kids if they are not performing. And you have to be the top, or you're not good enough."

Jennifer continued to underachieve in figure skating in comparison to her other pursuits, and eventually her dream to compete at a higher level was cut short. "I tried to go to Canadians [national figure-skating championship], and I had plans when I was near the end of my career — before

I tore my ACL — that I would be going to the [Vancouver] Olympics. That was one of the goals."

Not long before her switch to the new figure-skating club, Jennifer and her family moved north of Scarborough into the middle-class suburb of Markham. After years of hard work, her parents had finally saved up enough to take the plunge and make the move to the wealthier community. The house at 238 Helen Avenue, a new construction on a new street, was in accordance with two significant Chinese superstitions: it didn't have the unlucky number 4 associated with it (in fact, it actually benefited from the lucky number 8). And the home faced due south rather than north, which Chinese custom says brings ruin to a family.

But the catalyst for the move wasn't something positive. After years without any problems, the Pans' Scarborough home was burglarized days after they purchased a new TV. The thieves also stole some jewellery and gold the family had hidden away.

Bich was always convinced that it was the television box that had been left outside that prompted thieves to target their home. After working tirelessly for so many years and raising plenty of money to start fresh, the family decided the risk was simply too great to remain. Hann and Bich resolved to leave the neighbourhood Felix and his friends used to call "Scarlem." The Pans weren't alone. Markham was the community Asians wishing to improve their lot had been increasingly flocking to for years, and movement of Chinese families from Scarborough to Markham increased significantly around this time. When the Pans moved to Markham in 2005, the Chinese population in the town was just under 34 percent; by 2013 it had reached 53 percent.

Soon after the Pans moved north, the Luong family followed, buying a house less than a mile away. The Pan home soon became a hub of activity, with the family leaving their patio door open during the day so family members could walk directly into the eating area. At different times, young relatives also came to live in the home. Despite this, Jennifer also described the new home as a place where the family appeared to grow apart, explaining how her mother regularly slept outside the matrimonial bed. During dinner, the television was on and there was very little conversation around the supper table. Although Felix says he didn't want to move from his old neighbourhood, he stresses his parents were adamant and no longer felt safe in their Scarborough home. "It's where I grew up, so I did not want to move," he says. "My parents didn't like bad elements in Scarborough, and they did not like being broken into."

Hann had the benefit of being financially secure while looking for the house near Markham's historic downtown, known as Unionville. He finally felt secure in choosing a home that would best display the family's newfound image and the hard work they'd engaged in for almost thirty years, according to his son. "Impressions were important to father," Felix says. "Basically, my dad likes to keep a higher status, so we got a nice house, a nice car; we just got a TV. [My] dad had the greenest lawn and did buy the house because of the giant lawn."

Despite Felix's comments, it's important to understand the cultural instinct that might have led to Hann's behaviour. If taken in the context of Asian culture, it could properly be identified as an exercise in status fulfillment rather than an ego stroke. Hann was hoping the elevation would cement the family's status, help the Pans gain acceptance, and signal the family's class distinction in the wider community. That is to say, rather than Western displays of wealth — often referred to as conspicuous consumption — that might include flashy cars, high-end labels, excessive luxury, or gigantic homes, Hann's intention was that, with displays of status and wealth, his family would achieve acceptance in middle-class society. For Hann, keeping up appearances was all the more important for the sake of his children's future, rather than for his own purposes.

"We're a little bit lower in society than a lot of families we try to associate with," says Felix. "[He wanted to] portray to the community that success [with a big] lawn, [a big] house, and two nice cars. [He] liked higher status, big-ticket items." Felix explains his father's philosophy like this: "If my dad did better than his dad and I did better than my dad, it's just building up the family as a whole. So that's why my dad, although he's a tool and die maker, he kind of liked the image thing. He wants to keep it like a higher image. Because he wants me to hang out with a better crowd. So I was sent to private school. He just wants me to be successful." Felix adds that, although he had always wanted to be an engineer, as his father wished, he would often kid around with Hann that he might attend George Brown, a Toronto college, for culinary studies. "But it's just a joking thing," he says. And, although he adds that at times he didn't feel like his family was doing very well financially — including soon after his father and mother were let go from Magna years before — the Pans were always keen to project success. "The persona is that we're still doing well," he says.

In her online article "On Tiger Moms," Julie Park says that for many Asian families, rather than focusing on upper-middle-class cultural achievements such as visiting Paris and Rome, which Amy Chua was keen to do with her children, Julie's parents paid more attention to "bourgeois consumerism." "Instead, my parents spent money on objects," she writes. "A brand new house in a brand new neighbourhood was the ultimate purchase. 'Used' houses were inferior. To buy a used car was unthinkable. Luxury sedans — a Benz or a Lexus — were a non-negotiable necessity (we did live in Southern California). When I dared question this mentality, my mother patiently explained, 'The kind of car you drive shows the world the kind of person you are.'"

Of course, the type of car one drives goes far beyond Asians and is a commonality in many communities across North America, although it appears to be particularly pronounced in certain Asian circles. Julie's family weren't the only ones with a Benz and a Lexus. This instinct to show the world something that didn't necessarily exist went far beyond Hann and Bich. Jennifer also engaged in plenty of dishonesty to keep up appearances. "I was very good at putting on what I call a happy mask," she said. "Where everything in the world seems fine to everyone around me, but at the end of the day, I feel disgusted with myself. I feel miserable. I feel as though I was judging someone in my shoes. I wouldn't want them as my family or friend or anything like that. I tried looking at myself in the third person and I didn't like who I saw, but rationalizations in my head said I had to keep going. Otherwise I would lose everything that ever meant anything to me: my family — my mother, my father, and my brother."

Dr. Helen Hsu claims this is a common sentiment among children, especially girls, when leading a double life — outwardly showing they are happily obliging parents' wishes but privately suffering under the weight of expectation. "[Children] are expected to stuff it and endure and deal with it privately until they grow up," she says, explaining how their upbringing might lead them to believe this behaviour is immoral while simultaneously feeling they have little choice given the assumed repercussions of not following their parents' guidelines.

By this point in her life, eighteen years old and a senior in high school, Jennifer increasingly imagined a positive outcome to her deception. Her belief was that she'd end up in university with her mid to low seventies average and might either shape up or continue the deception, receiving average marks but bringing home report cards with an average in the high eighties. At the end of the day her thinking was: when she eventually graduated, all her parents would see was a shiny degree hanging on the wall, not the substandard grades. Once university was over and done with, she'd move out, having held up her end of the bargain, and be able to carry on without Hann and Bich's constant supervision. To achieve these goals, she honed her deceit. Instead of using the crude method of a protractor and X-Acto knife, she began to design her report cards professionally with Photoshop. In order to mask her whereabouts, she also lied about her activities outside the house each and every time she went out the front door. Jennifer used her piano lessons and employment as a way to escape the house and see Daniel. On other nights, when she couldn't escape, Jennifer played with fire, helping Daniel sneak through the home's rear entrance or even second-floor windows.

Their intimacy didn't happen right away. It took plenty of time before the pair finally went all the way. But when they did at last, which Jennifer said occurred after high school, Daniel could never get enough. Jennifer, meanwhile, tried to oblige his never-ending requests whenever possible. The pair, usually pressed for time and often without an appropriate venue, frequently engaged in sex in Daniel's car, either outside his work, at the end of a vacant street, or in other out-of-the-way locations. Sometimes they were a bit bolder, going at it in parking lots. Daniel was never satisfied, according to one person with knowledge of his sexual appetite. And when he didn't have access to her, he further encouraged her to sext him and share pictures and videos in which she was in various states of undress. One friend says more than anything, Daniel loved fellatio, telling his buddy it was like putting his member "in a hot bath."

The problem continued to be Jennifer's schedule and her improbably early curfew, which was still firmly set at 9:00 p.m. Jennifer later recalled the one time her parents extended that curfew so that she could attend her best friend Topaz's wedding reception. For that occasion, she was allowed to come home at 11:00 p.m. Despite Topaz being a straight-A student and a loyal friend, Jennifer recalled only being allowed to go to her house once.

Jennifer was also not allowed to attend school dances. "I even tried to go to my high school dance. My mom actually said yes, and that she would drive me and pick me up," she said. "But my dad was very much against it, and he told her I was not able to go, and made sure I didn't buy a ticket and that she didn't drive me. My father wanted me to focus on my piano or skating or school. He wanted me to focus on something productive."

In a written account, former friend and fellow flutist Karen Ho described the sort of upbringing Jennifer experienced as one foreign to many Western teens: "By twenty-two she had never gone to a club, been drunk, visited a friend's cottage, or gone on vacation without her family." Rather than spend time with her friends outside the home, she'd spend it with them inside. Like many teenagers her age, Jennifer spent much of her time in her room. Nowadays teens can reach the four corners of the globe from the comfort of their beds and, while Jennifer's father assumed she was studying, she was really chatting on Friendster or Facebook, which in 2006 began spreading like wildfire among young people, and playing fantasy games, one in particular showing her and Daniel's affinity for the service industry, Restaurant City. With Daniel, she whiled away many hours, often into the wee hours, texting or talking on the phone or just listening to each other breathe. It made her feel closer to him.

During those late-night calls, the two shared everything. Daniel called her "Munkie" or "Munk-Munk" because of her collection of stuffed monkeys, and he was "Mesa" or "Mr. Bubbles" — the name of her stuffed animal (sometimes spelled "Bawbos" in baby-talk texts). At times, Jennifer also referred to herself as "Mesa." The texts between the pair reveal endless baby talk during which they shared their emotions, usually when happy, sad, or excited:

> *dun worry munk-munk! supiman will get them.*
> *hang in there munkey, mr bawbos c u soon.*
> *me wuv u too.*
> *mama mesa fewing down.*

This style of communication is very popular in many cultures. Women might use it in relationships to demonstrate a feminine and innocent image, combining both softness and sexuality. For men, it can be used as a way to soften a tough exterior and share a sense of vulnerability with someone they feel tenderness toward, according to one blogger.

Although it's unclear who the initiator of this sort of communication was, we do know that Daniel maintained baby talk with Katrina after he broke things off with Jennifer.

Daniel and Jennifer spent endless hours in communication by cellphone. Regardless of whether they were talking, which Jennifer preferred, or texting, which Daniel favoured, the pair was rarely out of touch. As Jennifer's time outside her home became more limited, she often spent between six to ten hours on the phone per day, talking for a portion while sending hundreds of text messages, many of them to Daniel. The phone communication was so all-encompassing that the pair shared details of their lives, including when they were going to the bathroom: *Mesa dumping now*, Daniel texted her at one point.

Jennifer recalled how her seven closest friends visited her at the restaurant where she worked, and they would all eat dinner after Jennifer finished her shift. These were the times Jennifer relished the most, when she could be what she considered a regular young adult, away from the pressures at home. As she got older, she managed to convince her family that she was juggling her school work and extracurricular activities appropriately, so she gained more of a sense of independence. Quitting figure skating gave Jennifer even more time to pursue her personal goals. These were some of her happiest days. Her father's focus on her waned somewhat, and she had a loving boyfriend who she saw irrespective of her parents' wishes. Her depression fizzled, and she had a close network of friends that she could see on a regular basis, even though that time was always limited.

The problem was that this life she had crafted for herself wasn't sustainable. Jennifer failed to take steps to put an end to the lies constantly spilling out of her mouth. She wasn't proactive about her deceit, didn't keep up with homework in vital courses, and never took steps to ease her parents into a situation in which she could release herself of some of her dishonesty. Instead, she was doggedly determined to keep all her secrets from her family and most of her friends. She refused to disappoint them. So she became even more steadfast in her trickery, increasing the lies not only in measure but in scope.

Later, Jennifer implied that her family reinforced this behaviour on more than one occasion. "I felt guilty, but over time I tried to bring it up. There was just so much expectation," she says. The first time Jennifer was caught lying shaped her views about what happened when she played by her parents' rules. One day, after telling her mother she was doing other things, Bich saw Daniel drop her off at Pacific Mall. As she waited in the parking lot to pick her daughter up, Bich didn't just catch her getting out of his car, but also witnessed the two hugging and kissing as they said their goodbyes.

Jennifer's mother was incensed. She had never seen this kind of conduct from her little girl before. She didn't even know Jennifer had a boyfriend. When her daughter got in the car, Bich's eyes were wide with anger and Jennifer knew immediately what her mother had seen. "It did not go well," she said. And, although she yelled not only about her daughter's lies but also about how she could keep something like this from her family, Bich, ultimately, was sympathetic to Jennifer's situation. After all, Bich had also been the daughter of a strict and uncompromising father. To a certain degree, she knew Jennifer had little option except to lie about the relationship. When the tears stopped, Bich gave Jennifer the "one moment could ruin your life" talk.

And although Bich refused to keep Jennifer's secret from her father, she told her they were willing to meet Daniel. "She said to bring him over and integrate him into our lives like my friends had been." Even though she and Daniel had already been dating for years by this point, Jennifer agonized over the introductions. To ease the awkwardness, Jennifer decided to organize a Christmas party and invite a number of mutual friends. She also prepped her father, as only she could. In an attempt to ensure Daniel came off in the best possible light, she told Hann that Daniel was studying engineering at university — the most legitimate profession for a male in her father's eyes. She further explained that he was working as a manager at Boston Pizza, thinking that might show him what kind of diligent employee he was. Jennifer hoped her parents would see there wasn't much to dislike in Daniel. He was half Chinese and a Cantonese speaker, a hard worker with a cute smile. But it wasn't to be. Although Hann picked up Daniel and his friend and dropped them off later, he did little socializing. Jennifer held out hope that the meeting was going well, especially after Daniel and Felix bonded over video games. "I introduced him to my parents," she said. "He hung out. He really clicked with my brother. They were playing

Counter-Strike, and he was showing my brother tricks. Boys' stuff I guess you can call it." But in reality, the visit was a disaster. "When I brought him home," she said, "they automatically didn't like him, for no reason."

As it turned out, there were many reasons for the failure. Initially, Jennifer claimed Hann said it was the fact that Daniel wasn't pure Chinese that bothered him, and that he made reference to negative stereotypes. Hann denied this assertion. However, this sort of racism is common in many parts of Asia where cultures and nationalities have their own hierarchies. Filipinos are often hired as domestic help in other Asian countries and, in those places, can often be viewed as second-class citizens with their culture devalued.

When asked how common the issue of problems arising due to young people of different ethnic backgrounds dating, Jennifer's former friend J.B., an Asian male, says it's a regular occurrence, or was at Mary Ward. "It's not rare, it's almost common to hear these types of stories," he says. During the trial, Jennifer's lawyer also questioned Felix about whether Hann had ever talked about wanting to be associated with Chinese culture and not Vietnamese culture, because of the perceived associations with the drug trade. Felix rejected the assertion.

Jennifer also explained that her father didn't think Daniel's career aspirations were high enough, considering he worked as kitchen staff. "He wasn't going anywhere in life and he wouldn't be able to support a family," she later stated she overheard him say. In the trial, Jennifer said there were two separate issues. "They said boyfriends were a distraction, and they wanted my boyfriend to be the same family class, same working status; it'd be equal."

Felix, meanwhile, offered his interpretation, saying it was because his father believed the pair was sleeping together. Similarly, Daniel heard a variety of reasons as to why Jennifer's father disliked him: "There were so many different [reasons]. I asked her the first time, and she said it's because I don't make enough money. I was working at Boston Pizza, and she told them I finished engineering. The next time I asked her, she said it's not even about how much money you make, it's the fact that you're Filipino. And I'm like, how's that possible when your cousin just married a Filipino guy? And she said, well, no one in the family likes him. So there was always a reason why we couldn't be together." Although never mentioned in court, Detective Cooke later explained that a friend had told

Felix about Daniel's drug dealing, and Felix had told Hann. Both Daniel and Jennifer denied that Hann knew anything about Daniel's past; however, this would go a long way to understanding why Hann was so dead set against Daniel.

Regardless of the reasons why, her father reacted harshly and told her bluntly, "You are no longer allowed to see this boy." Her mother reassured her that, although it might seem hard, normal life would continue after a spell of heartache. Bich recounted a story about a boy she once fell in love with when she was a young girl. She wasn't allowed to carry on with the relationship. "She said over time, you will see him less, and passion will turn into a happy memory," Jennifer said Bich told her.

In telling the story, Bich clearly didn't grasp her daughter's devotion to Daniel. Jennifer further noted that Bich had told her that she had married to escape the family home. "[My mother said] she married to run away from her father," Jennifer said. Dr. Helen Hsu says this sort of reasoning is quite common in many Asian cultures, with her own mother-in-law advising her on her wedding day that the key to marriage was to "just endure." Jennifer explained that, in the Pan household, her mother backed her father's decisions no matter what her own feelings on the issues were. She indicated that if it had been Bich's decision, she would have been able to carry on with the relationship. "[My mother] had to have the same views as Dad. It's a cultural thing. Parents are united, and so must the children [be]," she added. "So, even though my mom told me [to] marry for love, not to get away from my father, she'd have to follow my father when she was home."

Up until then Jennifer's final year of high school had been going well. She was seeing more of Daniel, and at school she grew more comfortable within her own skin every day. She even secured an early acceptance into Ryerson University for the downtown Toronto school's science program. And, although it wasn't the University of Toronto pharmacology program her father had always dreamed of, she managed to convince him that with enough work, she could gain acceptance into that program after two years at Ryerson. Everything seemed to be falling into place for Jennifer, and she excitedly prepared with her friends, who were planning to go to schools across the Toronto area and beyond. Many of them were attending institutions highly prized by Asian Canadians, including the Universities of Toronto and Waterloo.

Although Jennifer dreamed of becoming a piano teacher and had already started teaching a number of children of her parents' friends, she found out very quickly that this was nothing but a pipe dream, at least for now. Even though she was offered a tryout at Queen's University for music, she said her father made it clear to her that while, she could attempt to get in, she wouldn't be attending. "I was planning on going to university for a music course ... I love music. I also love little children ... I applied to Queen's for music, York [University], Ryerson, and U of T," she said. "I got a [letter] from Queen's to go on an audition, and preliminary acceptance at Ryerson. My parents drove me [to Queen's for the audition], but my father said, 'You're not going to go there,' but said 'You can try that out and see if you get in.'" Because of Hann's declaration, she said, she "didn't even prepare for the audition."

While her father insisted on something in medicine, Jennifer once again came up with an alternative. "I wanted to do kinesiology, but my father was very adamant [with] me doing something in the medical field that was a little bit more, in his opinion, more successful, I guess you could say. So he wanted me to become a pharmacist." Hann was overjoyed to see his daughter crossing the threshold into higher learning, which he saw not only as an opportunity for her to gain her degree, but to secure stable employment. He might have also held out the hope that it would help Jennifer make a clean break from the past, surrounded by a slew of new and prosperous young suitors, ones who he might have accepted.

Neither was meant to be. Jennifer got the shock of her life after discovering midway through her final year in high school that she was failing calculus and she wouldn't receive the credit she needed. But this development went far beyond Jennifer not attending university; it put a kibosh on high school graduation, as well. This raised the stakes. Now the truth was far more troubling. She imagined having to tell her friends and family the entire truth: *I've been forging all my report cards since grade nine. I didn't graduate high school. I won't be attending university this year. I will have to take a year off to repeat my calculus.* So she made, as she later put it, the "biggest mistake" of her life. Rather than face up to the consequences of her actions, something many believe she still refuses to do, Jennifer took the easy way out once again. "I didn't know how they would react if they found out it [her acceptance to Ryerson] was revoked and the reason

why," she said. "So I started a new lie — that I was heading to Ryerson….
That was probably the most wrong decision I've made, to lie about that.
That was one lie I wish I could take back."

Failing to grasp the depths of deception she'd have to resort to over
time to pull this one off, she took the plunge. Pulling up her Photoshop
software for the umpteenth time, Jennifer set about forging a different
sort of document. This included an acceptance letter and then a $3,000
scholarship to Ryerson University. She also provided her parents with her
graduation photos, which had thankfully been taken prior to the school
discovering that she wouldn't finish high school. "I believed at that time
[everyone would wonder] *How could you fail when you were doing so well
in high school?*" Jennifer said. "*How could you not have enough attention to
realize, Hey, I'm going to be a credit short?* I believed that my parents would
be shunned … because here's someone that is supposed to excel in figure
skating, excel in piano, excel in school, but she can't get in to university?
That was something I didn't want for my parents to have to face the world
with. It would bring shame if I brought out the fact that I had been lying
for years now. It would make them into shameful liars, as well."

Jennifer later remarked how taking risks without properly assessing
the repercussions before engaging in serious regret became a recurring
theme in her life: "I tend to react on the spot and go back and think about
what I have done. I have memories from the past that haunt me, and, like
the lies, they all tumble in my head."

24

A DOUBLE LIFE

The metaphor is as common as it is poignant, in this case. A singular falsehood, given the right circumstances, can act like a snowball, rolling down a snow-capped mountain gathering ever more speed and heft as it descends. In Jennifer's case, it's helpful to picture her — a solitary figure standing alone at the base — sustaining it, too comfortable to slow its progression and too petrified to bring it to a shuddering halt. The hope was always the same: that by some magical happenstance, she would be spared its carnage.

The initial fabrication about university was intended to avoid the wrath and shame of the inaction and lies she had been fostering since grade nine. That original lie was contained, involving only her immediate and extended family. However, as the deception grew in size and scope, so did the consequences. The eventual impact radiated so furiously that its reckoning was endured by not only Jennifer and her immediate family but by her extended family and friends and complete strangers, eventually rippling out from there to damage countless lives, some of which hadn't yet begun. Like so many other details in her life, Jennifer thought she had it all worked out. Her mind worked feverishly, often into the wee hours of the morning, to come up with strategies and contingency plans as dilemmas arose.

In hindsight, it's clear that she failed to properly devise her exit strategy from underneath the weight of her dishonesty. It would seem that Jennifer's dedication to her original plan blinded her, prompting her to avoid decisive action or consider easier routes. She continued to put reward ahead of the consequences of confessing. Instead of realizing her failures and developing a new plan of attack, she stubbornly stuck to her guns. As time wore on, and her plan began to crumble, Jennifer tried to escape one lie with ever more, formulating a pyramid of dishonesty that leads one to question whether she properly grasped the consequences of her actions. Looking back, perhaps the most shocking detail of her twisted tale is how little Jennifer appears to have considered that her plan could, and most likely would, eventually come to a destructive end. It might have been due to Jennifer's youth and the slow progression of her lies that she failed to notice how big it was becoming and that the impetus had now shifted. Others suggested, an assertion she agreed with, that she had simply built a fantasy world, and her "plan" was actually a delusion. Still others say she didn't care what happened as long as she could remain with Daniel.

When Jennifer started telling her lies, she rationalized that she could eventually pick up her grades, avoiding detection. The problem with her new lie about university was that there was no going back to her old life without enduring the punishment she so desperately wanted to dodge. Rather than face her lies, she told more so that her scheme became more tenuous. But she felt that, as long as her family continued to force her hand, she had little choice, and she became emboldened, increasingly devoted to her deviance.

One can only assume that part of this misplaced confidence in her falsehoods can be chalked up to her successes in deceit up to that point. It's often this type of confidence in one's ability to fool others that can cause or reveal narcissistic tendencies. As time passed, Jennifer indulged in more selfish behaviour, eventually thinking only of herself — to the point where even Daniel became a victim of her fabrications. The feeling that she was so hard done by gave way to self-pity, even though the consequences were the direct result of her own poor judgment and could have been foreseen by any right-thinking person her age.

After reading her story, hundreds of people spoke out about their own run-ins with strict parents, many sharing their own stories of deceit. In almost all of those stories, though, the conflict inevitably reached a head and the ramifications were felt in varying degrees. Jennifer, on the other hand, never had the courage to face her parents. Instead, she repeatedly put off owning up.

In short, she appears to have approached deceit with the same will and dedication that so many of her teachers spoke about throughout her youth. The reality is that she never properly faced the consequences of her actions until she was found guilty by a jury of her peers for planning the horrible murder of her parents. Despite this, however, to this day Jennifer maintains her innocence.

When questioned about how her fictitious university career might play out, Jennifer later admitted she only thought in the short term. "I never thought that far [ahead]," she said. But reality dictates, especially given her parents' dedication to her schooling and career, that her plan was fanciful at best. "I thought once I finished my diploma that would be it, and I could go and live my life as an adult," she said. "I wanted to show my parents I could make it teaching piano, get my own place." But she also admitted she never imagined that snowball would grow so immense. "Honestly, I didn't think it would get as far as it [did]."

As her classmates set off for university, and her cousin, Michelle, headed to the University of Waterloo for science and accounting, Jennifer remained at home. Emboldened by her parents' trust and how easy it was to fool them, she decided to trick everyone else in her life, as well — except Daniel, of course. "I believed ... that if anyone knew, one person could tell another person ... and somehow this lie would come out and unravel. So, as terrible as it was, I lied to everyone."

In the lead-up to the school year, Hann and Bich were keen to show just how proud they were of Jennifer's achievements, showering her with money so she could buy anything she needed — school supplies, new clothes, and a new top-of-the-line $2,700 laptop. They also advanced her cash so she could focus on her studies without worrying about finances. Bich even co-signed a credit card for her. How many thousands passed between the two remains unknown. On that first day of school, Jennifer woke up early and dressed for success. Then, holding her new book bag filled with notebooks and highlighters, her head held high, she left the house. And so it began. Her destination, though, was not the frosh week festivities she had told her parents about, but rather a Toronto library. Once at a desk, she filled reams of pages and Word documents with notes she garnered from pharmacology websites. With her signature attention to detail, Jennifer also highlighted certain passages — with numerous school supplies she purchased from Staples — so that if her parents ever cared to look, the notes would appear genuine. "In the beginning, in my first year, it wasn't too hard because my family trusted me and they believed I was a good person, that I was a good student," she said. "I started looking around at what my friends were doing ... getting letters in the mail, saying that this was going to be frosh week, you will need to buy certain textbooks. [I bought] used scientific books, biology books, physics books. I pretended I attended, but came back home every night."

Her brother recalls her behaviour around this time quite clearly: "She always went to school, she always had a backpack with her; she had a laptop, she had books and everything." On certain days, Jennifer took the bus; on others she'd get a ride from her mother. And for the first little while she consistently spent her days at the library before growing more comfortable and eventually stealing away to visit Daniel at York University. She later said that it was only around him that she could relax during this frantic time. To fool those around her, Jennifer even created small anecdotes to share with her parents to give further weight to her lies, all the while engaging in hours of futile note-taking that consumed her daytime hours. "I started to make all these little lies to make it seem like I was going to university," she said. "It was a huge lie, and unfortunately a huge lie requires a huge amount of work ...."

One could argue that her lies took so much dedication that the effort far outweighed the effort it likely would have taken to simply right the ship — get the calculus credit and begin attending university. On the other hand, one might conclude that Jennifer simply hated school and didn't want to attend. This argument is strengthened by the date of the home invasion — almost exactly two months before her father was planning to force her hand, ensuring her attendance at the college laboratory tech course.

Regardless of her motives, the focus required to weave her web of lies remains one of the most fascinating aspects of the story. Imagine going to bed each night and waking up each morning always thinking of the same thing: how to trick people into believing you were doing something you weren't. Each day having to come up with bogus life details about who you met; what you did in class; what instructor you had that day; when your next test, assignment, or exam was; how many people were in each lecture; and what your professors' names were. It sounds easy — unless, of course, you had to remember it all. After all, these weren't details she could simply dismiss once they were spoken. Jennifer had to commit them to memory and build on them. And at the drop of a hat she could be forced to recall one specific detail in order to properly recount her supposed activities. To do this, she literally had to develop an alternate universe for herself. "In my mind I started making it seem like I was accepted [into university]," she said. "I started to make all these little lies to make it seem like I was going to university. From there, they trusted me; they believed I had a gradua- tion, that I graduated. They had my [high school] graduation photos. My mom kept them in her wallet for a bunch of years. So they trusted that I did graduate and I was going to Ryerson. They had that belief in me then."

Jennifer further admitted how the daily grind of lies and deception she was engaging in eventually caused her sense of reality and imagina- tion to warp to such a degree that she had a difficult time distinguishing between the two. "I had this fantasy world," she said, admitting that she had become so lost in her lies that, by the end, she had all but convinced herself she was actually attending university. Jennifer became so adept at creating the lies, and so in-depth in maintaining and then resurrecting them, that she became a fantasist.

Her acceptance of this theory came out in court during an inter- esting back-and-forth with Daniel's lawyer, Laurence Cohen, during which she admitted to having a "dual personality" and stating that she switched back and forth.

LC: My sense of your testimony is you had to create a separate life for yourself where you could be happy away from the pressure of your family, away from all these people that abandoned you, and you created like a separate life for yourself.

JP: I had a fantasy world, yes.

LC: You're so good at living this fantasy life that you actually take steps to convince people that (you are) living this life.

JP: Yes, I convinced myself.

LC: You're using this deception to protect yourself. You go to the library like you're going to university. People who would lie probably wouldn't have gone to the lengths you went to…. You went to the university, you went to the library, you went to Staples and bought supplies, right? You were living the life of a university student. You were so detailed in it you were almost able to convince yourself you were going to university.

JP: Correct. That's what I said.

When asked if she was a complicated person, she agreed wholeheartedly, noting that she was a Gemini.

One detail that allowed Jennifer to escape detection was her knowledge that her father didn't concern himself with the family bills. It was her mother who was the family banker, and it was from Bich that Jennifer wrenched control of her taxes.

But, over time, Jennifer started to feel the weight of her own lies. The resulting stress began to impact her behaviour. "It took probably most of my day trying to make up pretend notes and trying to travel from uptown to downtown," she said. "I sat at cafés or sat at the library and thought, *Where is this going?* I was exhausted. But there were times when I got time to myself … [when] I was somewhat relaxed."

Work had the ability to relax Jennifer as well as stress her out. Her job at East Side Mario's in Markville Mall was a sanctuary of sorts, a place where she could be around people her own age, experience independence, manage her environment and actions as she saw fit, and devote her time to a pursuit at which she really excelled. Jennifer was one of the best servers at the restaurant. It was difficult to find quality staff and, as a result, there was a very high turnover rate. Jennifer was a manager's dream, being able to serve seven tables at a time, always professionally, managing her time so the food came out promptly, and she made few mistakes. She took plenty of shifts and often worked five nights a week. "She was a strong server," says one former colleague. "She could take more tables, a bigger section, make bigger tips … she eventually became a supervisor and certified trainer."

However, two other members of staff agree that when Jennifer was "in the weeds" — server lingo for having too many tables/being overworked — she grew very bothered. One former server in particular says he recalls the intense focus with which Jennifer set about her job. He says he noticed that her stress levels seemed to mount over time. Others agree. "She was very focused when it was time to work, but when she was in the weeds she would stress," one of her former co-workers says. "She'd be running around trying to do everything."

Jennifer was well liked by her colleagues, who say she was "extremely normal," nice, shy, and quiet. After work, Jennifer and her colleagues either sat on the patio and caught up on gossip and news, or headed to the bar for a few drinks. Sometimes they went bowling and, on occasion, Jennifer drank alcohol during these outings, but never more than one or two. One disturbing detail garnered from Melissa, one of her restaurant co-workers, provides a small window into Jennifer's behaviour and the level she went to perpetuate her lies. Despite only tenuous ties to her parents (through Felix, who by that point had started working in the restaurant's kitchen), Jennifer went to great lengths to convince her colleagues that she was actually attending university. This, among other details, raises questions about the blurred line between Jennifer keeping up a lie to fool her parents and creating an alternate reality, a space where she felt comfortable and could project to the world what she wished her life was like. "Jennifer was a year ahead of me, and I remember sitting on the [restaurant] patio talking to her about graduation," Melissa says. "I even remember her, between shifts, studying with all the staff who were taking exams. We were all there. She had her notes out and books and was cramming with the rest of us." But her lies didn't end there. "She talked to me about being stressed, about having to maintain a certain grade-point average to keep her entrance scholarship," Melissa adds. "There was no reason not to believe her. She was your typical Joe. She was a typical Asian girl. She did figure skating and played piano like many of my friends in Scarborough. Music is always a big part of their lives. They are very obedient to their parents."

Melissa says that she distinctly remembers Jennifer being close to her mother, recalling when Bich purchased a pair of Lulu Lemon yoga pants for her, possibly the same ones she was wearing that fateful night. Despite these admissions, Melissa is clearly uncomfortable speaking about the kind of person Jennifer was, saying she still feels betrayed by her lies, many of which she remembers with great clarity and sometimes thinks about all these years later. "The girl I worked with doesn't exist. The person I knew doesn't exist," she insists, her voice betraying the anger she still has concerning Jennifer's dishonesty.

THE STRESS THAT Jennifer was experiencing began to take its toll on her, and Bich — the person who knew her daughter's emotional pattern better than anyone — started to notice. During one particular morning drive to Ryerson, Bich questioned her behaviour. Jennifer explained that it was the long commutes at the heart of her worry. Taking advantage of her mother's concern, Jennifer proposed a solution: she suggested that going to live with Topaz at her friend's small Toronto apartment between Monday and Wednesday would help avoid so much travel time. Bich, in turn, brought the idea to Hann and convinced him that it was in the best interest of their daughter. The leniency shown by her parents gave Jennifer a break from her never-ending worry for at least part of the week, but simultaneously added a further, much more perilous dimension to her lies. Instead of going to live with Topaz, who was herself under the false belief that Jennifer was attending Ryerson, the pair worked out a deal: if Hann or Bich called the apartment, Topaz was to tell them that Jennifer was in the bathroom and execute a three-way phone call, pretending to pass the phone to Jennifer when she exited. A reluctant Topaz, who had a fiancé by this point, might have been the perennial good girl; however, well aware of the circumstances Jennifer was living under, she obliged.

The new arrangements quickly became permanent, allowing Jennifer to live with the man she loved. At the beginning of each week, she ventured off to live with Daniel in his family's new home in the easterly suburb of Ajax (the Wongs had also left Scarborough after a break-in at their home).

"It was pretty relaxing," she said about the situation. "I got to see him when I wanted to, and I got to spend more time with his family. So between me and Daniel, things were okay." Initially, Jennifer slept in the large home's spare room. One thing Jennifer was insistent on was not betraying his parents' trust and sneaking into Daniel's bed at night. Daniel's parents, especially Evelyn, fell in love with Jennifer. And over time they repaid this trust by allowing Jennifer to stay with Daniel in his room.

For Hann and Bich, Daniel was clearly not the ideal match for their daughter. However, the Wongs took just the opposite view. Darwin and Evelyn saw Jennifer as their son's ideal mate and a positive influence — a partner they credited with Daniel refocusing on his education, getting gainful employment, and altering his group of friends. Dinnertime at the Wong household was likely quite different than meals at the Pan residence, and Jennifer's relationship with the family progressed with ease. She later explained just how much she relished the experience to interact so intimately with a family so different from her own.

After staying there for two years, Jennifer was firmly entrenched in Daniel's family life. Although, in hindsight it might sound naive, Jennifer, by then twenty-one years old, said Daniel's parents accepted at face value Jennifer's assurances that Hann and Bich were okay with the new living arrangements. And when they asked for the chance to take Hann and Bich out for dim sum, Jennifer shrugged it off as never the right time. To ensure her own parents didn't investigate further, Jennifer called them each morning. During these calls, she gushed about the lectures she was attending that day and how well she was performing. A second call was placed promptly each night before bed, explaining to her mother how late she planned to stay up finishing her work or studying for her mid-term exams. The rest of the week, and on weekends, she spent faithfully at home, so as not to raise suspicion.

During this time, her mother continued to put money in her account to help pay for Jennifer's portion of Topaz's rent. These funds remain unaccounted for. One investigator suggests the funds went straight from her bank account into Daniel's coffers — extra cash to help him in his drug business. Bich's employment wages were also deposited in Jennifer's bank account to avoid the government finding out — money Jennifer also had access to. While Bich seemed to harbour no suspicions that anything was amiss during this time, Hann felt something was up. Although he never knew exactly what, certain aspects of Jennifer's life weren't right, and he noticed inconsistencies in his daughter's story and behaviour. Hann was desperate to grill his daughter about his suspicions, but Bich placated him. "I was concerned something was not right … so many times I wanted to ask my daughter," he says, noting his wife had told him to go easy and stop pushing her so hard. "She's already grown … just let her be herself. Too much interference is not good for her."

Although Jennifer originally said she had long imagined that "a diploma" from Ryerson would have been enough to put off her parents and halt the lies, she eventually realized to her chagrin that it would not. Nearing the end of Jennifer's two years at Ryerson, Hann began to inquire about how she could best ensure success in the medical field, including bolstering her résumé with pharmacology experience. Despite worrying about signs that her plan was falling apart, Jennifer chose the path of least resistance. "I just thought, well, maybe if I did correspondence this year … I'll be accepted the year after," she said. "Honestly, I didn't really think too far ahead of that." However, much like her plan to work diligently to get her high school marks up after falsifying her report cards, she took no action to gain her missing calculus credit, powering on unabated.

It was only after telling her parents she had made the switch to the University of Toronto for her long sought-after pharmacy degree that her relationship with her trusting mother grew strained. This should have been the happiest time in her parents' lives — enjoying the fruits of their labours — but that was far from the reality. "When I moved over to U of T, it became a little more tense," Jennifer said, explaining how she told her parents she finished the two-year program at Ryerson and began attending the University of Toronto for pharmacology. "I was conflicted; I was confused. I was not really sure what to do. Part of me did want to come clean, because it was getting so complicated that even I was starting to lose track of every day's momentum. But on the other side, I knew … it would bring such shame and embarrassment to the friends and extended family. [My parents] would be ostracized from the rest of the family."

Despite this, her parents were overjoyed with her marks, considering she was consistently bringing home grades hovering around the ninetieth percentile. It was really quite remarkable, they thought. Out of the forty-two classes she claimed she had taken by the end of her U of T "career," she gave herself nine A+'s in classes, including statistics and chemistry, thirty-two A's, and only one A-. Yet, by this point, her problems had spread far beyond her grade-point average. Bich questioned Jennifer's repeated insistence that she complete her own taxes. This was especially true after Jennifer's cousin, Michelle, studying to become an accountant and helping with the Pan family's taxes, said Jennifer refused to allow her parents to claim her tuition credits like the rest of the family did and didn't let anyone see her tax returns.

As the pressure mounted, Jennifer fell back into some of her old high school habits, including self-harm. For this, she would use knives taken from her kitchen, preferring serrated instruments, she said. Although the incisions were never very deep, they were painful. She pressed down horizontally, hard enough to "feel release" and cause a trickle of blood. Unlike so many other parts of her life, she shared the details of this behaviour with the people around her, including Felix. It was her badge of honour. When questioned by police, she explained how it helped "relieve inner pain." Jennifer later explained to a police officer: "When I lose control, the only thing I can control is what I feel." But she passed off her self-harming as "embarrassing."

She told another police officer the reason for her cutting was distraction. "I was able to feel physical pain, so I didn't have to think about other pains in my life," she said. After she was arrested, she wrote to Daniel about her feelings toward herself, those around her, and the act of cutting: "Everyone needs to be wanted and wants to be needed," she wrote, adding that everyone preferred to believe she was an angel and "perfect." "They saw the cuts and bruises," she said, "but [not] one person clued into my self-hatred."

"Self-harm is usually a way of coping with or expressing overwhelming emotional distress," states the United Kingdom's National Health Service website. "Sometimes when people self-harm, they feel on some level that they intend to die. Over half of people who die by suicide have a history of self-harm. However, the intention is more often to punish themselves, express their distress, or relieve unbearable tension. Sometimes the reason is a mixture of both. Self-harm can also be a cry for help."

The intensity with which Jennifer was living her life, always having to be on her toes, ready to either create a new lie or conjure up old ones, found its way into her behaviour in other ways, as well. As her general happiness faded, her determination to succeed at piano morphed into an intensity that worried at least one of her music instructors. Fernando Baldassini, who taught Jennifer music theory, history, and harmony from an early age, recalls her musical ability and determined character as a child and young teenager. "She was one hell of a pianist," he says. "She won scholarships at school and many thousands of dollars as a result. She was amazing. She wanted a degree in piano so she could do something with it. She could have met any goals she wanted." He says he saw qualities in her he'd rarely witnessed in his female students. Years before, Jennifer had started working for the conservatory as a judge's assistant during the annual festival at the University of Toronto's Scarborough campus. "She would name the kids as they walked up. She took this role very seriously," he adds. "I remember the way she walked, with long determined strides.... She was very professional and always focused, even in this atmosphere."

Jennifer always loved playing piano. But as she grew older, the joy seemed to seep from her, not only in her mannerisms but in the way she approached her piano playing. Baldassini noticed that her rigidity intensified. He says by the end of her lessons with him, she appeared to have lost much of her zest for the piano and seemed to be going through the motions, something he'd never seen in her when she was younger.

"She didn't show much emotion and, as she got older, she got more stern and strict," Baldassini recalls. "To me it looked as though she developed a chip on her shoulder. By the end, she wouldn't engage in eye contact with me and seemed to be saying to me, 'Okay, teach me,' then when it was complete, 'Okay, thanks. I'm off.'"

At home, Jennifer faced feelings of jealousy and abandonment toward her brother. Felix explains their strong bond, noting that growing up, the two were "very, very close" and "as tight as can be." He adds that he considered himself, not only her friend, but also her protector. The pair talked about intimate parts of their lives they never shared with anyone else. Both Jennifer and Felix mentioned their "pact" — should their parents ever split, they both said they would go with their mother. This is how Felix describes one particularly memorable conversation between the pair: "I once asked my sister what her plans were for the future because clearly my parents weren't okay with my sister going out with Daniel, so I asked my sister if she was waiting for my parents to die and then get married with him. She didn't really say anything. She said that she loved him and … how … your parents raise you, and they're there for you a lot, but at the end of the day, your parents eventually pass away before you do, so she wanted to find someone she could grow old with…."

Although Jennifer felt a similar strong bond with Felix, she also talked about how she resented the way her parents treated him. In the Pan home, as in most traditional homes, there remained strict gender roles. As such, Jennifer explained how Felix always seemed to benefit from a separate set of rules. While Jennifer was expected to engage in the activities her father deemed important, Felix was able to forge a semblance of his own path, she said. He went to camp, played team sports like soccer, and took abacus, an ancient Asian form of calculation and accounting. These were all things she was never able to do. Felix was also able to go away to university, a liberty Jennifer said she was never encouraged to strive for. Felix also had a 10:00 p.m. curfew, while Jennifer's was 9:00. And while Felix explained that he was allowed to engage in these activities because he took the initiative, simply asking his parents if he could, Jennifer saw it as a double standard, in part because he was male.

Her complaints stretched beyond childhood. Felix was also able to bring his girlfriend around the house, and the couple even lived in the same residence at university. As the years passed and the in-fighting at the Pan home seemed to grow, Felix often just left, preferring his girlfriend's company and leaving Jennifer to deal with the situation on the home front.

Felix only partially agrees with Jennifer's assessment, admitting that the division of labour might have been skewed toward the men. He describes his father as "traditional," and says Hann often had double standards when it came to men and women. But, while Felix admits that his father rarely cooked and didn't encourage Felix to, he says that was because his father deemed certain chores more appropriate for males. "If no one is home, my mom's not home, my dad will do the cooking. But if everyone is home, then he won't. Just like my mom: if no one's home, she will do the [snow] shovelling, but on a regular basis she won't." He says his father raised him and Jennifer in this fashion as a means to an end — namely, to prepare his children for marriage. "My dad is a little old school by the fact that he doesn't cook, clean. He'll do it when he has to, but he doesn't like it. He tells me, 'That's the girls' job. The girl does that, but you never let the girl do hard [strenuous] work.' She'll never have to paint the house." However, when it's implied that his father was the "boss" of the house, Felix disagrees, saying this was only the impression. "No, my mom was the boss of the family. My dad just goes to work, comes home, and does whatever," he says.

Bich also took exception to her husband's views on housework. Jennifer said that especially after Felix left the house to attend Hamilton's McMaster University, she was often left to referee her parents' "bickering," which, she said, often revolved around domestic issues. "I missed him [Felix] a lot because we were very close ... it put a strain on me because of the dynamics within my family there was a lot of tension between my mother and my father. And that burden went on to [me], and I didn't have anyone to really share it with, because I didn't want to burden my brother at school." She said that while her father, a jack-of-all-trades, was always willing to help other family members in need of assistance, he let chores at home slip.

"My mother took on a lot of responsibilities, doing everything," she said. "Paying the bills, cleaning the house. She was just fed up doing it by herself."

But not all fights revolved around household habits. Jennifer said that, after her lies were discovered, it was often her own behaviour that sparked the arguments. "It divided the family ... I felt like part of it was my fault. It started with my lies.... The fights between my parents were usually about me, what to do with me, how to get me back on track."

As Jennifer's U of T graduation approached and Hann started questioning her about buying tickets, Jennifer knew she would have to come up with a whopper of a lie to weather the coming storm. And she certainly did. With Daniel's help, the couple paid $500 for a phony U of T degree, which they purchased on the Internet. But that was only half the battle. "That was a real crunch-time lie," she said. "Obviously, parents want to go see their kids graduate. My parents started to inquire when and where grad day would be. When would I have my grad pictures taken? How much to order one? At that time I was [trying] to figure out ways to fake it and lie." In the end, she decided to tell them that because there were so many people graduating at once, families were only able to buy one ticket. And because she didn't want to choose which parent attended, Jennifer gave her ticket to a classmate. "I told them spillage tickets cost a lot of money, [and I] didn't want just one parent there, and so I gave it away."

"Maybe I can stand outside looking in. Okay by me," Hann proclaimed. But Jennifer insisted and got her way, explaining that her parents were more likely to accept the lie because the degree had gone a long way toward proving that she had, in fact, graduated. When Jennifer got home from her supposed graduation, Hann requested any photos she had taken at the ceremony. In reply, Jennifer explained her friend had taken all the photos but was on a plane back to Hong Kong. Although Hann seemed resigned that one of his life's dreams — to witness his daughter walk across that U of T stage and grasp her pharmacy degree — wouldn't come true, he was still intent on seeing her succeed in the field. He immediately began advising Jennifer on how to best prepare for her eventual career, gaining experience and crafting her résumé to appeal to companies. Her curriculum vitae listed all her skills and abilities. However, there were two significant omissions: there was no mention of attending Ryerson University or her lack of a high school diploma. After sending out the document multiple times, she landed an interview with Walmart, but never got a callback. So instead of getting a real job, she created one.

Jennifer told her father that she'd been taken on as a volunteer at Toronto's Hospital for Sick Children (SickKids), Canada's foremost hospital for children. Conveniently, this work, supposedly in the blood-testing laboratory, took place on Friday nights and weekends. To her parents, she sold it as an endeavour during which she could do good things while collecting hours. Once her time sheet was full, she said university officials would verify them before she'd be given a practical test to prepare her for her career. This lie turned out to be a bridge too far. For Hann, something wasn't right — *Where was her hospital uniform, scrubs, and swipe key?* He might have kept quiet, but coupled with a number of worrying aspects of his daughter's life, he decided to find out the truth for himself.

One day as Jennifer was about to leave for work he demanded to drive her downtown and invited Bich to join them. Jennifer protested, but her father was insistent. "He noticed it in my behaviour," she said. "It wasn't like me to be so dysfunctional, disorganized. My head wasn't on straight about how I would be able to get into SickKids without actually being an employee there, having [swipe] cards. On the way, I'm pretty much sweating buckets. When we get there, my father instructs my mother to follow me out because I am trying to get out of the car quickly, so I could hide somewhere. I got through the emergency doors. I was just paranoid, so I stayed in the emergency waiting room for a few hours." And so, just as easily as Jennifer eased into her new reality, she came crashing back down to earth.

Bright and early the next morning Bich called a "groggy" Topaz and demanded to know where her daughter was. Forgetting that Jennifer was now supposed to be staying with her on weekends, too, Topaz said she wasn't there. "It started to unravel," noted Jennifer, now twenty-two. Bich then rang Jennifer and ordered her home immediately.

When Jennifer arrived home, she saw the fury in Hann's eyes. "I thought I would be disowned," she said. Hann initially threatened to kick her out of the house, but Bich quickly put a stop to that. Jennifer said a number of threats were issued at that time by Hann, including one that she said proved she was on the right track: he would disown her. He would hire a private investigator to follow her around to make sure she wasn't seeing Daniel. In the midst of the hollering, recriminations, and tears, a furious Hann came up with another threat that proved all the more poisonous. "I got mad and I said you have two options," he later said. "First you stay home and go to school. The second choice is go with Danny Wong and never come back." He then added what would become an ominous premonition: "If not, you'll have to wait until I'm dead."

Hann later contended that he meant none of these statements and only said them in a frenzied state. "It was in anger that I made the statement. I could not accept the fact that this person [Daniel] helped my daughter not attend school for four years. This does not mean I would have not cared about my children. All parents have deep affection for their children. When mistakes were made, I showed my anger, but she is my daughter; I do not always have anger."

As for her decision, she said a choice might have been presented to her, but really there was no option. "I wasn't leaving," she said. "There was no choice, because family always comes first."

Jennifer was so terrified of the truth getting out that, astonishingly, she lied again. In the face of her screaming parents, Jennifer quickly decided what would be acceptable to admit and what would be a step too far. So she admitted that she had been staying at Daniel's and that she had been lying about her work at SickKids, but she covered her tracks with regard to her Ryerson education and her failure to graduate from high school. About her fictional U of T career, she said she was doing correspondence, but not actually attending school. This was the first but not the last time she failed to grasp an opportunity to tell the whole truth.

In one sense, Jennifer had succeeded, for the time being at least. While she was grounded, it was only for two weeks. But this wasn't just another missed opportunity; it was also the beginning of an even more troubling way forward — half-truths.

In addition to the grounding, one vital thing was removed from Jennifer's life — the freedom to come and go as she pleased. This meant that her reasons for leaving the house became a subject of constant inquiry, bar two pre-approved activities: work and piano. Her methods of communication were withdrawn, including her cellphone and laptop. She was also forced to quit her jobs at East Side Mario's and Boston Pizza (where she had been picking up further shifts alongside Daniel). She said her father claimed that one in the morning (when she would often return home after her shifts) was no time for a young woman to be out, anyway. To his face, she accepted the terms of the agreement, not willing to try to live on her own. But inwardly she was defiant. She continued living in the comfort of her father's home, but refused to abide by certain rules he set down. At the heart of her defiance was the worry that Daniel might leave her. Jennifer knew this would spell disaster. She imagined herself as Juliet to Daniel's Romeo, the pair sharing a love that could never be rivalled. It was Daniel who could save her from her own deep-seated melancholy; it was only with him, she believed, that she could ever achieve happiness.

"I would say she hated herself less around him," says Allison, an associate of Daniel. "It was his presence and his unconditional love that was calming for her. That's why she wanted to be around him all the time, because she was incapable of feeling that way herself. She needed external validation."

All three surviving members of the Pan family describe this fight as explosive. Bich wept, and Hann screamed at Jennifer. But Felix and Hann both say efforts were taken in the following days to repair the damaged relationship. "They get upset, but it's one of those things where they're screaming for a day, everyone's really upset, but they're always trying to work it out somehow," Felix says, explaining how his parents controlled with isolation before eventually bringing the child back into the family fold. He adds that, although Hann and Bich wanted Jennifer to follow tradition, they didn't want to lose their daughter.

As part of Jennifer's punishment, Bich essentially became her daughter's babysitter, with the pair spending most days at home together, running errands, or helping to care for ill family members. Jennifer was also told to reconnect with her neglected piano training as she buckled down to get her Associate of the Royal Conservatory (ATRC) teacher's diploma. This comprehensive exam takes months if not years of intensive study and one must have the ability to perform multiple pieces by heart in order to pass. There are further requirements above and beyond that, including history and counterpoint. "I forced her to finish the theory part of the piano lessons in order to get a licence to teach piano," Hann says.

Almost immediately, Jennifer was back to her old tricks. Using the excuse that she needed her phone to check if any of the job applications she sent out had borne fruit, Bich capitulated and showed Jennifer where her father had hidden her cellphone. Jennifer used this time to check if Daniel had called and to touch base with him. "I did sneak a phone call here or there," she said. "She allowed me to have access to it for maybe a minute or two to check any messages ... I used it to check who had called me. Obviously, Daniel, being worried, would have sometimes called and I would see missed calls, and I would delete them so that my dad wouldn't see them." But when asked if she ever saw Daniel during that punishment, she insisted the pair held off. "I was housebound; my mother was pretty much beside me the whole time," she said. "[Daniel] was frustrated that he couldn't come over to his girlfriend's house when he wanted to. I had shared with him that my parents didn't think very highly of him and that he was a bad influence on me.... We loved each other and wanted to be with each other, but it was hard considering the restrictions. It put a real big strain on the relationship...."

Over time, Jennifer regained a measure of freedom. But she squandered it almost immediately. Jennifer was allowed to use her cellphone and computer again in their presence. She also began driving her mother's car to piano once more, although her parents clocked her mileage. But eventually, talking to Daniel at night, hidden in her room under the cover of darkness, Jennifer let her emotions get the better of her. One night, she said, he called her, said he "needed a friend," and felt an "emptiness" without her. She agonized over what to do, but the temptation was too great. Jennifer saw Daniel as the only person who could quell the inner frustration consuming her life. The only thing she believed could get her back to reality was her one true love. "I caved," she said. "I asked a friend to drive me over to his house ... in the middle of the night while my parents slept. I had tucked in my blankets to look like I was there." Afraid she was going to lose Daniel, she initiated a pact that night, which Daniel agreed to. If their relationship ever came to an end, they would remain friends. But fate, once again, conspired against her. It had slipped Jennifer's mind that her mother's wallet was still sitting in her room from the day before. And when her mother went to retrieve it early the next morning, she was shocked to find that Jennifer was nowhere to be found.

Bich called Jennifer immediately and ordered her to come home. It was on the long trip home that Jennifer would devise yet another lie. When she reached 238 Helen Avenue at 7:00 a.m., she explained to her exasperated mother that she had only just slipped out that morning to see Daniel at a nearby café. "I didn't think there was anything wrong with it, but with my restrictions I did feel very guilty for breaking that," she said. "For my parents, any girl my age, before marriage, going to a man's house and sleeping over is something that would look really, really bad on my family." After this, Hann and Bich began looking at other ways to straighten their daughter out, including sending her to stay with her uncle, who was a teacher in New Brunswick. "[I was to] cut him [Daniel] out of my life completely and to reapply to school and start a brand-new life," she said. "They even thought about taking me out of province and starting a new life, new school out there."

Faced with this possibility and realizing how determined her parents were, Jennifer became even more resolute. After this last transgression, it was her brother who took up the family cause, lashing out at his sister. "I had just found out that they were going out again," he says about that day. "My parents found out first, and then they were kind of arguing about it. I was upset about everything, so I was asking her why she's still going out with this guy when it's upsetting our parents. I was too angry to listen [to her response]."

"He thought I was tearing the family apart," Jennifer said about Felix's feelings that day. "[He didn't understand] why I couldn't drop one person for the sake of the family."

Dr. Helen Hsu says she often sees this type of behaviour among the young people she works with — situations in which a young female might have been unable to relinquish her relationship because of a poor relationship with her father. "Girls who have close relationships with their fathers are less likely to engage in premarital sex and less likely to have abusive relationships," she says. "If you don't [have a close relationship with your father], you have someone who feels very vulnerable, displays poor judgment in young love, feeling as though 'this is the only thing that will ever make me feel like this.'"

Stuck at home and becoming increasingly frustrated, Jennifer once again picked herself off the ground the only way she knew how — with a new set of falsehoods. In a doomed attempt to win more freedoms, she told her parents that she'd finally landed a job at a pharmacy located in the same Walmart where she had gone for an interview before. Her father, delighted by the news, advised Bich to let her use the car to drive to work.

To bolster her lie, she told everyone around her about it. "She needed the hours to finish her pharmacy [she told me] and she talked about it a lot," Felix says. To her cousin, Michelle, she said she was working at the back of the pharmacy, packing, unpacking, and labelling medications.

Melissa, from East Side Mario's, also explains how Jennifer would always talk about how many hours she was putting in at the pharmacy soon after she stopped talking about volunteering at SickKids.

For a discriminating Hann, though, it seemed too good to be true, and he once again wondered how a girl without a uniform and swipe card could work at a pharmacy. So one day, two weeks after Jennifer started, he approached her and asked if he could see one of her pay slips. She didn't blink; she made up lies to quell his concerns, saying she'd left her pay stubs in her work locker. The next day, she came home with a forged copy of a Walmart pay slip she'd found online. Jennifer said when he insisted on driving her to work the next day she obliged, this time having scouted the location beforehand. Lucky for her, someone was coming out of the employee entrance when she arrived and she slipped right in. She hid in the Walmart until her father left, and then went to the library. But this still wasn't enough to placate Hann. When she arrived home, he ordered her onto the computer and demanded to see the payment received from Walmart through her online banking statement.

Jennifer didn't let her repeated failure dissuade her and used her new-found tactics once again. She admitted to him that the hours were faked and used the opportunity to get other lies off her chest after explaining to her father that she hadn't actually graduated from U of T. However, she left out the deceptions regarding high school and attending Ryerson (something he didn't find out until after the murder). Hann also took this opportunity to confront her about a call he had seen on the family's call display from Boston Pizza. "[You're] a liar, a liar, a liar!" he yelled at her. After waffling about the next step to take following her last punishment, Hann quickly decided to take control of the situation. "Right: there's no way you're not going back to school," he told her.

Jennifer knew that she'd lost her father's trust forever; Hann never believed outright what his daughter ever told him again. "It made me feel no matter what I told my dad, the trust had been lost," she said. "It made me feel that I was not the daughter he wanted. That no matter what I would do or what I was willing to do. I was [never] going to gain back that feeling of what we did have between my father and me. The trust was broken and it would never be the same."

25

"HOUSE-ARRESTED"

After much of the truth had come to light, Hann sat his daughter in front of the computer and together the pair crafted an email to Daniel informing him that she was no longer to see him. Hann was so determined, that he even told Jennifer to blame the decision on him.

Obliging her wish to repay Daniel close to $3,000 she owed him, Hann cut a cheque on the spot. One investigator later called this little more than a "payoff" that Hann hoped to dispense to Daniel to keep him away from Jennifer. Afterward, Hann and Jennifer applied to three colleges, including a lab technician course at Centennial College for which she was eventually accepted. Hann paid a further $3,000 for her tuition. Jennifer later suggested that at this time the pair had released long pent-up emotions, crying together for the first time.

After this latest offence, Jennifer's two-week punishment, during which she was not to leave the house, was made permanent. Jennifer felt like a broken woman, and her excuses had worn so thin that even her mother had lost faith in her. "My mom was so disappointed. She had tried in so many ways and [had] given me so many chances. And I had blown them all. I still loved her, she still loved me, but she just had no more words and no more advice to give me." If there was any point when Jennifer's grip on reality started to loosen, this was the time. The happy mask that had been so firmly fixed to her face for all those years finally slipped. She felt defeated and her solemn mood began to show in her behaviour. Jennifer could no longer reach Daniel on a regular basis and her immediate family was at the end of their wits with her presence.

"I felt unwanted. I felt unlovable, unworthy," she said. "No matter what I do, [my father] won't accept it, no matter how hard I try, he won't accept it. It was a common theme in my life. That no matter how hard I tried when I was doing the right thing ... sometimes doing the wrong thing was the same repercussions or sometimes it gave me more ease." As the days passed, Jennifer felt as though she was under house arrest.

Her father, who had specifically rescinded her ban from using the car to help her get a leg up at work, decided she was unworthy of any trust. "I said, 'From now on you have no right to use the car, and you stay home,'" Hann says. "There was no more trust in me, and I also wanted my daughter to study and go back to school."

"It was hard to be home because I didn't have any more time for myself. It was so much expectation to go back to school, or always being watched by somebody.... Bedtimes being watched, surprise checks on my phone to see if I was calling Daniel or anybody, even the house phone display was being checked to see if anyone was calling that was suspicious. Everything was double-, triple-, quadruple-checked.

"I had no room to breathe, everything I felt was just squeezing down upon me," she continued, explaining how the monitoring became too much for her. The messages Jennifer's friends were seeing her post on Facebook during this time were also worrying. "Living in my house is like living under house arrest," she wrote, according to one friend. "No one person knows everything about me, and no two people put together knows everything about me ... I like being a mystery."

Friends explain that, around this time, Jennifer started to convey, both through actions and words, the extent of the situation she was living under and how it was making her feel. This was followed by countless efforts by those around her to encourage her to move out. "It's not an option to leave my house," she told them. "I felt I was still needed in my house and I would do whatever it took to keep the family face."

The stress she was under was palpable for her piano teacher, Fernando Baldassini, after Jennifer told him that although her cousin, Michelle, was allowed to have a boyfriend, she wasn't. "I told her she should go out on her own and that she can't have it both ways," he says. But Jennifer replied that moving out was not an option. And although she would later say that she chose not to move out due to her dedication to the family, Fernando says he believed Jennifer didn't want to lose all the comforts of home. He also got the impression that she had doubts about whether she could make it on her own.

Jennifer bolstered her story to Fernando with details we now know to be untrue. "She said her dad was following her around. She said she couldn't go out without having him follow her and not refusing to believe where she was."

Her friend, Melissa, also confronted her about her situation, repeatedly asking why she continued to live in her home if life was so difficult for her there. "When I asked her 'Why don't you just move out?'" she said, 'If I leave, I can't just come back. I'd be cutting ties, so there's no changing my mind.'"

Adrian, Jennifer's ex-boyfriend and one of her closest companions over the years, who was attending McMaster University with Felix, says he also saw through her facade. He was worried, so he gathered together a group of friends to discuss her behaviour and what appeared to be an increasing number of lies. "A number of things weren't fitting together in respect to work and her job," he says. "We were all curious and asking questions." But when he pressed her for answers, she told him she didn't want to talk about it or, as Jennifer would put it, she was constantly "changing topics" when friends asked her for details. "The topic in this case was *Why don't you move out?*" he says, referring to the "intervention."

"She did not like the restrictions and felt like she was being treated like she was still in high school," Adrian adds. [We said to her,] 'If things are that bad, you can just move out. We can probably help you find an apartment.' But she was worried about how it would affect her relationship with her parents. She had to support her parents." As to what Jennifer was doing during this time in her life, he says he recalls playing plenty of Scrabble. "I remember trying to distract her all the time. Just trying to be a good friend."

There were others who tried to intervene. Even Daniel stepped in, begging her to escape what he later called her "hellhole." He asked her to move out with him to his family's former home in Scarborough where his aunt and grandmother lived. But once more Jennifer refused. "I needed my family to be around me," she said. "I wanted them to accept me. I didn't want to live alone. I wanted to be a part of the family. I've always been a pillar of the family, when I was younger, and my family was pretty much all I really knew. I would also be ashamed if I moved out. You were expected to live in your house with your family until you're married."

About the possibility of marriage, Daniel said he just wasn't ready at the time. As for Jennifer, "I wasn't ready to marry him," she said. "But to move out on my own? I could have if I wanted to, but I didn't want to." Despite this response, one has to wonder, given her unfettered devotion to Daniel, whether she would have said yes if she'd been asked.

It was during this period that Daniel finally came to grips with the couple's reality and decided that enough was enough. He broke up with her. "You know what, you go figure it out on your own and come find me when you want to find me," Jennifer said Daniel told her. Daniel told police that by doing this, he was respecting her family's wishes that they not be together and that he "moved on."

Although he left the door open to a possible reunion, his comments plunged Jennifer even further into darkness. He'd made similar statements before, but this time he was "serious" and "frustrated."

"I was pretty much heartbroken, to be honest," she said. "Completely heartbroken. I thought we … would work things out together. [When we didn't], I felt more disappointment, more unlovable, more unworthy of people in my life. That's when we ceased talking … or communicating as often as we were. More of everything was being taken away from me. I came to the realization that … everything was crumbling around me." On top of this, the relationship with her parents pushed her even further away from the family. Instead of telling her parents the entire truth and letting out her emotions, Jennifer simply bottled them up. One night, as her mind reeled with dark thoughts, desperate new feelings crept into her mind. If she were ever going to act on her suicidal thoughts, that would have been the time. As far as she could see, there was no reasonable way out of her quandary.

Maybe a way out was to end it all. "I believed I was a failure. I had so many lies, and so much had happened because of my lies," she said. "I believed I was unworthy of anyone. The neglect I was feeling since no one needed me around or wanted me around … I didn't want to live." Jennifer said the overwhelming feeling from all the men in her life — Daniel, Hann, and Felix — was of abandonment. Clutching a vial of Tylenol 3s in one hand and a bottle of vodka she had fished out of the family's liquor cabinet in the other, she debated with herself: How far was she willing to go? The problem with her instinct was a simple one: Jennifer didn't want to die. She poured out a palm full of pills, and as her heart pounded, the moment of truth grew closer. "I stopped myself," she said. "I could have taken more, but I didn't." The prospect of a life with Daniel was too important to lose. She knew what happiness felt like. She knew what made her smile. Why should it be her that takes her own life? In the end, Jennifer relinquished the morbid fantasy that had haunted her since she'd first felt depressed back in elementary school.

After popping three pills and taking a swig of vodka, Jennifer started to feel sick. She then threw up and passed out. The next morning the room was still and the remnants of the night before lingered. She felt groggy with a mean headache. But she remained. This wasn't the last time, however meek her efforts, that she considered taking her own life.

The Internet is littered with stories of young and high-achieving Asian-American and Canadian teens, especially women, killing themselves. Jiwon Lee, twenty-nine, a dental student at Columbia University, killed herself after leaving a note saying she was "not living up to expectations." Kevin Lee, nineteen, studying biomedical engineering at Boston University, jumped to his death, and Andrew Sun, studying economics, committed suicide at the age of twenty. Luchang Wang, a Yale mathematics student, killed herself at the age of twenty at the beginning of 2015. The first three killed themselves in just one month — April 2014 — and are but three of the 150 or so college-aged Asian-American students who killed themselves that year, one-and-a-half times higher than the U.S. national average. According to the American Psychological Association, next to American Indian, Asian women have the highest suicide rates of all female racial groups aged fifteen to twenty-four (based on statistics from 2007).

In most cultures, women have suicidal thoughts more frequently than men but commit suicide less often. In China, though, women are 40 percent more likely than men to commit suicide.

In that country, suicide remains a particularly large societal issue. One set of statistics reveals that about 287,000 people commit suicide in the country every year, and another two million attempts are made — one of the highest numbers per capita in the world. It's the number one killer of young people between the ages of fifteen and thirty-four and between 6 and 10 percent of young people have attempted suicide at one point. In all, 56 percent of all female suicides worldwide take place in China. In 2013, a ten-year-old boy jumped thirty floors to his death after he was ordered to write a one-thousand-character apology for talking during an assembly. Jumping out of windows, seen as a particularly extreme form of suicide, is one of the most common ways young people commit the act. What follows is one Chinese student's description of her relationship with suicide while attending school in China. It appeared under an article about Jennifer Pan's story:

> I am Chinese. All the education I received in China was about cramming, testing and ranking. I've been through most of the "tortures" mentioned in the comments. I struggled the most when I was in middle school preparing for the high school entrance exam. There was only one prestigious high school in my city and every student was bleeding their life out just to get into that high school. And try to imagine the enormous population in China. It was insane. My middle school was pretty good and it always wanted to preserve its record of sending the most students to that high school, so it pushed the students to a limit that I couldn't stand. We started class at 7:00 a.m., stayed at school for most of the day. After a day of classes, night class started at 6:30 p.m., and we were finally discharged at 10:00 p.m. Then we returned home to finish the homework. On weekends and summer and winter offs, we had cram school scheduled. I repeated this routine for more than two years just for one damn test, and not to mention the whole monitoring thing by parents and teachers, and the public postings of our grade rankings of the monthly tests. It was such a torture, and I was super depressed. I thought eventually all the students would choose to kill themselves. Why wouldn't they? There was no meaning to continue living like that, living a life that you totally collapsed after, all the pressures and self-hatred, and all you earned was the privilege of not doing your homework for one day. I was sure that one day that I might end my life. But before that another student in my school committed suicide. His

parents came to the school and I saw how unimaginably
desperate they were. I never thought of ending my life ever
again. However, after I graduated, I heard that two other
students at my middle school committed suicide too.

Another result of this sort of pressure, for which there is far less pre-
cedent, involves outward-directed violence. There are some instances that
have occurred, although they are not very widely publicized. Dr. Helen
Hsu, acting president of the Asian American Psychological Association,
says that she knows of a number of incidents that have taken place in
Southern California in which children exploded with seemingly random
acts of violence against their parents (at one point with such frequency that
it almost became a trend). "Jennifer Pan's story is shocking in detail but
not shocking in the slightest that people lose it in this pressure cooker," she
says. "These are high-achieving, law-abiding people [who] suddenly have
a huge incident. These almost 'perfect' teenagers will go and stab a parent
or engage in other forms of family violence. Police are surprised when this
is what they are getting, but they are getting used to these families."

After "stuffing and kowtowing" it for so long, sometimes people reach
a breaking point. An eighteen-year-old Korean boy, known only as "Ji" in
the courts, was convicted of killing his "perfectionist" mother who was
obsessed with him landing a place in Seoul National University. He had
suffered regular beatings at the hands of his mother, had also been doc-
toring his grades, according to news reports. He stabbed her to death with
a kitchen knife before leaving the body in his house for eight months.

Esmie Tseng, sixteen, from Kansas, was an honour-roll student and one
of the state's best piano players for her age. The girl ended up stabbing her
mother to death with a knife after suffering relentless pressure and psychological abuse as a child. Other comments on Reddit's AsianParentsStories
posting board about Jennifer show murder has been on the mind of others.
"What the fuck?" one comment reads. "My folks are Asian and that kind
of pressure is normal for me. I sometimes get homicidal urges whenever
my parents are lecturing — or more like screaming — at me."

26

WALKING ON EGGSHELLS

The desire for carnal pleasures can grow overpowering sometimes, lead-ing a person to make bad decisions. But that's not the only desire that can skew a person's decision-making abilities. Sometimes equally powerful draws involve money, ego, friendship, and the respect of one's peers — a particularly pronounced reason for young males. Being close to Jennifer not only brought Daniel sex, but eventually led to an opportunity to pro-vide his friends with a scheme in which they could earn some serious cash. And there were few things in life that Daniel craved more than his friends' affection. He thrived when helping others and enjoyed being in demand by those around him, whether that was a buddy looking for a favour, a weed connection, or a woman seeking his attention. Had Daniel stayed on his path of hard work and diligence, he might have escaped Jennifer's grasp. But no matter how he tried, his efforts remained futile in the face of Jennifer's rabid determination to win him back.

The humdrum life of a hard-working kitchen manager might have kept his mind focused, but that reality was starting to wear thin. Daniel wanted more out of life. And he'd eventually get it, with plenty to spare. A year before the murder, Jennifer, at twenty-three, wasn't the only one experiencing a crisis of emotion. Daniel, a year older, also found him-self at a crossroads. After seven years with the same woman, someone he might have pictured himself growing old with, the relationship was now in tatters. The thousands of dollars he had been paid by Hann was cold comfort. Despite investing so much time and effort in the relationship (much of it trying to avoid her parents' detection), Daniel found that his hope for stability had been vanquished. His mind was finally made up for him — the Pans would never accept him into their lives.

Emboldened with new romantic options, Daniel decided to call it quits with Jennifer. To ensure this would truly spell the end of everything, he made sure he did it right. Knowing the dogged pursuit she might engage in to win him back, Daniel ostracized Jennifer from his life completely, letting her calls go to voice mail, and leaving her texts unanswered. "She tried to talk daily. She wanted the relationship to go on," he said. "She tried to stay in my life. She'd call me asking, 'How you doing? How's work? What's going on with your life?' I told her, 'We can try to work it out, but realistically it's not going to work out. Your parents don't want us to be together, and there's nothing really we can do about it.'"

Daniel had little idea how much more complicated his life was about to become. A crestfallen Jennifer soon discovered the truth about their breakup — another woman was involved. "I know I can't be with her, because I don't want to just get back with her to lead her on," he said. "It's obvious I don't feel the same, and I told her that. I started to move on. I met one of my friends, and I just moved on."

That friend was Katrina Villanueva, a former classmate from high school with whom he had been friends since he was sixteen. Her background was Filipino and she worked part-time at a grocery store. But things weren't completely smooth in this relationship, either. Katrina, who lived with her father after her mother passed away, had a son from another relationship. According to Daniel, she had a restraining order against the father of her son. Daniel's parents weren't too keen on his new relationship and missed what they deemed as the positive influence Jennifer had had on his life. "There's a big controversy," he later said about the relationship. "My parents don't approve of us being together." This would lead Daniel to spend much of his time with Katrina away from home, either at Boston Pizza or sometimes back at Club 300 (she loved to bowl). There were plus sides to the relationship, though. Katrina, three years older than Daniel, was much more mature than Jennifer and had more free time. And, notwithstanding his parents' feelings, the relationship didn't contain the hallmarks of his time with Jennifer — the never-ending tears and recriminations. *I'm always walking on eggshells with u*, he later texted Jennifer. Katrina had moved on from drama-filled relationships, and Daniel could see her whenever he wanted.

"My understanding at this point was that they had a strong bond and may be starting a relationship, but that they were not intimate or anything," Jennifer said, expressing feelings of resentment about their relationship. "I knew that she could make him happy and she had more [free time], so it wasn't so restricted. He had moved on. He had someone there for him 24/7 whenever he needed them, so it felt like I was replaceable, that I wasn't entirely going to be missed or that he'd entirely be alone. I felt that … I would be just a faint memory."

When asked to describe Daniel, Katrina tells me he had a "good head on his shoulders" and notes that he often used humour to mask his feelings during this time. "He was your regular funny guy," she says. "He never showed his emotions. He'd always be cracking jokes. To be honest, it was hard to get him to be serious. He was a goofball, but a very hard worker. His job was his main thing. Anything work-related, he'd do it."

By this point Daniel had quit university and given up his dream of becoming a high school music teacher or performer. Although Katrina knew Jennifer was still in the picture, she tells me she let her relationship with Daniel progress naturally and didn't try to put him off contacting his ex. "She [Jennifer] was always there for him. That's all he told me. But then other times he'd tell me she was bothering him. But that's what he was telling me. Whenever I met Jennifer she was always quiet, never outgoing."

Jennifer claimed to be at ease with the pair's burgeoning relationship — explaining Daniel's happiness was of utmost importance to her — but the reality was that she was fiercely jealous of Katrina. When asked during the trial by Daniel's lawyer, Laurence Cohen, if she disliked Katrina, she refused to answer, instead saying she "made him happy." She then added, "She was a mother and she worked," and eventually, through gritted teeth, settled on being "indifferent" to her.

Although Jennifer tried to display how much she had grown and how comfortable she was with the new circumstances, it was all a ploy; in reality the relationship between the two was tearing her up inside. That becomes clear when one reads several of the communications between them around that time. Jennifer knew better than anyone that all was fair in love and war. Over time she worked tirelessly to disrupt the feelings Daniel and Katrina had for each other.

One outlandish message Jennifer sent to Daniel's phone, implying all sorts of imagined behaviour, read:

> *This drives me crazy. If you want your space from me then fine. Just let me take all this stress away from you. If you miss her and her sex that much then just let me take this pain on my own, when I call and message you, just to be ignored and left on my own then let me fall. I have taken all this on my own all these past few days when it isn't even my fight with you, it's hers. If you're really fighting over something to do with marriage I don't know, but if you're fighting with her and punishing me because you prefer to sleep with her please just tell me. I am so broken that I can't do this anymore. I love you and worry my ass off, but try so hard to give you this space you want. They say you can still check in with her and not me then that really shows me that I don't even come to your mind. I was made to make you happy. I love you and everything about you, except when you forget me. It saddens me and makes me cry on my own like right now. I gotta go to the airport in a bit. Who knows what will happen to me.* [Although this text was sent partially in baby talk, partially in text lingo, it has been translated into English.]

Part of the problem for Jennifer was that, although she tried not to come across like a jealous ex-girlfriend, it was difficult when she had few other things to occupy her mind. She was on her phone constantly. No matter how he tried, Daniel wasn't completely ignoring her; he might not have been calling her, but he was still asking that his friends or friends' girlfriends were checking in on Jennifer on a regular basis. "Seven years was a long time, and I appreciated what she did for me," he said, explaining why he made that kind of effort. "We were best friends."

In the weeks following Hann's ultimatum, it wasn't just Daniel who was ostracizing Jennifer. Her family, weary from her constant lies, was also showing its disapproval. Hann was so livid with his daughter that he couldn't bring himself to speak with her. Jennifer claimed this went on "for weeks."

A fed-up Felix began avoiding the family home altogether, preferring to escape the tension by spending more time with his girlfriend when he came home from university. When he wasn't with her, Jennifer said he would head back to school early, claiming he had errands to run or social functions to attend. At one point, Felix texted his girlfriend, explaining just how desperate he was to get out of his house as Jennifer's mood took a turn for the worse: *I'm annoyed. I want to get [away] from my sister. Just need a break. I'm annoyed of how she's moody and slow.*

Bich, the eternal peacemaker, made her disappointment known and attempted to ease the conflict. But Hann's anger was just too great. "I felt that sometimes [my father and Felix] left the house without telling me," Jennifer said. "Even though before, I would be invited to go. When they were working on the cars — I'm actually into cars — they wouldn't involve me in it." Jennifer recounted a scenario in which she brought drinks out to her father and brother while they worked in the garage. She said Bich, who was trying to reconcile the trio, thought it might be a good way to break the ice. However, they spurned her attempts, choosing to show their backs to her. When she asked Hann if he'd like to invite his friends over for dinner so she and Bich could cook for them, he once again didn't respond, preferring to relay the answer to Bich via Felix. "[My father] had not spoken to me since he gave me all the restrictions," she added. "[He would speak to] someone so I could overhear the conversation, but not directly to me."

Although she had spent the past four years of her life fostering such a reaction, Jennifer found the behaviour unfair. "I was resentful, furious," she said. "I tried to be a better person, and I felt rejected, so I thought, *Why bother?*" Besides this, Jennifer was also suffering from feelings of inadequacy. "I believed I was a failure. I had so many lies and so much had happened because of my lies, I believed I was unworthy of anyone," she told the court. "The neglect I was feeling, since no one needed me around or wanted me around, I didn't want to live." Between her inner struggles involving her deep-seated anger toward her father and her wallowing self-pity, it was her indignation that prevailed, eventually consuming her entire life.

In China there is a myth that any child who commits matricide or patricide will be downed themselves by a strike of lightning by the filial deity Erlang Shen. The Chinese god has a third truth-seeing eye in the middle of his forehead. It's this myth that gave rise to the Chinese saying that translates as "Being smitten by lightning for being unfilial and ungrateful."

In Christianity there is also a saying that corresponds with this time in Jennifer's life: "Idle hands are the devil's workshop." In the ensuing months, both Jennifer and Daniel both got up to some nefarious activities. With no school and no clingy girlfriend, Daniel had plenty of time to pursue other things between working hours. If he was ever to achieve his new dream of owning his own Boston Pizza branch, he needed more money, so how long could he continue to ignore the numerous contacts he had still looking for marijuana?

During this time, he started reconnecting and making new links to those in the drug trade. He became closer friends with a man named Lenford Crawford. By that time, Daniel had ditched bowling and began playing paintball at two sites in Toronto, including Defcon Paintball, near Scarborough, and Sgt. Splatters, near Yorkdale, one of Toronto's biggest malls. One employee remembers Daniel hanging around Defcon for hours, just "shooting the shit" with customers and employees alike. Casting his mind back, the employee even remembers Jennifer hanging out, too, but can't quite remember Felix, who Daniel also brought along at one point.

It was during this time that Daniel also met Jeffrey Fu. When Daniel and Jennifer did speak via text, she said he often told her he was out "doing runs," which she took to mean he was delivering drugs. And, although she was disappointed at the development, she now had little control over the company he kept or his activities. Thoughts raced through Jennifer's mind as she spent her days studying piano, cooking, cleaning the house, and in her words, "taking people to appointments." That involved many in her extended family, including an uncle who had suffered a stroke and her ill grandfather, whose health was beginning to wane after he caught pneumonia at the age of 102. And while her father might have expected Jennifer to expunge Daniel from their lives, he clearly underestimated his daughter's resolve.

The reality was that, without Daniel, Jennifer was rudderless and sought somewhere to pour all the emotions besieging her heart. Fear of abandonment and insecurities surrounding her looks and her lingering wish to be wanted, loved, and cared for consumed her existence. It had been Daniel, along with her work, hobbies, and friends, that had kept these emotions at bay for so long. Jennifer replaced these pastimes with contacting people on her cellphone and a large amount of time spent on social media. One negative communication could ruin her entire day. But Jennifer wasn't a helpless girl. She hated to feel vulnerable and knew that what was good for the goose was good for the gander. Jennifer soon set about assembling her own gaggle of male groupies. Although she remained faithful to Daniel during this time, always believing he was the right one for her, flirting was fair game. This approach won her plenty of suitors, at least two of whom later admitted they had hoped to sleep with Jennifer, each believing he could beat the other to it. Perhaps the most ironic part of these largely telephone-based relationships was that they became as poisonous, if not more so, as her relationship with Daniel.

One of these men was Andrew Montemayor, a central figure in Jennifer's story. The pair rekindled their friendship after communicating sparingly over the past few years. If Andrew was her "bad-boy" replacement for Daniel, another man, Edward Pacificador, was a sentimental replacement. Edward was a former colleague from East Side Mario's and a man Jennifer said she began seeing for a few months. Although their time together was limited, the pair spent hours on the phone. Jennifer carried on a playful, flirty relationship with both men.

An online commenter says Jennifer piqued his interest around this time. Although he claims to be close friends with Daniel, he maintains he never knew the pair ever dated. "She was somewhat quiet in person, but smiled a lot," he writes about what he knew of her in high school. "Kept to herself, really. I always thought she was very bright with a lot of promise in her studies. Anyways, it wasn't till after high school, when I found her on MSN [Messenger], I noticed she opened up a lot. We actually used to flirt back and forth with one another. How she wanted to ... well ... you know. I'm glad I never followed through. She was manipulative and apparently lied about everything."

Try as she might, Jennifer couldn't bring herself to let Daniel go. He explained how Jennifer played on his emotions, ensuring the pair stayed in contact. "She would say 'What are you doing? Are you with Katrina?' that kind of stuff. Sometimes she'd cry and say 'Don't you love me anymore? Don't I mean anything to you?' After you hear that for a while and you're such close friends, you feel bad. You feel guilty. But I know I can't be with her."

Whether by coincidence or calculation, soon after Daniel ended their relationship, his phone was besieged with crank calls, threats, and cryptic text messages. "After we sort of stopped talking for about a month, then this problem started," Daniel said, referring to the phantom communications. Only Jennifer can be sure which parts were her doing and which parts were the actions of some mysterious caller. Initially, Daniel was just annoyed by the countless phone calls he was receiving both at home and on his cell. "I started to get more and more [hang-up calls] near the end of 2009. They never said anything," he said of the calls marked "private." "One night I would get a hundred; one night I would get seventy; other nights I would get just ten. If I answered, they would call back in an hour, and if I answered again, they would just hang up and call back. But if I rejected the call, they would just keep calling and calling and calling … at all hours of the night." Daniel said he did wonder if Jennifer was behind the calls and texts, asking multiple times to see proof, but in the end he believed her denials. "There's a lot of questions," he said about whether Jennifer was involved. "Because of how long I've known her and what we've been through together, I believe her. But in terms of seeing any distinctive hard proof of it, I haven't. She was with me during trouble, and she helped me out and stuff like that. I just trusted her that it was someone who was out to get her."

The disruption to his life didn't end there. The texts eventually progressed into messages advising him to stop talking to Jennifer altogether and focus on Katrina. At first he received messages like: *You don't need her, You're better off without her*, and *Don't be with her. Be with Katrina*. Before long, the texts became more personal in nature: *We're watching you*. The triangle became complete when Jennifer and Katrina started receiving messages, as well. Katrina says she received threatening messages like: *Be careful where you go*. Daniel was genuinely worried, but Katrina says she never considered them anything more than a nuisance. Jennifer said the contact to her phone was anonymous, but she claimed she also received emails from a hotmail address. She alleged the messages included: *Chrissy and Danny one forever*. Eventually, they became more stinging, involving petty insults: *Why would he want to be with you. You're stupid, You look like a man*, and *You're ugly*. Jennifer told Daniel that every time a car pulled up in front of her house, she received texts not only implying that Daniel was visiting her but that someone was watching her home. At one point she said she got a letter saying she was a "dead person walking" and then she claimed someone even called her: "We're watching you" the voice said before bursting into demonic laughter. "This is some pretty messed-up stuff," Daniel said, explaining how he grew concerned for Jennifer's safety. The messages to Daniel also began referencing sensitive parts of Daniel and Katrina's life. "[Katrina] has a kid, and the distinctive text message was *Do you like playing house?*" Daniel said.

Whether Jennifer was behind the scheme or not, it did succeed in reuniting the pair, with Daniel ensuring he was in constant contact with both women. Jennifer was milking it for all it was worth with messages stored on her phone, including *I'm scared that there r still ppl out there to get me, Becuz i am feelin attack and unsafe.*

Concerned for Jennifer's safety, Daniel started calling to check up on her himself. In return, hoping to promote communication between the pair but under the pretense of having him avoid the crank calls, Jennifer purchased a new phone with a new number for Daniel. The anonymous texts to his phone stopped for a while. Around this time Jennifer said the pair's relationship grew "stronger" as their communication increased. "Morning calls, afternoon calls, calls during the day, just little messages," she said. "Compared to most people, I use my phone a lot, so for me it was morning wake-up calls, okay, making sure you got to work, making sure whatever I was doing in the day that I was going to be okay. How I was feeling, and then what he was doing after work, and then also what time I was heading to bed."

The added communication with Daniel might have boosted her spirits, but Jennifer remained isolated and her behaviour became even more erratic. The suicide attempt and her cutting weren't the only worrying signs that Jennifer's grip on reality might have been loosening. Although the twenty-four-year-old always struggled with some form of insomnia, her sleeping patterns became even more varied during this period. The thoughts that so often coursed through her mind became louder as her stress level continued to increase. With very few responsibilities and very little reason to get up, Jennifer rarely needed to function at a level where sleep became necessary. If she felt tired, she could simply doze off. It tended to be at night that Jennifer got the chance to socialize with her friends, and most importantly Daniel, who had been working all day.

Another of the men Jennifer was contacting around this time was Otto Li. His relationship with Jennifer is shrouded in mystery. He was a hockey player at the time and appeared to have a crush on her, evident by the sheer number of times he contacted her with little reciprocation. Jennifer seemed to regularly give him short shrift, most often replying with one-word answers. This might have been the result of the way he tried to befriend her on Facebook. "He kept asking me questions ... I don't know if it's just his personality, but he asked me questions that I thought were too abrupt to ask someone you just met," she said, explaining that, although he said he knew her from high school, she didn't remember him. "He asked if I had a boyfriend, and if I was looking for a boyfriend, and if I engaged in sex and things like that." Their relationship appears to have hinged largely on his desire to know what Jennifer was doing at various moments of the day. He endlessly texted her the simple request for information: *What are you doing? Where are you?* If nothing else, the messages show how sparse her sleeping patterns had become. At almost three o'clock one morning he texted her: *Are you asleep?*

I hardly sleep, she responded. *I was never one to sleep much. Since I was young I had a lot to do and always and so much on my mind so sleep was never all that to me.* When asked how this affected her immune system and whether she regularly got sick, she told him she had been sick. *But I don't milk it like most girls. I hate to feel vulnerable.*

What do you do when you don't sleep? he asked.

Stare into the darkness, Jennifer wrote. *My life is so full of shot* [shit] *that most nights I am in thought.*

Another night he texted again at three o'clock to see if she was awake. Jennifer responded *Of course.*

By the following morning, she still hadn't slept. *What are you doing?* he asked in another text.

Laying in bed, came Jennifer's reply.

Jennifer also spoke about the tendency to inflate seemingly small issues so that they eventually consumed her thought processes, causing all her inner turmoil to bubble to the surface. When Daniel didn't respond to her texts or calls, she stewed about it, convincing herself he was with Katrina and ignoring her, at one point even suggesting he and Katrina were discussing marriage. This sort of behaviour is constantly discernible in her texts to Daniel. If Daniel didn't answer in time, her mind might go into overdrive. "I believe I overreacted," she said. "I thought way out of the bubble. I took things way too much to heart. Everything. I thought, I over-thought, and over-exaggerated in my head."

It was under this sort of emotional stress that Jennifer once again, however feeble her effort, tried to take her own life. This time she said she ditched the pills and picked up a knife. "I wasn't happy with any parts of my life," she said. "I tried to cut vertically one time. I was able to feel physical pain, so I didn't have to think about other parts of my life. But I like serrated knives over sharp knives because you can feel the pain more. It wasn't too shallow, but the more I went down, the more relief I felt, the more reality I felt, the more I knew how ridiculous committing suicide was." She said she never attempted suicide again after a friend she told her dilemma to said, "Don't be stupid." While this revelation might have dawned on her, the poisonous emotions she was feeling still consumed her and an outlet for those emotions remained elusive.

27

"OH, THAT'S THE BAD GUY"

It's easy to question the motives behind Jennifer's relationship with Andrew Montemayor and vice versa. After all, Andrew is the man Jennifer credits with giving her the initial idea to murder her own father. And, although he denies any such thing, Jennifer went one step further, saying he not only suggested a hit on Hann but followed it up by conspiring with her and another man to complete the task. The pair initially met when they were just kids in the same class at St. Barnabas Elementary School in Scarborough.

Andrew and Jennifer had a special bond if for nothing else but the fact that Andrew's father worked alongside Hann and Bich at Magna. According to Jennifer, Andrew was living in Mississauga in 2010 with another man. She said that after high school he'd struggled but had seemed to come out on the other side, landing a job at HomeSense in his mid-twenties. However, she also said he'd been bragging to her that he and his roommate had been busying themselves with armed robberies. More specifically, Jennifer said that Andrew had told her he'd been terrorizing people with a blade in parks, relieving them of their wallets and cash along with his roommate, Ricardo Duncan, a.k.a. "Ric." It was during this time that Jennifer said Andrew had a crush on her. And he admitted that both he and Ric had a bet going to see who could sleep with Jennifer first. It's clear that Jennifer didn't shun Andrew's attentions. Instead, she brought him closer, despite harbouring no interest in being with him intimately. When I contacted Andrew to discuss the relationship, he refused to speak to me. But in court he denied ever telling Jennifer about any armed robberies, as did Ric. None of these allegations were proven in court; neither man was ever convicted of any involvement in this crime or any others, and both acted as witnesses for the Crown.

Jennifer claimed she initially reached out to Andrew to seek advice, knowing he'd had a confrontational relationship with his own father at some point. The pair eventually found each other again on social media, starting with Facebook, then MSN Messenger, and then on a now-defunct social media app called Friendster. Jennifer said Andrew had lived through a rocky spell with his father and ended up dropping out of high school. However, Andrew had carved out his own path and ended up landing on his feet, working as an apprentice at an insurance company. As their telephone conversations continued, he shared with her a few options to relieve herself of the pressures she faced. Jennifer said the first idea he proposed involved running away, which she told him wasn't possible, claiming she wanted to remain with her family. His second was even more extreme, she said. That idea involved having her "kidnapped" — another plan she rejected because she said she didn't want to "leave her mom." However, his third scheme set her mind racing, she said.

It was this suggestion that Jennifer said caused her to begin contemplating something she'd never thought of before: that it was her father who was the problem all along. She said Andrew recounted how he had once tried to kill his father during a physical altercation. "When I confided in him, he understood my feelings.... He said, 'You know what? One time I even tried to kill my dad,'" she told the court. "It kind of felt like something clicked between what he was saying and what I was feeling, because my dad was the one making me feel isolated. My mom made me feel home and warm. As bad as it sounds, when he said he wanted to kill his dad at that point, that triggered something inside that was like maybe, maybe life would be better without him. We spoke about it sometimes. Reality would hit me, and I'm like, that's ridiculous." However, over time and further conversations, Jennifer said her feelings began to shift, slowly coming around to the idea that killing her father could be the solution to all of her worries.

"Were you serious? Did you go and have someone plan something out for yourself?" she asked him. "And he had said, well, he'd actually got in a physical altercation with his father, which surprised me." It was at this point she said that Andrew handed the phone over to his roommate, saying, "You know who could help us … Ric." After a brief conversation about the struggles she faced, which he sympathized with, she said the pair organized a time to meet near her piano school in Scarborough. It only dawned on her what she was getting involved in when she first saw him. "My first reaction was wow, this guy looks really gothic…. He was wearing a hat, black nail polish. His eyes were always kind of shifty. He looked … like one of those really serious gangsters in movies," she said. "I was never opened to any of this, and I didn't think it was real life…. He looked very much like one of those predators you see in the movies and you're like, 'Oh, that's the bad guy.'"

The negative impression didn't put her off one bit. Instead, Jennifer said the pair then went for bubble tea. It was at this time that Jennifer said she laid out her parameters. First, she said, she wanted her father to be alone, ideally near his workplace. But beyond that she didn't know much else and needed advice. In response, Ric said the hit would cost $1,300 and that he would need to find a gun. "I don't have the tools to do the job yet," she said he told her. "I wanted to see if this guy was for real," she added, explaining that she was suspicious that Ric might have just been trying to help Andrew get laid. "Or if he was just helping Andrew to boast about something."

About a week later, she and Ric met again. By her own admission, Jennifer finally committed herself to the murder. Armed with $1,300 she had allegedly earned teaching piano — the instrument her dad had encouraged her to dedicate her entire youth to — there was no turning back. When asked why she'd given him the money, Jennifer responded without flinching, "To kill my dad." It was in a local Tim Hortons coffee shop that she handed over the cash and discussed with him how the scheme would be executed. "The plan was going to be that he'd go to my dad's workplace and shoot him dead in the parking lot," she said. Before departing, she said Ric asked for another $200, which she gave him, something bank records later confirmed. An inexperienced Jennifer said the pair agreed on a plan, and she gave him a Google map of Hann's workplace and the area surrounding it. However, she added that Ric told her that, before anything went down, he had to arm himself. "He hadn't found a gun yet," she said. "So we hadn't verified a date and time." If Jennifer's version is accurate, the three were engaging in conspiracy to commit murder, punishable by up to fourteen years in prison. It was during this meeting that he unlucky pair was spotted by Jennifer's uncle.

After that meeting, Ric all but disappeared, Jennifer said. Although she spoke to him a few more times to see if he had managed to purchase a gun, he eventually stopped answering her phone calls. And when she finally got hold of Andrew to inquire about Ric's behaviour and ask for her money back, he told her that Ric had moved out and stopped answering his calls, as well. "He just kept making excuses for Ric," she said. "I realized that Andrew and Ric had ripped me off ... I realized it was a sham."

Ric's version of events stands in stark contrast to Jennifer's. He insists that, after a number of conversations over the phone, the pair met three times; however, he says, it was simply to get to know each other. Ric says he initially had romantic intentions with Jennifer, explaining the bet he and Andrew had to "hook up" with Jennifer. He details a number of stories she told him, including how she graduated with an accounting degree, same as her cousin, Michelle. Jennifer also told him, he says, that she was locked away in her house because her parents were afraid for her safety, considering she had been receiving messages from a jealous ex-girlfriend of her boyfriend. Ric adds that she told him she was "pissed off" about her parents' rules at home and explained this, along with their meddling, was the only reason she wasn't able to be with her ex-boyfriend. He denies the existence of any plot, any Google map, and any talk of guns. He does admit she gave him money but says the $200 was so that he could go out with some friends for karaoke.

Ric says the last time he and Jennifer spoke, she told him she had tried to move out of her house but that her parents found her and brought her back. He says she was screaming mad on the phone before she asked him to kill not only her father but both of her parents. In reply he says, he considered her request "racial profiling," since he's a black male. He adds that he then told her to "fuck off," hung up the phone, and never spoke with her again. That last communication between them took place on July 8, 2010.

Despite believing Andrew had ripped her off, Jennifer said she remained friends with him and continued to speak with him over the next few months. "We've known each other for a long time," she responded. "Forgive and forget. Money comes, money goes."

Around this time, Jennifer's relationship with Daniel had progressed beyond phone calls and checking in on each other. She started sneaking out of her house to visit him at work, often bringing him and his colleagues breakfast and lunch from McDonald's. Sometimes the visits lasted ten or fifteen minutes, sometimes longer. Jennifer was also using this time to entice him with sexual pleasure, someone close to the case says.

And when he didn't have access to her, he encouraged her to sext him and send him pictures and videos of her in various states of undress. Material later discovered on her cellphones included multiple short videos of her shaved vagina, one of her buttocks while she bent over and spread her cheeks, showing, as police later put it, "very intimate areas," and bondage pictures with her arms tied behind her back. "I have been in similar positions when you're dating someone older or someone you don't feel you deserve, whether they're saying I'm not going to love you if you don't put out. You feel that pressure; you put that pressure on yourself. She felt she had to," says Allison, who knew the couple. "I can totally imagine she would feel she needed to do that stuff in order to keep him interested, and maybe [she] regretted it. If you don't like yourself, your body is a very easy way to get affection. *Of course, he likes me. I know he likes this. I feel very close to him right now. He must love me, he's making love to me ...* It's a really common tool that girls with low self-esteem rely on because at least [the men] are demonstrating their affections."

Jennifer and Daniel engaged in sexting, and she sent him what were often sexually suggestive pictures of herself.

This renewed relationship was an important turning point in Jennifer's life. Up to this point, she had been lying to every person in her life except Daniel. But that changed. Whether he chose to believe her fabrications because she'd never lied to him in the past remains unknown.

As time passed, the crank calls and messages received by Daniel (now also on the cellphone that Jennifer had purchased for him) became more bizarre. Jennifer had devised a new plan to leave her house even when her parents were at home. At night, a friend of Daniel's quietly picked her up and delivered her to the pair's favourite sushi restaurant so they could have dinner together. After one of these rendezvous, Daniel received the following messages: *Doesn't she ever learn. You didn't listen to us, she's going to have to pay.*

When Daniel texted Jennifer later to make sure she was safe, he received the reply: *You don't need to know where she is, we have got her.*

"When I tried to call back to make sure … it was okay, maybe about a half an hour later, there was no answer, so then that's when I drove by her house to see if she was okay," he said. "I kept calling her and eventually she picked up and said, 'Yeah, I'm fine.'"

Another night after they went out to see a film together he received the following messages: *Why are you guys watching a movie, I thought you were just friends?* and *You shouldn't be seeing each other like this if you guys are just friends, You should be with your girlfriend.*

On another occasion, he took Jennifer to Dave and Buster's, an adult arcade, only to receive a message after they left that said: *Why would you be walking around there* [Dave and Buster's] *with her?* Daniel began to notice the messages stopped when they were together and included details no one else could have known. "When I went out with her, there were no messages, no phone calls," he said. "But as soon as I dropped her off and she went home, probably within ten to fifteen minutes, I started to get messages of what happened when we were together or where we went. It led me to think, is she behind it, or is someone else behind it? Whenever they sent me a message, they'd tell me exactly what we were talking about. It's as if they were there. But there's no one around. If it's not me, then … it's got to be her."

Jennifer, meanwhile, always laid the blame squarely at Katrina's feet, but Katrina denied sending the messages. Before long, though, the messages got even more threatening — something Jennifer did admit was her doing. One day Daniel received the following message: *We've sent something to her house. The next time she opens it ... Boom!* Then a follow-up text arrived that read *Bang, Bang.* When he called to check in, Jennifer explained she had received a package at her home but that she hadn't opened it and had given it directly to police (something we know she never did).

Soon after this incident, Jennifer told Daniel that while she was out on a walk she dropped her phone. She said that the person who had been harassing her had discovered it and was using the information garnered from the phone against her and Daniel in these messages. Jennifer said she then received a text from the person saying *Look in your mailbox, we have something for you.* In it she found a bag containing her phone and some white residue. Jennifer lied to Daniel again, explaining that the police had analyzed the substance and found it was itching powder. Her lies eventually grew even more outlandish, almost as if she wanted to be caught in them by Daniel. The only problem was that he never called her out. After this incident, she told Daniel the police had grown so worried that investigators were sifting through her mail and following her around. At one point she told him how police conducted a takedown of a man who had tried to swap her water bottle after she got up to go to the bathroom while studying in the library. Eventually, the stories reached a crescendo. Soon after Jennifer said her father chased away five masked Asian teenagers who had repeatedly knocked at her door one night. She told Daniel that she'd received a voice mail one day with muffled screaming, something that made Daniel very nervous. Then she explained how after returning home from a jog, five Asian teenagers had pushed her in her home and raped her in her bedroom, covering her eyes while they performed sex acts on her.

Allison, Daniel's associate, says: "Instead of saying 'Daniel I need you in my life. I need you, I miss you, I feel abandoned,' she said *I've been attacked and raped by Chinese gang members.* She has told herself *I can't tell the truth because the truth won't be accepted, so I have to find other ways.* She was using his sensitivity, care, and worry for her against him."

Jennifer told him that her mother took her to the hospital and that the police were looking into the incident. But when he asked how he could help, she insisted she wanted to deal with it by herself.

"There was so much controversy in it that I really didn't know how to take it, but I would rather be safe, right, so I just took her word for it," he said. "One thing I kept thinking about is that, if there was a sexual assault, it would be all over the news, just like everything else. Some guy just sexually assaulted a woman in the park recently. It was all over the news. But her case wasn't." By this point, Daniel didn't know what to believe. The last thing he wanted to do was accuse her of lying, but he found the details so shocking as to be unbelievable. "I asked her for some sort of proof, like … the blue card or the wristband [you're given] when you get admitted to the hospital," he said. "[But] she'd say, 'My mom got it, and I don't know whether she kept it.' When I started to get these phone calls and these messages, I asked, 'Can I see your phone bill to see?' and she said I'll bring it to you next time I see you [but never did]. Because of how long I've known her and what we've been through together, I believe her. But in terms of seeing any distinctive hard proof of it, I haven't."

Daniel said he believed Jennifer because of her uncanny ability to make those around her believe what she was saying, despite evidence or lack thereof appearing to show otherwise. She was able to conjure up intense emotions at the drop of a hat to manipulate those who loved her. Now, no one was safe from her trickery. "At first, honestly, I thought she just wanted me to get back with her," Daniel said. "She was seeking [an] attention sort of thing. But when she told me something like that [about the rape] and I heard it in her voice even though I couldn't see her. It's not like I could call her parents and confirm whether it happened or not. From then on I told her to just keep reporting it and keep calling and keep the contact with me so I know that she's okay. After that point … I believed her."

Daniel later explained that he thought about going to the police with the issues but was reluctant given his criminal record. Although counterintuitive, the messages and lies resulted in a marked improvement in the pair's relationship. By this point, Jennifer said they were once again communicating daily.

28

DEADLY BETRAYAL

Jennifer's version of events as they unfolded was examined, and the jury soundly rejected it. Hence, it will be the Crown's theory that we will explore from this point on.

The five months leading up to that terrible night in November were agonizing and terrifying from the outside looking in. The distress was only intensified by the nonchalance with which Jennifer seemed to manage the roles in her life, from doting daughter to loving niece, to caring friend, to calculating, cold-blooded murderer. She seamlessly switched between those roles, simultaneously texting with murderers to plan her parents' assassination while handing out candy to toddlers at Halloween with her mother. When what Jennifer called her initial plan fell apart — whether because it was rejected or it was just an elaborate rip-off from the beginning — she was left undeterred. Rather than reject the idea and allow it to fade from her mind, she pushed on using her scant resources to find a group of men willing to carry out her scheme.

Crown lawyers contended that over the next month Jennifer honed her plan to rid herself of her parents. Her instrument of choice was not a knife or a match but her cellphone. At all hours of the day and night, in hushed tones and darkened rooms, she forged ever onward on her path of destruction. All the while, her unwitting parents carried on with their daily tasks and chores, earning money to keep a roof over her head, making her food, and trying to plan for her future.

During this time, Jennifer didn't seem moved by the day-to-day machinations of a normal family household in which someone might hate their parents and want to be free of them one day and the next make up and forgive them. Rather, she spent three months planning without ever once, as far as any evidence showed, giving any indication that she had second thoughts about carrying it out. In fact, it appeared the only time she might have felt some remorse was after her mother's passing, but even that was questionable. Her scheme spanned half of the summer of 2010 and into the autumn, while her parents remained blithely unaware of the doom that was about to shatter their lives. In fact, Hann later remarked that right up until that most awful moment, he thought his family was content, even joyful.

What made the plot even more unnerving was, as far as we know, there was never anything other than acquiescence from Jennifer toward Hann's or Bich's demands — not the slightest outburst of anger or violence, as seen in other murders by young people who find themselves under intense pressure. Jennifer bided her time under the pretense of the good daughter, all the while conniving her way toward her ultimate goal. It was during this summer that the twenty-four-year-old was wracked with feelings of revenge and bitter alienation that gave way to the most callous and shallow of acts — murder. One can only assume that Jennifer felt all her options had been exhausted. So surreal was the evidence that one might conclude by this point she had either turned wicked or was losing her mind, but both are mere assumptions. It was her love for Daniel and her refusal to give up on their future together that continued to propel her forward. In fact, the adoration of Daniel was the one and only thing Jennifer appeared concerned with throughout much of this time, oblivious to anyone else around her. This apparent detachment from any sort of reality carried on right up until the moment her parents were brutally shot and well beyond the death of her mother.

At some point during their relationship Daniel certainly was in love with Jennifer. However, after they broke up and he started a new relationship with Katrina, there seemed to be a switch in the impetus behind the pair's dealings. Daniel tried to keep his distance from Jennifer but was brought back into the fold by her duplicitous ways.

After entangling himself in Jennifer's net again, Daniel sought a way out. But it was too late. Jennifer lashed out. This was his chance to be done with her, but for some reason or other it was now Daniel who reached out, reuniting with Jennifer once more and professing his love for her mere days before the killing. The question was: why? Why did Daniel want this crazy scheme to go ahead? Was it for Jennifer's insurance money? Was it so he wouldn't lose face in front of his friends? How could Daniel have gone along with this plot?

Did he really want to be with Jennifer in the end? We may never know. One lawyer involved in the trial has a theory, implying these feelings are born in the male ego. In his decades working murder and armed robbery cases, he's seen similar scenarios play themselves out almost exclusively with men time and time again. "Things like this have a snowball effect," he says. "The idea is this: the conversation [about a crime] happens ... then someone is introduced to the original pair ... the expectations go up. That person then goes and talks to another person.... At some point a hardened criminal is approached. When serious boys come to play, it reaches a new level and at that point they each have a role to play. [When the time comes], they've assumed these roles and they are roles they have to play. The reality is that none have the guts to say, 'I want out of this.' They didn't want to look foolish having gone so far. Daniel was certainly compelled by his self-image and reputation."

Perhaps most grievous of all from an outsider's perspective was Jennifer's behaviour with co-conspirator Daniel in the lead-up to the murder. They engaged in nervous yet excited baby-talk conversations via text right up until her mother was executed. Their communications continued in the days following the murder and until Jennifer finally stopped writing Daniel love letters from her prison cell. By August 2010, Jennifer started using two separate cellphones. While she continued to call and text from her older Rogers Wireless flip phone, Daniel had also given her another phone to use, this one an iPhone 3 registered with Bell Mobility, which he paid for. "Jen had two phones," he said. "After the [rape], I gave her the phone. I said, 'I need to contact you all the time so that I know that you're okay,' and 'If your parents are going to keep taking your phone away from you, then at least try to hold on to this one so I can contact you.'"

In court, it was suggested this was her "secret murder phone," used for more treacherous purposes, including planning the hits. And the data bears this out somewhat. Between August 3 and November 8, the

Bell phone accounts for three thousand calls and texts, 74 percent of all communication. Jennifer never used the Bell phone to call her friends, Adrian Tymkewycz and Edward Pacificador but did use it to call Andrew Montemayor on occasion, Homeboy, and Daniel. And this was the phone David Mylvaganam's phone called a number of times prior to the murder.

Jennifer began plotting her parents' deaths in June while her relationship with Daniel was on the rocks. Initially, she proposed it to Ric, always using her Rogers phone to contact him. But after that plan disintegrated in July, she bided her time. As Jennifer and Daniel's relationship blossomed anew, she presented a tweaked plan to him. On August 3, Daniel gave Jennifer the iPhone. She was using this phone when the pair shared a marathon phone conversation on August 16. It was during this call that she first presented her plot to Daniel. It was simple and sophisticated, and if it worked, ingenious: hired hit men would break into her home, tie her up, and go on a rampage through the house.

During the invasion, they would do their best to make it look like a robbery, flipping beds, rifling through drawers, and demanding cash with guns pointed at both Jennifer and the homeowners. In the ensuing minutes, after finding little or no money, other than Jennifer's, the men would kill her parents under the pretext that they'd grown infuriated with their lack of loot. It would all happen very quickly, and the armed men could be in and out of the house in less than thirty minutes. There would be only one person remaining, the only witness — a poor defenceless girl named Jennifer. Jennifer would then use her penchant for dramatics to place a 911 call from her Rogers phone, which would be conveniently placed in the waistband of her yoga pants. During this call, she'd remain so frightened and helpless that she'd have to be untied by police themselves. When investigators arrived on the scene, they would have no one to interview except Jennifer. As for any remaining evidence, gloves and hats would ensure there would be no DNA left behind, the clothes and weapons would be properly disposed of, blankets would be used to avoid blood splatter, and the SIM card from the Bell phone, which contained evidence of the plan, would disappear before police could get their hands on it.

The plot would leave Jennifer alive and her parents brutally gunned down. Clearly, this was the weakest part of the scheme for three reasons, which Jennifer clung to until November 22. One, she co-operated by giving the thieves $2,000, money she'd been saving for a new phone. Two, her parents didn't co-operate by "lying" about the money available. Three, the murderers ran out of time and were suddenly forced to flee, leaving Jennifer tied up one floor above and alive.

Sure, there were flaws in the plan, but Jennifer believed these were calculated risks, considering the lack of witnesses and cellphone evidence. Anyone who's ever escaped a murder rap has always had a partially deficient defence, but as we all know, finding the suspects is the easy part, proving it is not. Even if investigators had suspicions, there would be no one except Jennifer present to call into question her version of events. No contradictory information would be available if everyone followed the plan. Police might have their doubts and uncover inconsistencies, but they would never risk accusing the victim of trickery and deception on this scale without proof, especially when that victim had just lost both her parents in a double homicide.

As with so many plans throughout history, Jennifer's plot looked bullet-proof on paper. Any investigation without the weapon, DNA evidence, or witnesses is severely hampered. Theories, motives, and suspects are one thing, but Canada's judicial framework is based on proof. Without witnesses, a case relies on forensic evidence such as footprints, hair follicles, a murder weapon, cellphone records, wiretaps, or ideally a confession. In Jennifer's plan, police would have none of these. Of course, there were countless mistakes. However, had those responsible been just a bit more careful, it remains an open question whether the police would have seen the men eventually convicted and had enough evidence to charge Jennifer, or whether the Crown would have had enough ammunition to convict. All investigators say they would have gotten Jennifer regardless, but that's certainly up for debate. If two or three details had turned out differently — if Hann had died, it died, the iPhone didn't store messages, and to a lesser degree if Telus didn't store text messages — the case would have been much harder to crack. At least one lawyer says it would have been very difficult to prove the case had "everything gone according to plan," especially considering Jennifer's Samsung phone had little or no evidentiary value other than perhaps the communication with Andrew.

Detailed phone records show that one month after her last phone conversation with Ric, Jennifer placed what would become a fateful call. On August 16, Jennifer used the iPhone to call Daniel at 1:21 a.m. The two had a five-hour talk. But it wasn't the length of the conversation that was the most telling detail; rather, it was what occurred during the ensuing forty-eight hours. After this call, Daniel's cellphone communication with Jennifer was muted. But Jennifer's frenzy didn't stop. In the hours following that conversation, Jennifer called and texted Daniel forty times from her Rogers phone, family landline, and her Bell phone. But the attempted communication didn't cease there. The following day, August 17, she called and texted Daniel a further one hundred times between 1:00 a.m. and 11:30 p.m., again using all three phones. On August 18, she sent four texts and called fifteen times, but all her calls went to voice mail. Then, between 5:53 a.m. and 8:00 a.m. she sent five texts and called another seventeen times, all of which went to voice mail. In the next thirty-five minutes, she called him twelve more times before Daniel finally answered her call at 8:47 a.m. In the follow-up to this call, Daniel eventually capitulated and sent her the bit of information she was seeking — the phone number of a friend. Jennifer didn't call Daniel back after this until the following day. Instead she began texting a new man, Lenford Crawford, a.k.a. Homeboy. He returned her call at 11:09 a.m., and the pair shared a four-and-a-half-minute conversation.

There are only two outside sources who have described Jennifer's odd behaviour during this time, namely, the two people she was in constant contact with — her piano teachers, Ewa Krajewska and Fernando Baldassini. The latter says he saw her in the spring of 2010 in the lead-up to a counterpoint exam the pair were working toward in May. "She was already going through a lot," Fernando says. "When she came in, she didn't feel all that well. She wasn't completing her work, and I confronted her. I gave her hell. Jennifer broke down. She said her father didn't approve of her boyfriend — that he was a cook and her dad didn't approve.

Ewa saw her even closer to the murder. "I saw her in September," she says. "She returned all my textbooks to me and told me she had passed [her piano teacher accreditation exam]. I noticed her face was different. I taught her a very long time and I never saw her like that. It was like she was hiding something, or very sick."

There is no evidence that Jennifer passed her exam. A former co-worker, Melissa, says she saw Jennifer a week before her mother was murdered but didn't notice anything out of the ordinary, and that the pair had agreed to meet for lunch in the near future.

Unlike her first foiled plot, Daniel assured Jennifer that if anyone was capable of bringing in the players to execute such a brutal act, it would be Homeboy. Jennifer would be responsible for initiating contact over the next ten days, which she did. The two texted back and forth before having relatively brief conversations that usually lasted only a few minutes.

The sum of money agreed upon remains a bone of contention. While there is no direct knowledge of how much was paid by Jennifer to those involved, there are three clues that hint at the deal that was negotiated. In her version of events, Jennifer admitted that Homeboy said it would cost $20,000 for a murder, but for her he'd do it for $10,000 to $15,000. Daniel told police that someone could be killed for $10,000 on the street. These weren't the only instances in which the sum of $10,000 was thrown around. Although this might not seem like much to split between the five men, including a number of others on the periphery, investigators said it is, in fact, a lot of cash to certain segments of the population. One investigator in Toronto, speaking on condition of anonymity, says murders in Toronto can be carried out for much less — as little as $500. Furthermore, there have been suggestions by seasoned investigators that those involved would have hoped to swindle further funds from a naive Jennifer after the murder. A number of police officers and lawyers say the men could have easily used their knowledge of the crime or threats of violence to gain access to Jennifer's newfound insurance riches.

One vital part of Jennifer's plan revolved around her connections to the murderers, or better yet, the lack thereof. This strategy is often employed in Hollywood plotlines. Reminiscent of the movie *Reservoir Dogs*, in which six complete strangers use aliases such as Mr. Blonde, Mr. Pink, and Mr. Brown, the Markham plot was dependent on the fact that Jennifer had no direct links to the intruders. This approach would ensure silence through ignorance. It was simple, really: if she didn't know her co-conspirators, she couldn't rat them out or implicate them in other ways. Police can't pressure a suspect to give up names or identities if they're unknown, and if or when police make connections, it's harder to prove their existence.

As far as her four co-accused go, Jennifer only plotted directly with one man she actually knew: Daniel. She came to know his associate, Lenford, only by his nickname. They spoke over the phone and texted only a handful of times. Jennifer knew the name Homeboy, his telephone number, and the sound of his voice, that was all. As for the other men, all of whom Lenford independently recruited and coordinated, Jennifer would have ideally never met or spoken to or contacted them, with the exception of the few minutes they spent in her home committing the act. If all the communication between the plotters was destroyed, police would have few options other than what one might say or do in the aftermath. Although Daniel knew both Jennifer and Lenford, both men benefited from indisputable alibis on the night of the murder. Furthermore, all communication between the three was supposed to be destroyed the night of the murder. If police were to check Jennifer's Rogers cell, they'd only find "clean communication." The men who broke into the Pan home wouldn't have alibis, of course, but by virtue of their anonymity, they wouldn't need them.

It all comes down to degrees of separation. If everything went according to plan, police could prove that Jennifer knew Daniel and maybe that Daniel knew Lenford, but considering both men had concrete alibis on the night of the murder, police would have a difficult time getting warrants for much beyond that. Of course, there were countless mistakes made. Lenford was using a phone registered to himself, which police easily tracked from Jennifer's cellphone records. These they extracted from her iPhone, a device that stores messages to the SIM and the phone itself, which was discovered out in the open in her room. David Mylvaganam's phone was used to contact Daniel and Jennifer in the lead-up to the murder, likely by Eric Carty. Daniel had sold drugs with Eric in the past and they had shared texts, later recovered, about those transactions. Jennifer didn't manage to destroy her iPhone records or even to delete sensitive messages from her phone. Daniel admitted to police that Jennifer had asked him to murder her parents. Furthermore, Jennifer confessed to a plot involving Homeboy and then seemingly told Detective Cooke that Eric was Number One. It's hard to imagine police becoming wise to Eric and David's identity had they just purchased a new burner phone to be used only that night to call Jennifer. Unfortunately for them, both were broke.

Had all this not gone wrong, Jennifer's suspicious behaviour, the fact that nothing was stolen from the house, her dodgy call while tied up, would have been simple suspicions, nothing more. One thing the evidence does bear out is that as Jennifer and Daniel delved further into the plot, their communications doubled, increasing to levels not seen since before their breakup. Between August 3 and September 26, a period of just fifty-five days, the pair shared 969 calls and texts. But the majority of the communications originated from Jennifer (809, compared to a paltry 160 from Daniel). Between September 27 and November 8, that number jumped to 1,754 calls and texts — 1,067 from Jennifer and 687 from Daniel. They shared another 3,000 calls and texts on her Rogers phone between May and November. The communication with Lenford paled in comparison. After their initial conversation, Jennifer texted Lenford on six separate days until the end of August; they had one conversation in September, three in October, and twelve in November, totalling forty minutes.

There remain no psychological evaluations about Jennifer's mental health. However, it's clear that her behaviour is beyond the realm of what our society deems normal. She was not only lying to everyone in her life, including her parents, for almost a decade, but she was also forging documents, cutting herself, and experiencing suicidal thoughts. Some might conclude this was due to the depression she suggested she was struggling through, questioning whether she wanted to continue living. However, according to Barbara Greenberg, a well-known American therapist, this is just what Jennifer wanted those around her to think. According to her, this was a ruse designed to portray Jennifer as the victim when in reality she was predatory — a selfish young woman who had become an expert at manipulating those around her. Furthermore, she describes Jennifer's depressive behaviour as "impression management" by a very intelligent, decisive, "creative and crafty" young woman.

Barbara, a clinical psychologist practising in Connecticut and specializing in the treatment of young people and their parents, often deals with cutters, those suffering from intense depression and a range of personality disorders. She says Jennifer's behaviour is more consistent with that of a sociopath than someone who is suicidal, depressed, or struggling through the symptoms that lead to cutting. "There appears to be some narcissism involved, but I think the more accurate diagnosis is anti-social personality disorder," she says. "She started lying in her teen years early [around age fourteen] … a characteristic of ASPD, and she clearly had an impaired moral compass. Most people who are narcissistic do have a moral compass and do have a sense of what's right and what's wrong, but it's when narcissism overlaps with ASPD that you can start to have the makings of a young woman like Jennifer. For a person who is narcissistic alone, even malignant — the worst type of narcissist — it would be unlikely that they'd have the heart and the mind for this type of behaviour."

Greenberg says that one particularly worrying tendency was not only Jennifer's penchant for creating large-scale lies from a young age but how those lies grew in size and scope over time. She says Jennifer managed the lies effectively, perfecting the behaviour associated with this type of disorder, with her story only falling apart because it simply grew too big for her to maintain. A good example Greenberg gives of this type of escalation is a boyfriend who first verbally insults his girlfriend during a fight, then punches walls, and finally physically assaults her. Each time he gets away with the behaviour, he is emboldened and takes it a step farther until it is too late. These are the criminal deviants, often men, who show progressively aggressive behaviour, that police most fear. An example of this is a sexual predator who gropes unwitting victims before escalating to violent physical assault such as trying to remove their clothing. It's at this point that investigators redouble their efforts to locate the suspect because there is a heightened risk the perpetrator might escalate his attacks. Greenberg says that, while minor deception might be ever-present in homes with high expectations, those lies might be characterized by children as not divulging information or merely forging a few signatures. Jennifer, on the other hand, started with fraudulent report cards and then escalated with further forgeries — first, a university scholarship and then entire transcripts.

The same goes for the scope of her lies. They began with her parents and then eventually widened to everyone in her life. "This behaviour is above and beyond what you'd expect in a child from that culture who wants to please," Greenberg says. "I think a lot of the kids in those homes are more likely to withhold information than actually fabricate. She was starting to become anti-social or sociopathic at a young age. Her behaviour was very calculated, very planned and deliberate, also signs of anti-social — forging report cards, scholarship letters, then creating a new existence for herself."

Greenberg suggests that, while her upbringing might have led to a variety of deceptions, it wouldn't have caused this magnitude of lies, adding that Bich might have actually contributed to Jennifer's sense of infallibility by siding with her over Hann. "When you look at the childhoods of people who develop ASPD, you can see tremendous inconsistencies between the parents in terms of how they treat the kids ... that's a good predictor of the development, and you will often see that in their histories. Kids need to get consistent messages of what's okay and what's not okay. And kids who get messages from one parent who say that's okay and the other parent that's not okay, those are kids who have a harder time developing a good set of clear ethical principals because they are getting inconsistent messages. So while her mother was maybe her supporter and her rock, her mother wasn't doing her any favours by being more permissive." As for why her mother would then be a target, Greenberg says, "Love and hate are not mutually incompatible. Think crimes of passion."

When it comes to Jennifer's self-harm, Greenberg says evidence that she was sharing this behaviour widely among those closest to her, and also with complete strangers, such as police officers, indicates that she was doing so to paint herself in a certain light. "My impression was this was not a depressed girl. Clearly, she was a very serious girl. I work with a lot of cutters because I work with a lot of teenagers, and they say the same thing that Jennifer did: 'That cutting grounds me, allows me to feel again.' I would suspect that Jennifer may have known other girls who cut, probably did some reading about it. However, she doesn't fit the personality of a cutter. These girls who cut themselves are very depressed. Not only can they not handle their daily lives, they certainly don't have the energy to fabricate transcripts and plan murders. I think this was just part of her scheming. [My guess] is her suicide attempt was a manipulative gesture to try and portray herself differently. It's just impression management. She was trying to give an *impression* of a depressed girl is my guess. She was a planner. When this girl wanted something done, she went out and did it. I hate to say it in this way, but if she really wanted to kill herself, she would have done it. Frankly, if she was really so depressed, it's surprising she didn't kill herself before or after the murders. I'd say the cutting was no more than a ploy to make it look like she was a depressed girl who couldn't handle her feelings."

As for how psychologists treat ASPD, Greenberg says this sort of disorder can be the most difficult to treat, in part because the subjects often end up fooling even the therapist concerning their true intentions and feelings. "ASPD is the least treatable psychiatric illness because the people with this diagnosis have the ability in therapy to really present themselves very differently than they are," she says. "They're often very charming … they can fool therapists. Furthermore, it's very hard to treat someone who feels very little anxiety or empathy. Quite frankly, they're not working with the same moral system that the rest of us are."

What makes Jennifer's case so astounding, according to Greenberg, is how out of the norm it is for a female to act in this fashion. "More men are diagnosed with ASPD and, secondly, men are more likely to commit crimes like this," she says. "Men are more likely to act out aggressively against others, and women are more likely to act out against themselves. Women tend to be torturers of themselves, and men tend to be torturers of others."

Finally, Greenberg says she ran the symptoms Jennifer displayed through a diagnostic test from the *Diagnostic and Statistical Manual of Mental Disorders* (*DSM*), which offers standard criteria for the classification of mental disorders. Although someone only needs to show a pervasive pattern since age fifteen, from what Greenberg can tell, Jennifer fits each and every criteria, barring only the physical violence suggested in the fourth item in the following list:

1) Failure to conform to social norms with respect to lawful behaviours as indicated by repeatedly performing acts that are ground for arrest.
2) Deceitfulness, as indicated by repeated lying, use of aliases, or conning others for personal profit or pleasure.
3) Impulsivity or failure to plan ahead.
4) Irritability and aggressiveness, as indicated by repeated physical fights or assaults.
5) Reckless disregard for safety of self or others.
6) Consistent irresponsibility, as indicated by repeated failure to sustain consistent work behaviour or honour financial obligations.
7) Lack of remorse, as indicated by being indifferent to or rationalizing having hurt, mistreated, or stolen from another.

When asked how Jennifer might rank on a scale of one to ten in terms of severity of this disorder, Greenberg says she'd be at the high end of the threshold. "[Jennifer would] be a ten," she says emphatically, adding that an easy way to consider how narcissism comes into play is to imagine someone with great power. "Like politicians who have all these affairs and think it's okay for them. Jennifer doesn't appear to think normal rules apply to her." Greenberg says that the cutting, the suicide attempts, and if it was, in fact, Jennifer behind the messages being sent to Daniel, it truly shows how deranged she really was during this time. "Again, this is all about fabricating and manipulative behaviour," Greenberg says. "She's very crafty and creative. This is really a disturbed girl."

There have been two suggestions of the sorts of mental health issues Jennifer may have been suffering from in the lead up to the murder. Two lawyers suggested that she was a pathological liar, a person who lies compulsively or impulsively on a regular basis and is unable to control him or herself despite foreseeing inevitable negative consequences or ultimate disclosure of his or her fabrications. Therapist Barbara Greenberg on the other hand suggested Jennifer is a sociopath, someone who lies incessantly to get his or her way and does so with little concern for others. Sociopaths are often goal-orientated (i.e., lying is focused and is done to get one's way). They have little regard or respect for the rights and feelings of others.

29

"SHE'S NOT MY MAMA"

For juvenile and flighty Jennifer, the alleged plot might have simply blown over had those around her seen the twenty-four-year-old and her ramblings for what they were — an immature girl trying to find an illogical way out of her problems. This would not be the case. Although the plot seemed to get short shrift at the outset, it eventually gained more steam, with money eventually trumping good sense. After the flurry of communication between Jennifer and Lenford in late August, there was radio silence between the pair for about a month until Jennifer finally called him on September 13. Even then there was little conversation until a month and a half later on October 28. There would be little waiting after this day, with armed gunmen breaking into Jennifer's home eleven days later. The Crown's case continued.

So what changed? Why did the plan kick into action so quickly in and around this date? Only a handful of people might have the answer to that question. What we do know is that at least one man around this time needed money — badly. In the days leading up to October 22, Eric Carty texted Leesha Pompei and complained about a lack of "doe." In the texts he told her that he felt like a "waste" because he was unable to afford a birthday present for his daughter, bearing in mind he was on the lam at this time and couldn't carry on business as usual. However, it was also clear this wasn't the first time the couple had discussed the subject. The pair went on to argue about her insistence on paying Eric's dinner bill while out for a family meal at the Mandarin. Leesha continued to reassure Eric, explaining how good a father he was, irrespective of whether or not he could buy his child a gift. Eric eventually replied by making four significant requests of Leesha in two communications, but never mentioned the reason why. In the first message, he told her he needed a new cellphone and a rental car. Within a week he made two more requests: black gloves and a black hat. *I found 2 different winterish gloves, but [they're] black if that helps,* Leesha eventually responded, blithely unaware of the reason behind Eric's requests.

For Jennifer, October was a busy month. Hann later testified that it was around this time, as Jennifer prepared to attend college in January, that he made a conscious decision to "bring [Jennifer] closer" to the family. October 8 was the last day Felix saw his mother alive. After he returned to school, Jennifer travelled to Boston for a wedding with Hann and Bich. The following weekend she, Bich, and Bich's sister, who had flown in from the United Kingdom for the wedding, took a "Chinese bus tour" to Ottawa and Montreal. During this trip, Jennifer repeatedly sent Daniel selfies of her stuffed animals posed in front of monuments such as Montreal's Notre Dame Cathedral. It was on October 24, back at home in Markham, that she withdrew $500 from a nearby bank.

Five days later, on October 29, Eric sent the following text to Lenford: *u gd* [good] *and can dat gwan* [go on] *2night.* There was no response. Undeterred, Eric was back on the phone soon after, when he tried to recruit a friend for the job. To a phone registered to another fake user, Duane Stephenson (the name of a Jamaican reggae artist), Eric texted: *I nd u 2day gt a money ting 4u.*

On October 30, Eric finally got the phone he'd been asking Leesha for the week before. However, it appeared someone else might have picked it up, since it was registered to Silvia Powell's address. Halloween 2010 proved to be a pivotal day in the evolution of Jennifer's master plan. On Sunday, October 31, between 6:30 and 7:12 p.m., Lenford's phone could be seen travelling east until it ended up at the Scarborough Town Centre shopping mall, about halfway between Rexdale (where Lenford lived) and Ajax (where Daniel resided). Daniel's phone arrived at the same location. By 8:50 p.m., both cellphones were using the tower closest to Jennifer's house. It was the perfect night — they were both off work and the children out trick-or-treating through the dark Markham streets provided them with the perfect cover to scope out the neighbourhood in preparation for the murder. Although he was supposed to have been there, Eric was unable to attend. He wasn't idle, though. He left multiple voice mails for David Mylvaganam, his young associate. In the end, the pair discussed the contract by text message:

> **DM:** *Yo Pop.*
> **EC:** *10 stacks.*
> **DM:** *Ya … Wen u ready k.*
> **EC:** *Ya 5 each ting.*
> **DM:** *Me u.*
> **EC:** *Ya bt u all da way and all ten 4u.*
> **DM:** *Easy ting.*
> **EC:** *Awo.*
> **DM:** *De ya a bill link.*

In essence, the exchange was translated by one expert as meaning the job would be for $10,000 — $5,000 for each body. If David shot both, all the money would be his. The roles and contracts were now cemented. Eric, David, and a third man would be the perpetrators of the violence. Lenford and Daniel were the middlemen, communicating information between Eric and Jennifer.

Before leaving Markham, Daniel met Jennifer in the alleyway behind her home. During that fleeting moment, an exchange was likely made, but whether it was the $500 Jennifer pulled out of the bank days before remains unknown. After showing Lenford the Pan home and its surrounding area, including the route to the highway, Daniel and Lenford left.

Lenford made one more trip before heading home. He stopped by the home of a man who knew Eric well, and it was the only time he was ever at this address. Whether he was there to drop off a down payment for Eric is yet another plausible but unproven detail. A date for the plan to be carried out was then allegedly confirmed. The murder was to take place on November 3.

The eight days leading up to the murder were manic for Jennifer. She was on her Bell iPhone constantly, her mind boiling with feelings of envy and gluttony. However, there is also evidence of lust and wrath, with Jennifer experiencing an enraptured feeling, the thrill of the plot, the fearful excitement of the unknown, and at least for a while, a renewed sense of hope regarding her relationship prospects with Daniel. Her text messages from this period also contained worrying references to "sweaty palms and heart palpitations," revealing a woman racked with worry over Daniel's feelings for her or lack thereof. Perhaps what was most evident was her callousness and seeming disregard for her parents' lives. For many people this juxtaposition is hard to fathom and comprehend. How could a daughter be so caught up in her love life and so detached from the havoc she was preparing to unleash on those around her — the very people who loved her more than anyone else?

On November 1, two days before the murder was originally supposed to take place, Eric was harassing Lenford via text for Daniel's phone number. Lenford, attempting to adhere to the plan, which was not to involve any communication between Eric and Daniel, didn't respond to his messages. However, after applying just enough pressure, involving at least one profanity-laced text and a voice mail, Lenford eventually relented and texted Daniel's number, scolding Eric that he was texting Lenford like his "gal."

The intricate web of phone use by a sly Eric to avoid detection can be seen in the next sequence of events. Eric used Silvia's phone at her Mississauga home to receive Daniel's phone number. Then he drove to David's house in Rexdale. Once there, he used David's phone to contact Daniel. Although it's unclear what Eric wanted to talk to Daniel about, the financial terms of the contract might be a good guess. At 5:15 p.m. David's phone and Daniel's phone shared these texts:

> **E:** *Can we meet up nw bro u kno who it is call me nw?*
> **D:** *Who is this?*
> **E:** *U kno who it is call me man?*
> **E:** *Yo man i was 2c u yesterday* [Halloween] *wit roy man fuck call me.*
> **D:** *Oh u were to c me wit roy yesterday.*
> **D:** *Nows not a good time to talk.*
> **D:** *Call u wen it is.*
> **E:** *When bro im ready nw.*
> **D:** *Nows not a good time to talk man.*
> **E:** *So what nw?*

The exchange made clear a number of things. First, Eric was supposed to attend the meeting near Pan's house on Halloween but wasn't able to. It also showed that Daniel remained very aware that his phone shouldn't be used to contact anyone involved in or carrying out the plan. Daniel never did call Eric back. In fact, other than a conversation about drugs when Eric berated him in July, this was the only contact between the two men. The following day, November 2, involved further preparations, and a series of texts in the lead-up to the murder gave the police their first insight into Homeboy's true identity. The late-night conversation began with Daniel asking Jennifer to come and see him at work the following day. Daniel refused to call her, knowing that sometimes meant hours on the telephone satisfying Jennifer's insatiable need to hear the sound of his voice. Meanwhile, needy Jennifer was clearly not happy that the pair hadn't talked for some time.

D: *Mama mesa* [I'm] *fewing dwn* [feeling down].
D: *And dun wanna talk on the phone.*
D: *Any chance u can come tomolo?*
J: *I will try. Fine.*
J: *Wat time?*
D: *Idk* [I don't know].
D: *Come over for breakfast.*
D: *Contact homeboy.*
J: *I will in the morning. Runs aways boohoo.*
D: *Pls tke care of my monkie mr chipmunk and mr bawbos.*
D: *Good nite.*
J: *Good nit monkey head.*
D: *Y u down munkey head?*

Then, the following morning, there was this from Jennifer: *Sad u pomiss to call. I kno wat u said but still sad. No seep fo me.* After calling Homeboy, she texted Daniel again: *Homeboy said he hadn't talked to you yet.*

It was only by cross-referencing Jennifer's contact with Homeboy (who promised to call "in the morning") and Daniel's calls to him, given the text that Homeboy "hadn't talked to you yet," that investigators were able to identify Lenford as Homeboy. It was also on this day that Lenford's phone made initial contact with the phone of Tim Conte, a friend of Eric's, whose phone number reappeared on November 8.

Later that evening, for some unknown reason, a day before the murder was supposed to take place, Daniel decided to drop an atomic bomb on Jennifer's hopes. Throughout the plot, Jennifer never wavered in her belief that once her meddling parents were out of the picture the couple would be reunited, with the promise of love, devotion, and money. But Daniel clearly had misgivings:

> D: *I'm really down right now jen :t.*
> J: *What's wrong??*
> D: *I'm talking to you as a friend because I have no one else I can talk to like this.*
> D: *I feel the way u feel.*
> D: *But about her.*
> D: *I'm sorry.*
> J: *What do you mean? Can you please clarify for me because I think I am misunderstanding.*
> J: *What do you mean when you say that you feel for her the way I feel about who?*
> J: *What are you sorry for?*
> J: *Hello? This delay isn't making feel very good. Can you please answer?*
> J: *Do you feel for her what I feel for her? Or you feel for her what I feel for you? Which is why you would be sorry? I'm trying to clarify. The suspense is making me all clammy hands and heart racing.*
> J: *Pls hurry to answer me.*
> D: *I dunno how to say this.*
> J: *So you feel for her what I feel for you. Then call it off with Homeboy.*
> D: *I enjoy chilling with her she's one of my closest friends and now I can't even be that bcoz of the ppl* [those crank calling and threatening].

D: *What do u mean I thought u said u wanted this for u?*
J: *I do. But if I have have no where to go.*
D: *Call it off with homeboy? U said u wanted this with or without me.*
J: *But if you want her how are you going to protect me from them* [those threatening her].
J: *I want it for me.*
J: *But what are you trying to say? You want to be with Katrina?*
J: *I am in a very dark place right now. Please just tell me everything so I can deal with what I need to. Do you love me and want to be with me?*
J: *Sorry. Totally lost it there. This is about you. Please go on. Ignore what I said. I'm trying to b a better person.*
J: *Sorry. That was a slip of habit. I didn't mean that. I'm so sorry please forgive me. Please go on. She is one of your closest friends and then?*
J: *Why not? These people want you to b with her right? Then how does that top* [stop] *you from being friends with her? Do you want to be with her with her?*
D: *My parents and everyone in the world do not want us to be together* [he and Katrina].
D: *Its not even about her its just I don't' have to hide anything and worry about her feelings like I had to with u.*
D: *I was always walking on eggshells with u.*
J: *I asked if you do. And not everyone. These friends of hers* [the ones allegedly threatening Jennifer] *obviously want you to be.*
J: *Just be straight with me then.*
J: *What is it then?*
D: *I dunno pls don't force me u know I love u.*
D: **Sniff**
J: *I'm just trying to help you here.*
J: *I'm not forcing you. I think I can help you. I won't be second choice again.*
J: *I'm sorry.*

D: *Its not even about that.*

[Break in time of an hour and a half.]

J: *So I have thought about this all day. Read and reread everything. You kno you want to b with her so go. At the end of each day it's not my choice and it's not your parents. If she can make you happy then I have no other choice but to find a way to let you go. You say nothing but praise for her and only things that make you feel like you need hold onto me like walking on eggshells and your parents don't like her. So as a friend you sound like you have made up your mind. As this pains me to say good bye my love. May god watch over you where ever life takes you.*

J: *I won't be getting in your way anymore and please tell these people to leave alone. Let me rest in peace.*

D: *Huh?*

D: *Did u really txt me all that from both fones?*

J: *Sorry other message was t intended for you. I leave u alone. Sorry for not making you happy and making you walk on eggshells.*

D: *Huh?*

D: *Pls dun be like that.*

It was the dramatic text *You feel for her what I feel for you? Then call it off with Homeboy* that showed the murders were so that Jennifer could be with Daniel. In sending it, she tacitly admitted the simple reasoning: *If you don't want to be with me, there's no point in killing my parents.* This text also remained the only shred of evidence that Jennifer might have thought twice about the murder or pulled back on the plan. But was it really a pullback? One might reasonably conclude that Jennifer wasn't reneging on the plan at all; rather, this was just another ploy to ensure Daniel knew the repercussions of dispensing with their relationship. This was just a part of the ongoing manipulation she concocted. Her fears were that Daniel would abandon her. His fears were that Jennifer wouldn't go through with the plan after calling it off one night: What other reason would there be for Daniel re-professing his devotion to her — *She's not my mama* — two days later?

One might further assume that with her parents' murder on her plate Jennifer would have had enough to worry about, but with her relationship with Daniel falling apart, she felt as though she might need to re-engage his cellphone with anonymous texts. As Daniel began to pull away from Jennifer, he received this message from her Rogers phone: *I hate you, I don't ever want to see you again. You and Katrina can be happy together. I hate you. Don't ever call me again. I can't believe you don't care what happened to me, I tried to come see you at work and I got shot at.*

However, when Daniel said he called Jennifer back to see if she was safe, she acted surprised and said she was fine. When Daniel told her why he was concerned, that she had been shot at, she responded, "How did you know?" Jennifer explained that she had received bullets in the mail, but that the police, who had been sifting through her mail because of the previous alleged threats against her, "intercepted" the package.

When Jennifer denied sending the message, Daniel sought out the advice of his most tech-savvy friends. They advised him that it was indeed possible for people to send messages using another person's phone number, a technique known as "spoofing." "They're spoofing, they're using [Jennifer's] number to send me the message," he explained. On November 3, the original day of the planned home invasion, Jennifer and Daniel began texting bright and early. At 7:47 a.m. Daniel wondered where Jennifer was. He'd expected her to stop by for breakfast after the pair coordinated the meeting over texts. When he asked why she hadn't arrived, she wrote: *waiting for homeboys call and waiting for my mother to leave.*

By the time she did arrive, just after 9:30 a.m., Daniel was too busy and was unable to meet with her.

> J: *U cudn't come out I see.*
> J: *There is a note on your car. I hoped you'd see me one last time. But u you can't.*
> J: *If you want m to leave so you can smoke then feel free.*
> D: *I can dun leave.*

Some fifteen minutes after this text, Jennifer sent three more text messages — two to Daniel and one to Lenford. But unlike many of these others, she deleted them and they were never recovered. Daniel's replies showed, however, that the texts could have been about the murder.

> **D:** *Be safe.*
> **D:** *Please.*

That same day, Eric texted Lenford *2 would be nice*, an indication that he wanted $2,000 up front as partial payment. Eric also appeared to be asking for gas money — between $20 and $40 to do the job — from Ayan Mohamed, another one of his girlfriends. Later Lenford texted Eric *When do we want to go to work* and again *Today at 7 p.m., u good?* A reply was registered from David's phone saying *Gusi fo sho.* This text was much debated during the trial — the defence saying it was a reference to a character named Gussy from the Jamaican crime film *Shottas* (of which Eric was a fan) and the Crown arguing that it meant "Go see for sure."

By the time Daniel and Jennifer reunited over text, Jennifer, angry and bitter at Daniel's recent behaviour, made her feelings clear. It seemed as if Daniel's initial stance about wanting to be with Katrina had softened.

> **D:** *What u doing?*
> **J:** *Just taking time for myself curled up in bed. What's up?*
> **D:** *Just checking up on u.*
> **J:** *U dun need to check up on me. She won't like that.*
> **D:** *I dun care ur still my friend.*
> **J:** *If u allow me to be.*
> **J:** *It's not my choice. You can be happy with her. I don't want to cause any problems. I will take care of you but I'm heart broken.*
> **D:** *I know and I'm so sorry for that.*
> **J:** *No your not. I told you this would happen. No matter I went through it doesn't matter.*
> **J:** *But don't worry I soon will b free and you can live happily without me.*

J: *I trusted you with the only thing I never gave anyone in this world and you played with it and broken it over and over. I have to go now but I know what I am going to do. I'm sorry for never being good enough. Good bye.*
D: *Please.*
J: *Forward this to Katrina. Congratulations to you and your friends for winning and putting me through not only emotional pain but physical. They raped me and beat me and yet you win the only person that meant anything to me. Please just tell these people to leave me alone so that I may rest in peace and so that I may go easy. I have suffered enough and I don't want to suffer in my last days. Good luck and take care of Daniel for me. He is everything to me but sadly I was never enough for him to love.*
D: *I didn't expect this to happen.*
J: *I knew it wood. Good bye.*
D: *I didn't u gotta believe me.*
D: *I did everything and lined it all up for u.*
D: *Please. Mesa gonna be alone.*
J: *You have Katrina. You won't be alone.*
D: *I told u no matter what I need u.*

In saying *I didn't expect this to happen*, Daniel was explaining to Jennifer that he didn't expect to fall in love with Katrina or have to end his relationship with Jennifer. However, when Jennifer rejected this, he reinforced his point, insisting *I didn't u gotta believe me ... I did everything and lined it all up for u.* This can be easily translated as "Had I known I was going to fall in love with another woman, there's no way I would have helped you plan the murder of your parents." When Jennifer wrote she would "take care" of Daniel, she was just admitting that when the deed was done, he'd benefit from the windfall. Only hours before the plot was supposed to reach its climax on that November night, though, Jennifer called it off with a simple but possibly worrying text to Homeboy: *Today is a no go. Dinner plans out so won't be home in time.*

Surveillance video across the street from the Pan house showed a car leaving Jennifer's home at 5:54 p.m. and returning at 7:14 p.m. It was thanks to this meal — a night out with the Luongs — that Bich's life was spared for four more days. Coincidence or not, the reality was that Jennifer cancelled the plan thirty-three minutes after she and Daniel ended their text argument. One has to wonder whether Jennifer really thought the plan couldn't happen that night or if she was manipulating Daniel again, essentially using her parents' lives as a brokering chip, wishing for more respect from Daniel in the future. Regardless, the tone of Daniel's texts after this moment certainly changed. Hours after calling off the hit on her father and mother, Jennifer remained racked with anxiety over the status of her relationship with Daniel. Just after midnight she called him before writing *Sorry, it's late. You are probably on your call with her now since she is your closest friend. Sorry and good bye.*

The next morning, November 4, Jennifer was still miffed at Daniel for failing to stay in touch with her. It also appeared from Daniel's replies that someone might have been up late sending Daniel errant text messages.

> **J:** *What's up?*
> **D:** *What u up to? Did u txt me those msgs last night?*
> **J:** *Huh? I think I just msgd u once.*
> **J:** *I passed out at like 4 or 5 waiting for you. Guess u had to mug [much] of a good time.*

Hours later, at 1:25 p.m., tower records showed Jennifer was at a bank machine pulling out another $500. Her phone then travelled to Daniel's workplace. Twenty minutes later she sent this text to Daniel: *Open door pls?*

Was she at Boston Pizza to hand over another payment for the murders? It was only after this action that Daniel began re-engaging in baby talk with Jennifer and even implied he preferred her love to Katrina's.

> **D:** *Mesa dun have my monkie.*
> **D:** *:(*
> **J:** *You have a mama better than munkie making you happy. No one wants a munkie that isn't good enough.*

J: *I love you though.*
D: *She's not my mama.*
D: *She dun take care of me like u do :(*
D: *Mesa sad.*
J: **Kiss forehead be happy.*
D: *Hmph.*
J: *You don't like that? *Hangs head low**
J: *See not good enough. :(*
D: *I do but me missy u.*
J: *Mesa miss you more.*

That night Jennifer also finally got her long-awaited wish, and the pair shared an hour-and-a-half conversation. The following day, November 5, seemed to show that now that the money had been dropped off, Eric and David could get into the particulars. Before trying to interpret the following conversation, Detective Jansz explains that when translating texts or phone conversations involving codified language it is vital to know the context. After all, he says, deciphering the meaning calls for an understanding of the manner and situation of the text message. For example, the following exchange took place between Eric Carty and David Mylvaganam:

D: *Me need a new new.*
E: *I hear u.*
D: *Cheap new.*
E: *Mmmmm.*

Jansz says *new* is a reference to a firearm. *New* suggests the gun had to be undetectable by the authorities so that it couldn't be traced, he says. *Cheap* is used to explain that the gun shouldn't cost too much, since it would have to be disposed of immediately after.

On November 6, Eric searched for further funds. For this, he contacted another girlfriend, Heather Martins, in London, Ontario, a university town about two hours southwest of Toronto.

HM: *Is something wrong?*
EC: *Money mama.*
HM: *Is it just survival money or you need a lot?*
EC: *Not much, just to get me by mama, I'm coming them ways this week. My word, I miss you.*
HM: *Aw babe, I told you I'm doing really good now, I can take care of that kind of shit for you, I miss you too.*
EC: *OK mami is there anyway you could western some money today for me please.*

Meanwhile, Jennifer remained bitter over Daniel's comments from a few days earlier and continued to punish him through texting. In the exchange that follows, she complained about seeing a picture of Daniel and Katrina at Dave and Buster's. She notified him that she would be putting all his Dave and Buster cards, used at the adult arcade to store credits for the games, in an envelope in order to deliver them to him.

J: *Well all your d&b cards will be put in an envelope. I will drop it off at bp* [Boston Pizza] *maybe tomorrow if I can. I can't pretend that it doesn't bother me when that d&b was the happiest I have ever been, and now all I can see is that picture of the two of you together. On a double with charlie. I'm sorry but cant get it out of my head. I loved going there with u so much …*
D: *Then we can still go there.*

Hours later she wrote again:

J: *I knew that my time wud b over. And that her time was nearing. Didn't expect you to cut me off like you did.*
D: *I'm not talking to her. I'm talking to my parents.*
D: *Just talk to me when u get out of ur hellhole.*

With this last comment Daniel appeared to once again be opening the door to a relationship when Jennifer was out of her home, a.k.a. her "hellhole."

On November 7, Eric stopped using his Larry Davis phone and started using a phone given to him by Silvia Powell, registered to Tanyka St. Louis.

Meanwhile, Daniel continued to try to make up to Jennifer. But she still seemed angry that he wouldn't spend as much time as she wanted him to on the phone.

> **J:** *Mesa really tired of being replaced. I was quite* [quiet] *today. Did what you asked. Didn't bother you. Still Mesa don't deserve you :(*
> **D:** *U do u do!*
> **D:** *Nite nite munk munk.*
> **J:** *Nitey then.*
> **J:** *If you can you visit me? No one home. Peas u haft come.*
> **J:** *So you can't stay on the phone with me but you can stay on the phone with her? Fuck this.*
> **J:** *Have a nice life. Here I was thinking I am going crazy and I should give you a break. I'm so stupid. You could never love me the way you love her.*
> **J:** *You know how hard yesterday was for me? To know that time was running out. I was up the whole night. And you hung up the moment you needed to talk to her. You wanted to "watch your movie." I'm so mad at myself right now. I believed you. Again.*

30

GAME TIME

November 8 was just an average Monday for the Pans, but it was far from normal for the other five players involved in the plot that unfolded that night. At 10:05 that morning, Jennifer received a text from Homeboy that changed the lives of each of them forever: *2 after work ok will be game time.*

This text was sent after a flurry of communication between Lenford and Eric. In simple English, it meant the job would go down that night after everyone was home from "work" and settled in their homes. After Jennifer got that text, she and Lenford had a four-minute conversation. She then deleted a number of texts from her phone that she and Lenford had shared. November 8 also signalled the entrance to the plot of another man, Demetrius Mables, a friend of both Eric and Lenford. Jennifer spent part of her day texting back and forth with Andrew Montemayor. Between 4:30 p.m. and 5:06 p.m. the pair exchanged more than fifty text messages, each of which were deleted from her Bell phone. Why did Jennifer take the deliberate steps to delete each of the fifty texts she shared with Andrew and only a few from Daniel? Is it possible that Daniel got a twenty-five year sentence because of Jennifer's penchant for reading his texts over and over alone in her bedroom long after they communicated? We'll probably never know, nor will we know what Jennifer and Andrew were discussing in those texts that Jennifer was determined to keep secret.

Hann Pan returned after work and then left again on a trip to Home Depot to pick up a USB pen and ventilation covers. First, Jennifer and her mother would eat — Bich's last meal. Hann arrived back home at 6:03 p.m. — a neighbour's surveillance camera witnessed his return. At 6:12 p.m., Lenford called Jennifer and they shared a forty-three-second phone call. This was the final time these two phones were in contact.

All the players' roles were finally cemented. Now, it was really game on. At 6:23 p.m. Andrian Tymkewycz arrived at the Pan home to visit Jennifer.

At 6:51 p.m. Eric was in Rexdale at his girlfriend Ayan Mohamed's home, and he was using her phone.

Bich left home to go line dancing. While Jennifer and Adrian sat together watching television in the basement, Jennifer received a phone call. Adrian testified she didn't say who it was but that she chatted for about one minute. It was Demetrius Mables's phone calling, and the conversation lasted twenty-eight seconds. The Crown alleged he was passing on information from Eric, who knew better than to relay the messages with his own phone. According to Adrian, Jennifer acted completely normal that night.

"This was act one in the long bloody play that was going to unfold that night," said Crown prosecutor Michelle Rumble. At 8:32 p.m., Ayan had her phone back and Eric was mobile. Adrian left the Pan house, after which Jennifer and Daniel, both nervous but giddy about the imminent attack, engaged in ridiculous, verging on disturbing, text conversations, when one considers what would occur just a few hours later.

> **D:** *What is it munky?*
> **J:** **Pokes munkie side**
> **D:** *Huh? Watsa rong?*
> **J:** **Squishy face* craving attention.*
> **J:** *Pokepokepoke* runs around with arms flapping around like a chicken.*
> **D:** *Haha wats up?*
> **J:** *Chickens go cluck. And munkie say …?*
> **D:** *Oooo ooo oooo mmmeeee meeee meee!*
> **J:** *Mesa no sues munkie make meeee sound. Maybe no mmm.*
> **D:** *Mmeee meee mooo ooo!*
> **J:** *Munkie no make mmmeee sound silly!*
> **D:** *Monkies go e e e o o o!*

Phone records showed that Eric and David met up around 9:00 p.m. Prior to this, Eric was dealing with an "explosive domestic situation" at home as two of his worlds collided. Two of his stable of girlfriends, it seemed, were on to him. His girlfriend, Megan Johnson, aided by his other friend, Silvia Powell, were texting seventeen-year-old Ayan, who the pair had discovered was sleeping with Eric. At 8:56 p.m. Silvia's phone, commandeered by Megan apparently, texted Ayan. The two girls' only connection was Eric. Megan tried to call Ayan, but she didn't answer, so the pair texted her instead.

> **AM:** *Who de fuck is dis?*
> **MJ:** *What does you man look like?*
> **AM:** *Dark skin short thick body shape billed niggah y.*
> **MJ:** *No disrespect but can I ask ur name?*
> **AM:** *Y?*
> **MJ:** *Didn't not know he had a lady how long you been around?*
> **AM:** *I'm tired a de lies n fakery i'm gone to my bed.*

During the drive to Markham, Eric used David's cell to call both women to try to keep the situation from boiling over. Jennifer spent the rest of her night in her room, chatting to Andrew Montemayor and Edward Pacificador. Although she had been exclusively using her Bell iPhone to call Andrew since July, she used her Rogers phone that night. The reason? She had to keep her Bell line open; after all, she was expecting a call on that line. This call was to take place twenty-six minutes before the murderers burst through her front door. Bich got home at 9:28 p.m., put on her Winnie-the-Pooh pajamas, filled a bucket with warm water, and soaked her feet in front of the television as she watched the Chinese news. Hann was already in bed sleeping.

In her police interview, Jennifer said she crept downstairs to unlock the door, above which hung a picture of Bich and herself, under the pretext of saying good night to her mom. The pair shared a fleeting good night.

Back in the car, Eric wasn't the only one dealing with domestic issues. David Mylvaganam was in touch with Denise Brown, his ex-girlfriend.

The two were in the midst of trying to reconnect after a trial separation following the discovery of David's infidelities. He was trying to make things up to her and hoped the money he was to earn that night would go a long way to showing her he'd grown up. Much of it was earmarked to be sent to Montreal to take care of the couple's son. As he and Eric and one other man sped east along the Highway 401 on their way to Markham, the pair constantly passed the phone back and forth, with Eric calling Megan and Ayan and David keeping in touch with Denise. At 9:34 p.m. David's phone, likely being held by Eric, called Jennifer Pan's Bell phone.

That call, intended to advise her how close they were, lasted one minute and forty-two seconds. Calls to Megan and Ayan were placed right before and right after. Eric then used David's phone to call Lenford, letting it ring for exactly sixty-one seconds — a signal to Lenford no doubt that "we're closing in on the targets." At 9:42 p.m. David and Denise shared this revealing text conversation:

> **DM:** *In a meeting with Kimble. I will text you to call k love.*
> **DB:** *OK, was that who I heard cussing, tell him I say whatup.*
> **DM:** *Ya ya u now go to sleep for now.*

The pair were in a "meeting" — a.k.a. on their way to "work."

At 10:02 p.m. the light in the window in Hann's study was switched on as a late-model Acura drove past Jennifer's home and turned onto Dodds Gate, a street running north two doors up from 238 Helen Avenue. Two minutes later, David's phone contacted Jennifer for the last time. Jennifer, who was talking to Edward at the time, hung up on him and said she'd call him back. The call from David's phone to Jennifer's lasted three minutes and twenty-three seconds. *Is your dad sleeping? Where's your mom? Is the door open? Are the lights on? Are you ready?"* were questions the Crown suggested were asked of Jennifer during that call. There were three men in the car, and three guns, at least one of which was loaded.

At 10:08 p.m., Jennifer called Edward back, betraying nothing of what was about to occur, according to Edward. "Given what we've seen of Jennifer

Pan ... that's not so surprising," the Crown later asserted. "She was ready for her plan to be carried out." Partway through the second call, she interrupted Edward and said she heard something downstairs and that she'd call him back. The time was 10:14 p.m., and the men were now in her home.

Hann Pan's testimony recounting what happened next was quite literally a homeowner's, not to mention a father's, worst nightmare brought to life. Hann was roused from his slumber with a gun in his face held by a man he later all but confirmed was David Mylvaganam. Money was repeatedly demanded, but none was actually sought. Hann managed to catch a glimpse of what he later described as "brown splotches" on the man's clothing. "There were some dirty markings on the sweater," he said. "Looked like the ink from a paintball gun. I have seen it previously. One time I drove my daughter and son to a shop that sold it [paintball gear] near Yorkdale Mall. Same kind of dirt as people who went in there to play that game. It was light brown. I did realize it was the marks from the paintball." (It was the police's theory that Daniel had stolen the clothing used in the home invasion from one of the paintballing sites he frequented.)

Hann said the man wore a black turtleneck and had a black baseball cap pulled over his eyebrows and the tops of his ears. After managing to stand, the father of two was led from the bedroom without the benefit of his glasses. When they emerged from the bedroom, Hann saw the one thing that was even more terrifying than a man holding a gun to his face. Surveying the hallway before him, he opened his weary eyes wide with dread when he saw two figures in conversation at the opposite end of the second floor, next to his daughter's bedroom door. One was Jennifer and the other was the man Jennifer later said resembled Eric Carty. Although the glance was only momentary, Hann said the conversation between the pair was familiar and spoken in hushed tones. "I could not hear what was being said because it was being spoken softly," he said. "It was like a friend, softly." He said throughout the conversation his daughter wasn't restrained.

As he descended the staircase, his sobbing wife came into view, her feet still in the bucket of water, a gun held to her neck by another man. Hann's mind reeled, trying to understand how what he was experiencing could be real. Rather than panic, though, he pushed the rising tide of fear down. "I thought they wanted to rob my house, not kill my wife," he said. Hann had no idea of the fate that awaited them.

Once on the couch, Bich asked how their front door had been breached without a sound. Hann had no answer for her. He was then told "Shut up! You talk too much!" by one of the men towering over them, making him seem larger than he was — at least six feet, Hann later estimated. (In reality, all of the home invaders were in and around five feet eight inches.)

"Where is the fucking money?" the third man demanded. When Hann told them he had only $60 but had plenty of goods the man might be interested in, he was called a "liar" as the butt end of the gun descended swiftly onto his skull.

Bich screamed, "Please, don't hurt my husband!"

When the intruder ordered Bich to turn down the blaring Chinese news, she was too nervous and fumbled with the buttons, so Hann assisted her. Bich was asked how many people were in the house. Although honest, mentioning Jennifer, Bich quickly added that she was sleeping. The invaders called upstairs to their partner to check if the $60 was there and to bring the girl down.

Bich's trusted daughter was led down the stairs, unhindered by tether or the grip of the man accompanying her. First she walked to the kitchen, illuminated by the light from the fridge. Next she ventured to the dining room table as Hann held his head, blood dripping between his fingers as he cowered in fear next to his wife. Jennifer and her "captor" then stood and spoke quietly for a minute, again too softly for Hann to overhear the exact words, before Hann's tormentor ordered Jennifer be returned upstairs. As Jennifer left, Bich cried out, "Please, you can hurt us, but please don't hurt my daughter!"

The reply was cold enough to give any parent the shivers. In court, after attempting to make the assailants response clear a number of times through the interpreter, Hann, fed up with the confusion, finally blurted out in heavily accented English: "Don't worry. Your daughter is very nice. I won't hurt her."

Hann and Bich were then ordered to stand up and were led downstairs into the basement by two of the men. The third ran from the house. Hann and Bich were forced to sit down on the couch, and Hann heard one of the men ask the other: "Should we tie them or tape them? Exit by the front or rear door?"

The reply was succinct and cold: "Shoot and exit via front." The directness of his command would have raised alarm in Bich as she realized in that moment that she and her husband were as good as dead.

The men threw blankets over each of their heads. Hann didn't fight back, resigned to his fate, but Bich lost control. "My wife was opposing ... she did not want the blanket to cover her head," he said in court.

The men shot Hann first, pumping two bullets from close range into him. He ended up hunched over, apparently dead. Next, their attention shifted to Bich. Their attempt to place the blanket over her head ultimately failed, and she was likely hysterical as she begged for her life. *"Pop, pop!"* — Bich's screams went silent. There was one more shot for good measure. This time the pistol was placed so close to the back of her skull that the entry wound featured a ring around it due to proximity and force. *"Pop!"* Blood was splattered on the far wall of the basement and possibly on the assailants' clothing.

Ultimately, it was Hann's placid acceptance of the men's order to place the blanket over his head that saved his life, the fabric obscuring the target so that the shots weren't fatal. Both bodies slumped onto the cold basement floor.

The men then bolted upstairs and out of the house to the waiting car, speeding off into the night at 10:33 p.m.

After they were gone, Jennifer fished her phone out and called 911. While doing so, Hann awakened to a nightmare. "I saw my wife was lying at my feet," he told the court haltingly. "I shook my wife, and I realized my wife had no movement." Somehow he made his way upstairs and ran from the house and waited for his neighbour's garage door to open, frightened the killers were still present as his daughter screamed his name. "I went out of the house," he said. "I called for help. My neighbour at that time was preparing to go to work. He opened the garage door and saw that I was standing outside. I told him please call 911; my house was robbed, and I was shot."

Before he was taken away in the ambulance, Hann described the three men to police — two black, one white.

THE MEN IN the car gave themselves fourteen minutes to calm down before they carried right on doing what they had been doing prior to the murder. At 10:46 p.m. a call originated from David's phone when it was in the vicinity of Highway 401. That first call was to the phone of Tim Conte and lasted one minute and eight seconds. Conte's phone at the time was bouncing off the cell tower near Kik Custom Products where Lenford Crawford worked. The men then drove to Rexdale. At 11:33 p.m. David called his girlfriend, Denise, in Montreal and the pair spoke for four minutes. She later testified that she didn't detect any signs of anxiety or trouble in David's voice and that the texts he sent right after were quite loving. That could be because he'd just shared with her the news that he had made a lot of money and would be sending her some of it the next day. Denise said nothing made David happier and prouder than sending money to her to take care of their son.

An hour later, at 11:53 p.m., Lenford called Jeffrey Fu — "Tell the kid everything's all right," he told him. At 12:49 a.m. and 1:20 a.m. Demetrius Mables was called by Lenford. Then Eric called Ayan. Next, David responded to Denise with the good news.

> **DB:** *Good night, sweet dreams, talk to you in the morning.*
> *love you.*
> **DM:** *Same here always love you, in the morning K mama.*

With his portion of the $2,000 booty sitting in his lap, one wonders if David's reference to something happening "in the morning" was about the money he promised to send Denise during the couple's conversation about an hour after the murder. His text early the next day seems to make that clear. On November 9, David messaged Denise that he was "going to da Western," Western Union, that is. Other than the money Jennifer may have handed over in the lead up to the murder, and a small amount of marijuana fronted to Lenford and Eric by Daniel after Jennifer's arrest, this $2,000 was the only cash ever to exchange hands in return for murder. Small potatoes for the havoc wreaked on so many lives.

PART FOUR

CONCLUSIONS

LIVES FOREVER CHANGED: IMPACT STATEMENTS

HANN PAN

When I lost my wife, I lost my daughter at the same time. I don't feel like I have a family anymore. On the day Bich-Ha died, I feel like I died, too. My life totally changed that day. Some say I should feel lucky to be alive, but I feel like I am dead, too. I can't work anymore because of my injuries and I have given up all of the things I used to love to do, like gardening, working on cars, and listening to music. There is no joy in any of that for me.

I miss my wife so much. She knew me better than anyone and cared about me. I am so lonely without her. We were married for almost thirty years. Bich-Ha was a good wife and a good mother. She always put her children first and rarely spent money on herself. She loved music and loved to go line dancing; she took care of our children while I worked. She had always wanted to go to Vietnam, and I always said we have to spend our money on the children's education first, but once they are finished school we can focus on doing the things we want then. But that time never came for her. I don't find any joy in holidays anymore. I am sad and lonely all the time. Sometimes when I see my friends I try to pretend I am happy but struggle with being jealous of my friends' families and their happiness. My only hope for the future is that Felix will get married and let me live with him. Right now I live with my two sisters and my elderly mother as I can't stand being in my home because of all the bad memories of what

Hann Pan and Bich-Ha Pan. Undated photo.

happened there. There are repairs that need to be done on the house, but because of my injuries I am unable to do anything. I don't like going to my house because my neighbours ask me what happened and I am ashamed. I can't sell the house because it is in a Chinese neighbourhood [with superstition] and no one would want to live there because of the murder.

I cannot sleep at night and have constant nightmares about what happened the night we were shot. I feel panicked all the time, especially when I see a group of young men in the street. I am not racist at all, but black men really scare me if I see them standing in a group. I am in a lot of pain and take medication for pain every day. I have no appetite as food is not pleasurable to me because I know I will never be able to taste my wife's cooking again. I am also on medication for diabetes and high cholesterol as I cannot exercise as it is too painful. My life has totally changed. I attend my wife's grave with my brother and sister-in-law on the anniversary of her death and on other special holidays and it is so very hard on me to remember how she died and what my life has become.

I am a very lonely person and have no one to share my feelings with as my son, Felix, does not want to talk about what happened and just wants to forget. It is very hard for Felix; he doesn't want to hear his sister's name and doesn't want to know about what happens in court. Felix has become very separate and is a very different person; he doesn't want to talk about the family, and he is very closed down, distant and too sad. He says he doesn't want to remember and won't look for a job in Toronto because he feels like he has a bad family name because everyone knows about his mother's murder. I would like to thank the following people who have been involved in this case through this very difficult time with me: Michelle Rumble, Jennifer Halajian, Rob Scott, Detective Bill Courtice and the York Regional Police, Justice Boswell, the members of the jury, Karen Binch, and Dianne Blair. I hope my daughter, Jennifer, thinks about what has happened to her family and can become a good and honest person someday.

FELIX PAN

Four years have passed since the incident on November 8, 2010, and although many things have changed, some of the things I hoped would change didn't. I can't recall how many times I have been told "Time will heal all." As much as I wish this were true, I can't say it has for me. It dulls and fades over time as periods of depression brighten up to give me hope and drive me to try to change things in my life. Supportive family, encouraging friends, and happy Internet videos make me want to stand up and make a difference in this lifetime. Not only for my family and me, but for the world we all share. But in an instant it is all gone. A comment from a stranger, sad news on the radio, an awful day. Sometimes all it takes is a whiff of a long-forgotten smell to send my mind spinning back into the darkness. My heartbeat races and I'm thinking about every breath because my brain has completely forgotten how to breathe. Like a dark shadow it's something I cannot hide from. The best I can do is try to keep moving. I can be the first to admit running away from my problems is not healthy, but it is the only way I know how to keep going. I don't have an issue talking about feelings or have issues trusting people around me. I have people who I can tell everything, but when it comes to this one thing, nothing comes out. Even trying to piece words together now feels like mission impossible. I keep telling myself I have to do this for the ones who no longer can. Now I am stuck. This is where I want to start to talk about how I lost my emotional support, my foundation, my mom. This is where the pen stops, the flood gates open, and I can no longer continue with this topic. Unfortunately, this is not where I stop losing people. News of this incident spread fast like wildfire through friends, family, and all throughout Facebook. Everyone knew. From then on nothing was the same. Everyone's reaction toward me was different. The way they asked me, "Hey, how are you doing?" Or sometimes it's just a "Hey" and a long pause, not sure if they should carry on. Some friends could take it, some friends couldn't. At the end of the day I don't blame anyone for bailing. I, if anyone, should know how draining this can be. For those who stuck around, I am grateful yet pity. Being associated with me doesn't come without consequence. I recently invited someone and their friends over for New Year's. I had to watch them squirm and suffer as they tried their best to refuse without admitting to the fear of explaining to friends how they ended up at a home of such darkness. I've had to deal with this long enough to know it's happening before it happens. I once had a friend who simply wanted to Google directions to come over [to my house], but instead of a map, received pages and pages of news articles — my name, where I went to school, my major intersection. Any one of these things is enough to warrant the question, "Hey, did you hear about the Markham home invasion a few years back?" Unfortunately, four years doesn't give me enough experience to dig such a terrifying question. For four years people have been telling me, "You have stayed so strong" and "You are the strongest person I know." I honestly cannot agree. To me being strong is a choice. Being forced through a tough time is just surviving. For the longest time I would keep telling myself *I have to keep moving forward.* That it was the only way not to let this define me. I worked hard, studied hard, did everything I thought I was supposed to, reminding myself that I wasn't just doing it for me. I was doing it for everyone who ever loved me. Believe me, it's a lot harder than they make it seem in the movies. Fast-forward a few years and I'm a brand-new graduate. The worst is over, time to build a new life, or so I thought. Starting a new career, I thought I could finally leave some of this baggage behind me. Little did I know it's not so easy. In the unforgiving world of social media, nothing gets left behind. I can have a perfect résumé and perfect LinkedIn, but it's always overshadowed by what happened in 2010. Any employer looking for Felix Pan over the Internet is first welcomed with punchlines such as "Brother Believed Sister's Lies, Murder Trial Told — *Toronto Sun*." Not a great start. I guess hard work doesn't always pay off. Sometimes no matter what you say or do, no matter your skills or personality, it's impossible to see through the past and give someone a chance. When first asked to make a statement regarding how this case has impacted me, I didn't know what to expect. Now that I'm writing down my last few thoughts, I'm questioning if this is what everyone else expects. It's been a while since everything happened, but I am still barely able to think about, let alone write about, how I feel for others to read. There are many things I would rather not discuss and some things I couldn't even if I wanted to. We have barely scratched the surface of what is going on in my life. I just hope this allows you to get what you are looking for and gives you a glimpse of what it is like to be me.

AFTER THE TRIAL, the Crown requested that there be a no-communication order placed on Jennifer so that she couldn't contact her family. Although her lawyer, Paul Cooper, argued against it, it was put into force by the judge. Jennifer remains committed to reconnecting with her family, but so far that hasn't occurred, and unless the order is removed, it won't occur for more than two decades.

WHERE ARE THEY NOW?

Daniel Wong is being held in Collins Bay Institution in Kingston, the oldest prison facility in Canada, located about two and a half hours east of Toronto. The jail is sometimes referred to as "Disneyland North" because of its château-style main steeple. When a friend visited him at the prison in Lindsay, Ontario, prior to his being moved, Daniel, sitting behind a thick Plexiglas pane, was still "happy and cracking jokes." Wearing an orange jumpsuit, he told his friend he had bonded with some Cantonese inmates in his block and that they were helping him ease into prison life.

He now spends part of his time composing music and has requested that visitors bring him staff paper. One friend said that, although she wasn't sure if he was putting up a front, Daniel seemed "normal" when she went to visit him. Daniel told another friend that thinking about "what-ifs" would drive a person mad. He is very focused on his appeal, which is currently working its way through the courts, though it is looking increasingly unlikely that it will be heard. He refused a chance to speak to me about this book, but it is understood he vociferously denies his guilt in the case. Barring an appeal victory, Daniel will be released from prison at age fifty.

David Mylvaganam is currently incarcerated in New Brunswick at the Atlantic Institution, a former ammunitions depot in Renous, about two hours northwest of Moncton. It's unclear what David is doing behind the walls of the facility that holds about 240 inmates. He turned down an opportunity for an interview with me.

Lenford Crawford currently resides at Kent Institution in Agassiz, British Columbia, home of Robert Picton, one of Canada's most infamous living serial killers. Although it's unclear if he still maintains this role, Lenford's mother said he was very involved in prison activities and worked in the kitchen while at Millhaven, where he was previously incarcerated. Lenford refused to speak to me himself, but his parents openly spoke about their firm belief in their son's innocence. His mother also expressed her anger at Corrections Canada for moving her son so far away from her Toronto residence. Lenford is appealing his conviction.

Eric Carty is serving his time at Millhaven Assessment Unit, which houses inmates recently sentenced to federal time in Ontario, though he is currently scheduled to be moved. He was granted the chance to serve his time in Atlantic Canada or the West. Furniture for federal government offices is fabricated in Millhaven. Inmates receive a small weekly wage for working there, about $20. It also houses Paul Bernardo, Canada's most infamous convict. Eric is appealing his conviction in the Kirk Matthews conviction. If that judgment is overturned, he could be out of prison in nine years. He turned down the opportunity for an interview with me.

Jennifer Pan is being held at Grand Valley Institution for Women in Kitchener, Ontario, about an hour and a half west of Toronto. Many of the offenders in this prison live in residential houses and living units, but overcrowding has often been a complaint. In one letter to Daniel, Jennifer explained that she spent much of her time cleaning the "range" — the living quarters she shared with her cellmates. She complained about the food, about being alone, and she said she missed Daniel. "I get really depressed, the beds are not comfy." She described her cellmates and how she braided one woman's hair and that she kept busy by cleaning, hoping this might keep the more aggressive inmates from harming her. Jennifer said some people call her names, and she's scared of fights occurring or getting hurt. She added that when her close friends, including one woman named Kay, leave, she's worried how the others will react when there's no one there to protect her. One lawyer says perhaps the most ironic thing about the trial is that Jennifer will be serving the easiest time by far than any of the men. She maintains contact with at least one of her former friends.

Jennifer maintains her innocence and is appealing her conviction, which is also unlikely to go ahead. She refused the opportunity to speak to me on a number of occasions. As part of her sentence, she is no longer allowed to communicate with her co-conspirator, Daniel Wong. However, in her final letter to Daniel, Jennifer signs off simply but tellingly — *Love Always*.

AFTERWORD

BY DR. BETTY KERSHNER, PH.D., REGISTERED PSYCHOLOGIST

How could a young woman arrive at the point of wanting to kill her parents and cold-heartedly attempt to carry out the plan? Was it nature or nurture? Was Jennifer Pan somehow born with "a bad seed," a defect in her mental health that would turn her into a monster? Was it the way that she was brought up by demanding "tiger parents"? Jeremy Grimaldi's narrative contains many fascinating details and insights from the public record, the court testimony, and interviews with some of the people who knew her. I have not met Jennifer Pan nor have I conducted a psychological assessment of her. However, there are psychological factors and profiles generally associated with certain kinds of experiences — the sort of background, upbringing, family, and social life that Jennifer had.

Based only on what is reported second- and third-hand, I can speculate about the personality and mental health associated with that kind of life and this kind of murder and how the situation might have developed. I cannot say specifically that this is what happened with Jennifer Pan: I do not know her or her family. I can only offer informed speculation.

I WILL START at the beginning.

Jennifer's parents were immigrants to Canada from Vietnam, where the rural population was bombarded during the war and the middle, upper, and educated classes in the cities were devastated in the immediate aftermath. The entirety of their childhoods took place during wartime (1946–75), and their young adulthoods were experienced in the aftermath of war as the country was being rebuilt. Hann would have been twenty-two during the fall of Saigon.

We do not know if they or their families were exposed to fighting, relocation, re-education, or whatever else, or how people in their social circle suffered. We do know that Hann attended college in the former Saigon after the war, but there would have been few opportunities for him there. We do not know about Bich's education or otherwise. When they departed Vietnam, they left behind and lost whatever they had. Certainly, there was trauma all around: in the war on the ground, and on the water in the boats they travelled in to get away. We know that severe trauma in one generation often finds a pathway of effects down to the next and even successive generations.

If Hann and Bich themselves did not face or were too young to be aware of danger, most likely their parents did. Parents who have faced horrific experiences and demonstrate resilience often do so at the cost of shutting down aspects of their own emotions. Scars harden over tender spots, making people less vulnerable but also less aware of and sometimes less responsive to their own emotional needs or the needs of others. Recognizing emotional need can sometimes be too risky, threatening to open the floodgates and allow emotion to overwhelm. Often, parents who have been exposed to trauma want to keep it from their children to protect them. They do not talk about it. They do not share it.

Children in such families can feel that something is missing, that there is something bad, threatening, amorphous, unknown, and not labelled, but is part of their environment, creating in those children a vague sense of apprehension. The very wish to protect children can lead to unanticipated, unintentional fears and worries in them because they sense something is wrong but no one talks about it and they do not know what it is.

We do know that Jennifer was afraid to be alone, afraid that she could die, and that she was asthmatic. Jennifer met Daniel, the "love of her life" and co-conspirator, when they both travelled to Europe as part of the school band. Asthma can be triggered by environmental factors such as the smoke in the auditorium where the band performed but also by emotional stress. This was the first time that Jennifer was away from her family. Who knows what that meant to her? Much as she wanted to go,

Jennifer was accustomed to her family's constant monitoring and supervision. The separation might have left her feeling exposed and vulnerable. When she suffered an asthma attack, it was Daniel who stayed with her. He comforted and calmed Jennifer and helped her to breathe. Jennifer believed that Daniel saved her life that day, and she began to love him.

Both of Jennifer's parents worked hard and were determined to make a better life for their children. Following Chinese/Asian cultural norms described in tiger parenting and endorsed by Felix's testimony, Hann and Bich may not have believed in praise as a form of child guidance. Instead, they appear to have criticized and demanded more. It has been said that in that cultural form of parenting, children do not get emotional support but only demands and expectations. The paramount goal is the creation of the necessary credentials to build a future. There is also the matter of appearances: the family must look successful. To that end, Hann and Bich worked hard. Money went to the children and to keeping up appearances: a nice home and high-end cars. Energy and time went into jobs, the home, and providing transportation for the children's activities. While Jennifer sometimes came home from hours of skating practice only to practise piano and do her homework, staying up late into the night, she would not have been the only one in the family with little or no time for a personal life. Neither of her parents, especially her mother, seem to have had much unstructured time — no moments to just relax with Jennifer. There might have been little opportunity for the kind of "quality" time that allows people to really get to know one another and really feel intimate on a deep level: open, shared periods together.

Jennifer's father and Felix did some of the chores together; her mother was kept busy with the household. In those circumstances, Jennifer might have felt she was not really known by her family — she talked about being a mystery and no one knowing everything about her. She might not have felt loved for herself, intrinsically important to them, since she stated they did not really know her; but rather, as she said later, that she was important to her parents only for what she could achieve. How could they know her when she herself apparently did not believe she really, solidly existed as a person in her own right? Her fear of being alone suggests that Jennifer did not know how to self-soothe and also that, during her early childhood, her normal childish fears were not, or not adequately, addressed. Infants left to "tough it out" and "deal" might manage, but some will not and will be left with feelings of vulnerability and danger that are beyond their capacity to cope.

Little children might experience fear of annihilation: that without someone strong to protect them, someone who cares enough to bother and to be there, they might die or simply disappear. Thinking of their parents as all-powerful, infants can develop the misperception that if their parent is not there to see them and validate them, if they are not present in their parents' eyes and can see themselves reflected, they do not exist. This is why "Peek-a-Boo" so delights a young child: they are just at the point of figuring out that someone continues to exist even if they are out of sight, and are thrilled to be proven right when that person comes back. But if a parent does not come when the child is afraid and calls out for them, that infant/toddler can be left with a sense of doubt and insecurity, apprehensive that the parent really has vanished into thin air and so might they. This can create a deeply held, even unconscious feeling of vulnerability and a kind of hole in the beginning sense of personhood.

Jennifer's descriptions of her adult feelings suggest the possibility of a childhood where, at least sometimes, she was left on her own with her infant fears beyond her capacity to handle. Her mother might have comforted her at points here and there, but in those moments of childhood terror, that childhood crisis, comfort might not have been dependably available. Jennifer seems to have thought in her heart of hearts, curled up in the fetal position as she did at times, such as under the heavy stress of police interrogation, that she did not really exist, that she was alone and helpless, might disappear, and be nothing substantial.

Similarly, if Daniel did not love her, withheld that validation, she was "nothing." On top of that, if Jennifer believed she did not exist in her own right rather than as an appendage and at the discretion of her parents, she might feel she existed only to fill their image of what she should be. Otherwise, she might think she would be hollow inside. In this kind of situation, people tend to feel insufficiently separated from their parents — enmeshed. Forming a core identity as distinct from the parent is something that normally happens for a child in the early years. If it does not happen successfully, the person tends to become entwined with their parent, caught in a tangle that keeps them close, at least emotionally, and interferes in the development of a freely chosen life.

Jennifer might have failed in a primary task of normal child development: the development of a solid sense of oneself as separate from her parents. Her sense of herself during her elementary school days and into high school is described as dependent on her parents' perception of her and a growing sense that she was "not good enough" — tellingly, the very phrase she used later with Daniel when he told her he cared for another woman. This suggests that her very being was shaped to please her parents. It might have felt like freefall when her performance fell short and she displeased them, as if she would be destroyed or disappear.

We know that Jennifer suffered from anxiety and learned to cover it with her "Happy Mask" — at first for the outside world and later for her family. The known facts suggest that from the beginning, from earliest infancy, Jennifer might have felt it was all or nothing — her parents' approval or she was gone.

If Jennifer had had the foundation of a solid sense of self, she likely could have withstood her parent's criticism, and for a while she did, as long as she believed she was capable of living up to what her parents wanted. She took it constructively and tried harder. But people who knew Jennifer in elementary school say that her academics, while among the best, were not the very best. While she had friends, Jennifer was described as "cold" and "driven." It reportedly upset Jennifer deeply that she was not awarded any significant prize at the end of grade eight. That unexpected outcome overturned her world. No matter that she had worked so hard; she was not sufficiently rewarded or recognized. Her intense efforts failed to result in prizes that would gratify her parents and validate her personhood.

By grade nine in high school, with stiffer competition, Jennifer realized she did not have what it took to get that very top mark. Many students, faced with the prospect of trying and failing, decide that it is better not to try so that they can console themselves with the thought that if they had tried they would have succeeded. Better to abstain than to risk trying and failing. Consistent with her developmental age and stage, Jennifer turned attention to her peers, now that she had lost the motivation for all-consuming study. She spent time socializing instead. In grade nine, Jennifer began her string of lies. Having earlier conceded the right to create her own sense of herself and given it over to her parents, Jennifer next lost the identity that they had created for her. Lacking a sense of who she was to fall back on when she realized she was not going to be the girl her parents wanted her to be, Jennifer had nothing in its place. She would have been primed to fall hard for someone and to see that new person as everything for her, filling the empty spaces where her self-esteem and sense of personal identity should have been.

It was not long after this that Jennifer met Daniel. His rescue of her during her asthma attack put Daniel in the place of a surrogate mother for Jennifer: a life-giver and saviour of her body and soul. She believed her life depended on him, just as an infant's does on its first caretaker. He had soothed and calmed her breathing, the stuff of life itself, and stabilized her body the way a mother calms an infant. Daniel was simply with her, an attentive presence. It might be that he became Jennifer's primary attachment figure: the person she believed most able and likely to protect her in times of danger, to look out for and care about her, so that she transferred that feeling from her parents to him. With Daniel around, Bich might have become replaceable for Jennifer — perhaps eventually expendable. It seems that Daniel became the repository of Jennifer's sense of herself once the identity her parents had created for her was shattered. Jennifer might have been starved for someone to pay that kind of close attention to her. Much later, Jennifer could spend hours on the phone with Daniel while they both lay in bed in their separate homes, just listening to his breathing. This suggests the possibility that when she was very little, that kind of connection through silent, attentive presence might not have been forthcoming from her busy parents, that during those foundational early years, there might have been repeated times when Jennifer felt alone, fearful as children can be, and her parents were busy elsewhere and not available to her. Bich likely was busy with housework; Hann likely considered that kind of thing woman's work.

Jennifer also loved her stuffed toys: she and Daniel talked about them as if they were real, even in her twenties. Jennifer shared that, as a child, she felt affectionate and nurturing to Felix, who was three years younger. When in elementary school, she enjoyed helping the teachers by looking out for the younger children. These are nurturing activities and can sometimes represent the wish that a person had enjoyed that kind of care and attention for oneself. Jennifer's stuffed toys appear to have served as "transitional objects." These are things that young children become attached to, which offer comfort when parents are not available. They hug their bunnies or their blankets to feel safe when uneasy. As the child grows up and matures, that feeling of safety moves from the transitional object to inside themselves. The successful child can comfort herself and learns to feel safe on her own — that she can handle being alone. She no longer needs her mother or her toy to protect her. She knows that she herself has what it takes.

It seems that Jennifer did not make that transition and failed to develop the ability to soothe herself. She continued to rely on her stuffed toys, even as an adult, giving them names and talking to Daniel about them. This fits with the baby talk she and Daniel indulged in together for hours at a time. With Daniel, Jennifer might try to elicit the kind of attention an attentive parent would give to an infant to calm childish, unnamed fears. As with an idealized parent, Jennifer might have come to believe that Daniel's purpose was to be there and take care of her. Little children do not recognize that their parents have needs of their own. They believe parents should be right there whenever they want them and make everything better. Otherwise, the children can become enraged. This is another part of infancy that Jennifer does not seem to have outgrown but appears to have projected onto Daniel: that she should be the girlfriend who was good enough for him as she tried to be good for her parents, and that Daniel should recognize her value, be committed to her protection, and fulfill her wishes the way every infant believes a parent should do, leading to the inevitable disillusionment when the parent is not omnipresent and omnipotent. Jennifer stated that Daniel could make her calm, and that she needed him in order to be calm. He, on the other hand, talked about walking on eggshells around her, always being worried about her feelings. It sounds as if he monitored Jennifer's emotional state. Her devotion to Daniel might have derived, at least in part, from his ability and willingness to manage her feelings for her.

My impression is that Jennifer was vulnerable. She could be angry, she could be cold and calculating, but she could not soothe and calm herself. Her interior world seems to have been in a turmoil of anxiety. Jennifer needed someone else to regulate her feelings. Indications are that person was Daniel. The kind of behaviour that is attributed to Jennifer with her parents when she was younger is sometimes associated with disorganized attachment. The attachment system is a relationship between two people, originating when one is a vulnerable infant who could not survive on her own, and the other is older, usually a parent, who is inclined to want to keep that infant alive and therefore protects and nurtures her. In humans, when that infant realizes the protective figure takes the job seriously, keeps her safe, fed, and loved, the infant becomes *securely* attached. If instead the infant experiences that sometimes that figure is not around, is not dependable, wanders off or is too busy, lets her get hungry, cold, or in danger, that infant becomes *insecurely* attached. Such an infant puts effort into developing a way of handling things alone or clings close to parents, trying to be one with them so that they will not forget about her. Either way the infant develops organized strategies for coping.

It seems that, when she was younger, Jennifer focused on her parents, not herself, trying to give them what they wanted from her. She existed in their sphere of influence and seems to have been distracted or even prevented from developing her own personality and style, likes and dislikes. But at the same time, Hann and Bich Pan are described as having been critical, dismissive, and rejecting of Jennifer, teaching her that other things such as academic achievement and superiority in individual activities were far more valuable than anything else that might have interested Jennifer — more important than friendships or relationships, for example. Jennifer's parents wanted her close and paid close attention to what she was doing, but at the same time she felt they rejected her as "not good enough" — pulled her in, pushed her away. This type of experience tends to disrupt a child's ability to develop a coherent style of relationship, due to the inherent contradiction: "disorganized." Often, it leaves the child, and later the adult, likely to have confused, unsatisfactory relationships.

When Jennifer met Daniel in grade ten, after the disappointments of grade eight and the beginning forgeries of grade nine, it was within the context of ditching her old routines and old identity that her parents had crafted for her. She had seen that focusing exclusively on hard work had not led her to something satisfying, so she was open to change and experimentation. Jennifer was spending time with friends and had a casual boyfriend, but that changed when Daniel "saved her life." Here was someone she could give her all to, turn toward, pleasing him the way she had tried to please her parents. Here was someone she might have hoped would give her the affectionate, dependable attention she craved. With Daniel, Jennifer was surrounded by marijuana and eventually got into sex and good times. The Happy Face mask she had previously shown to the world outside the family, she now showed to her parents. They did not know what she was doing or feeling. It was only with Daniel that Jennifer could relax — and she stated that she needed him in order to relax. Otherwise, during those "university" years, Jennifer drove herself to create the world of lies and to document the false life she presented to her parents, to prove to them that she was the daughter they wanted when, sadly, she knew she was not.

Having grown up with "acceptable pretense," described as putting on a show for the sake of appearances, people acting as if something was true while knowing that it wasn't, Jennifer pushed that concept further. She seems to have developed the ability to decide that she would behave as if something that she knew to be true simply did not exist. To that end, she decided that she simply "refused to know" that Daniel was dealing drugs, or at least that is what she told the police. She knew, in other words, but was able to repress that information so thoroughly when she wanted to, that she could react as if she really did not know. There are indications that Jennifer helped Daniel distribute his drugs. But with this type of thinking, there would be moments when she might really feel that she did not know. This kind of behaviour was demonstrated later, under questioning by the police, when Jennifer was so shocked by the insinuation that she was lying, that her spontaneous body language made the officer apologetic for the suggestion. Of course, at the time Jennifer really was lying. Perhaps she did not let herself know in that moment. She convinced herself of her victimization and repressed acknowledging to herself her perpetrator status.

Some people have described Jennifer as a consummate actor. I suggest an alternative possibility that she was not acting all the time: sometimes, yes, but not always. She had divided her thinking, had "split" her mind, and one part did not know what was going on in the other. This is a defence mechanism when things are too hard to handle. This type of "splitting" conceivably might allow the person to feel and act innocent when they are guilty. Once someone develops this type of coping, they can use it for many things in daily life to bolster self-esteem and feel good about themselves. They can use it to keep away thoughts about the bad things in their life done by others or by themselves. It might be that this helped Jennifer deal with the burden of her snowballing lies during what her parents thought were her university years. On some level she might have believed those lies, made herself not think about or forget the distasteful truths. She admitted to the police that she half or sometimes fully believed in her fantasies. As she said, Jennifer did not think about the future, or how it would all work out in the end. She took things day by day, moment by moment. This kind of defence mechanism is considered "primitive" because it cannot work over the long term. Reality comes crashing in sooner or later.

I have to wonder about the nature of the relationship between Jennifer and Daniel. She said that not even Daniel knew everything about her. At the end, she spun out quite a web of deceit in order to try to get Daniel away from his new girlfriend, Katrina, who thought that Daniel used humour to mask what he was really feeling. Were Jennifer and Daniel really open with each other? How emotionally intimate was the relationship, really? They spent hours baby-talking on the phone. That kind of conversation would not likely get very deep or thoughtful. They seem to have related on the level of little children seeking comfort at bedtime. And there was sex. Police have suggested that Daniel was in the relationship for the money that he got from Jennifer, but for him there was also her adoration and Jennifer's wish to be what he wanted. She would be the "best" girlfriend for him, just as when younger she wanted to be the "best" daughter for her parents. Daniel was increasingly into a criminal element. Did Jennifer think she would enhance her attractiveness to him by becoming a gun moll? A Mata Hari? A master criminal? A murderer? Would that give Jennifer street cred with her man?

On her side, the attraction might have been that sense of almost maternal acceptance and nurturance from Daniel — his close attention to her moods and feelings, his regulation of her anxiety. These suggest a wish to repair a maternal bond gone astray. If Daniel was a type of replacement for her mother, her mother might have felt disposable to Jennifer. It seems that Jennifer withdrew her focus from her family and gave up the hope of having her parents meet her emotional needs — that she poured out all that need onto Daniel.

Daniel urged Jennifer to leave her parents and move in with him, but she refused. Daniel would live with her but would not, at least at that time, marry her. Perhaps she could not bring shame on herself and on her family by living common law. Friends attempted an "intervention,"

believing that the restrictions her parents placed on Jennifer were draco-
nian and she should leave them. They offered to help Jennifer find a place
of her own. But she would not. Was it because she simply wanted the crea-
ture comforts of her family home, the middle-class existence her parents
had worked so hard to provide? I think not. By this point, someone with
this type of upbringing would most likely have incorporated the values
of her family, and Jennifer's sense of personal esteem likely by now was
dependent on public success, presenting a "correct" image to the outside
world. She would not be likely to settle for living in a place that she would
consider substandard, or in a public relationship that lacked social status.
Status was non-negotiable. In a real sense she had already lost her family.
She had "killed" their image of the kind of daughter that they had, and
the kind of family that they were, but only in private. If she moved out,
she said, she "would lose everything that ever meant anything to me, my
family, my mother, my father, and my brother" because it would become
a public shame. Jennifer knew that she could not survive on her own.
Alone, she did not feel real to herself. She felt empty, "nothing."

The extreme of this was demonstrated during police interrogation.
Jennifer shook violently, visibly, when questioned, and also when alone.
She asked for someone to come in with her whenever the investigating
detective stepped out. At first she was accommodated, but not later, when
suspicion against her was gaining momentum. Jennifer had a "meltdown."
She paced, "manically" stroked her hair, rambled to herself, and became
dizzy, needing to lean on something to keep her balance. At times, she took
the fetal position, rocked, covered her face, and wept. Many guilty people
would not be able to rise to the occasion under police interrogation. But
Jennifer's reaction was extreme. Under pressure, on her own, it seems that
there was nothing inside her to fall back on. Having felt rejected and abandoned by her family, Jennifer next was rejected by Daniel when he took
up with someone else. Even worse, Jennifer was losing the competition to
another woman. Losing was intolerable for Jennifer. She had to win with
Daniel, just as she had to win those competitions and prizes for her parents.
Sometimes a suicide attempt such as Jennifer alluded to can be a call to activate the attachment system, to bring running that person who is supposed
to care, to get them to demonstrate their concern and bring them close. If
Jennifer actually did self-harm (she had scars) and considered suicide when

younger (she told Felix), it might have been in the service of trying to get her family to show affection to her and about the "real" Jennifer. Her fabrications to Daniel about phone calls, texts, threats, rape, et cetera, fantastic as they were, might have similarly been intended to activate Daniel's attachment and pull Daniel back to her — and they were partially successful.

Jennifer used what her father had nourished in her, that dedication and perseverance, to disrupt Daniel and his new girlfriend. Daniel got back in touch, involved, to ensure Jennifer's safety. She successfully activated the attachment system. For Jennifer, the murder plot provided another reason for Daniel to stay in contact. She had to hook him and keep him. With a shared murder between them, Daniel would not be likely to abandon Jennifer, even if he wanted to. She presented the idea to Daniel in a five-hour phone conversation followed by his silence and then massive communication attempts from her to him. Jennifer bombarded Daniel with calls and texts, suggesting that he needed persuading.

Eight days prior to the murder, Jennifer was engaging in endless baby talk with Daniel. On the day before the original date set for the home invasion, he confessed his love for Katrina. Why would he bring up this potentially destabilizing news at just the point when he and Jennifer most needed to rely on each other? When the transcript of those texts is read, it seems as if Daniel is naive about Jennifer's motives, and innocently trusts in the goodness of her character. My interpretation is that the intensity of the planning made him feel close to Jennifer; that he was performing the murder for her benefit — a gift for an important friend. I suggest that he thought he was doing so much for her, that Jennifer should be able to do something for him: to recognize and acknowledge him as a true friend and be happy for him about his feelings for Katrina. This reveals Daniel's naïveté. His function to Jennifer was to provide her with unconditional love, not to develop his own desires and pursue them. Jennifer might have felt that she was replaceable to Daniel and that she was not going to be missed. Again, she did not exist. She existed only in the image that someone else had of her. Jennifer needed to be first and constantly on someone's mind in order to keep her reassured that she was real, hence the need for constant texting and contact with Daniel.

When Daniel told Jennifer that he loved Katrina, Jennifer asked, "Who will protect me from 'them' if you're not in the picture?" Jennifer knew there was no "them," having fabricated "them" herself. But my impression is that Jennifer really did not feel safe and had decided on Daniel as her protector from her chronic fear of annihilation, her fear of ego death — the loss of a workable image of herself. Possibly, when Jennifer decided to continue with the murder plot even after knowing about Daniel's affection for Katrina, the plot actually became just for her own sake, as she had claimed all along. Perhaps at that point Jennifer felt she could manage alone in the family home, with her parents gone and Daniel with someone else, temporarily. She probably assumed she would get Daniel back.

With Daniel's admission that he loved Katrina, Jennifer, who to that point had pretended acceptance of their relationship, texted Daniel: "I'm sorry for never being good enough." This is exactly what she said about her family. Jennifer saw herself as "not good enough" for them and then for Daniel. Rejection of this sort was not something Jennifer could accept and move on from. She seems to have responded to perceived rejection by focusing her considerable effort and skill into trying to change reality into what she wanted it to be, even if that meant getting rid of people who did not see things that way. She congratulated Daniel (and Katrina) for "winning" — and hinted at suicide, likely another ploy to activate his attachment to her.

Her testimony that the intended plan was for the murderers to kill her, not her parents, a kind of suicide, was true in a way. With her parents gone, so also would go the vision of the daughter that her parents had wanted. It might have seemed a necessary sacrifice so that Jennifer could "come out" as a different kind of person. On one level, killing her parents was the ultimate way to protect them from the shame of her failure: they would never know how far down she had gone and the world would never know that the family was not a smooth-functioning unit of hard-working high achievers. In a way, murder would have fulfilled her cultural responsibility to take care of her parents. They would die with some remaining shred of belief in her and would not have to face the shame of social exposure when Jennifer did not return to school as they expected. In a way, she tried to take ultimate care of them, killing them to remove them from a life that would not be to their liking. Her mother, at least, did not live to witness public exposure and shame, something her father and brother now have to deal with.

Then there is the factor of "ultimate" winning. Patricide cannot be topped for extremes. This dramatic event could have been Jennifer's

Olympics, demonstrating the stuff that she was made of and her determination to win. Had she developed Hann's stubbornness and rigidity? Was Jennifer, after all, faithful to her father — internalizing the characteristics of determination and persistence that he wanted her to have? With the murders, Jennifer would prove to herself and would show those who knew, such as Daniel, how exceptional she really was. The murders would be proof of her mettle, the most forceful display. For Daniel, it would show him how much he meant to her, and how "ultimate" a person she was: someone of extreme value that he should want to be with. If tiger parenting claims that the one who shows the most drama wins in the family competition, then that was Jennifer, with this ultimate play. She showed herself and others that she was not a "loser," that she was capable of going to much greater extremes than anyone else to win: her father's girl, after all.

One detail from the murder enactment is striking. Jennifer had no final words for her parents. Helpless, with guns pointed at them, Jennifer could have told her parents off with anger and impunity. She could have had the final word. She could have tried to explain herself or apologize. But there was nothing. She kept up the pretense that she was also a victim of the home invasion. This was an opportunity that I do not think Jennifer would have passed up if revenge had been her primary motive. I believe Jennifer really wanted her parents to die thinking well of her. She wanted to preserve what she could for them of the illusion that she was a good daughter and that they were a good family together. Jennifer also wanted to preserve it for herself, giving herself memories that she would revisit to think well of herself.

With the type of disorganized attachment that I think Jennifer might have had, with the ability to split off and repress from her awareness what was really going on, it might be that Jennifer was already focused in her head on her fantasies for what her life was going to be, how she was going to think about herself, and that the real-life flesh and blood of her parents held little meaning for her. Was this inborn in Jennifer? As I hope to have made clear, I think not. In my view, Jennifer did not have the type of upbringing that she needed to help her learn to cope with her vulnerabilities. It was not a good fit. She made, as they say, bad choices. Those kinds of choices and experiences take root within a person and become who they are. They are not easy to change, sometimes impossible to change. They can become a personality disorder, but that is not an excuse for murder.

BIBLIOGRAPHIC REFERENCES

Barlow, D.H. et al. *Abnormal Psychology: An Integrative Approach.* 2nd ed. Toronto: Nelson Education, 2009.

Berling, Judith A. "Confucianism." *Focus on Asian Studies* 2, no. 1 (Fall 1982).

Chao, Ruth, and Vivian Tseng. "Parenting of Asians." In *Handbook of Parenting: Volume 4, Social Conditions and Applied Parenting.* 2nd ed. Ed. Marc H. Bornstein. Mahweh, NJ: Lawrence Erlbaum Associates, 2002.

"Children and Lying." The Truth About Deception website: www. truthaboutdeception.com/lying-and-deception/children-and-lying. html. Accessed in 2015.

Choi, Yoonsun et al. "Is Asian American Parenting Controlling and Harsh? Empirical Testing of Relationships Between Korean American and Western Parenting Measures." *Asian American Journal of Psychology* 4, no. 1 (March 2013).

Chua, Amy. *Battle Hymn of the Tiger Mother.* New York: Bloomsbury, 2011.

Lam, Andrew. "The Education of a Vietnamese American Writer." *The Huffington Post*, January 29, 2013.

Park, Julie. "On Tiger Moms." *The Point* (2012). Accessed at https:// thepointmag.com/2012/examined-life/on-tiger-moms.

Reappropriate.com. "Let's Talk About On-Campus Depression and Suicide." (May 9, 2014). Accessed at http://reappropriate.co/2014/05/

today-is-aapimentalhealth-awareness-day-remembering-jiwon-lee-kevin-lee-andrew-sun-others-apahm2014.

Tan, Amy. *The Opposite of Fate: A Book of Musings*. New York: Putnam, 2003.

Truthaboutdeception.com.

AUTHOR'S NOTE

I have tried with this book to write a story that involves several people's lives. That was difficult largely because only a handful of people involved or associated with the case directly chose to share their stories with me. Despite being a public institution, the Crown — a very political office — and its representatives rejected my repeated overtures to speak, missing out, in my humble opinion, on an ideal opportunity to educate Canadians about their very own public justice system. With this book, my goal was not scandalize, vilify or shame those convicted. In fact, I did my best to speak about the people they truly were outside of this one very negative event. As such, I attempted to approach this tale not in the traditional sense — delineating between right and wrong, reviling some and sanctifying others. This is a story really about humans making mistakes, some for the right reasons, some for the wrong.

Having said all that, I do realize the information in this book, especially regarding ethnicities and their values and belief systems, is understandably a very sensitive subject and can be taken in many ways. So, in short, I just want to say: I come in peace. I've done my best to keep my personality out of this story, but for anyone interested, I felt it important to say that I consider myself a traditionalist and raise my children as such, much like my parents raised me. It wasn't my purpose to cast aspersions on either culture or tradition — two abstracts I have great respect for. Nor was I attempting to publish salacious details about people's private lives. My wish an accurate account and educate people about the relationship ... parents and children. It was intended as a means to an end; what that is exactly I'm not quite sure — perhaps just a better understanding of the world we live in and our fellow man, as clichéd as that sounds.

On a more personal level, I wrote the book because I wanted to share a tale of love gone so horribly wrong — a story of relationships and family, of fathers, mothers, and children, wives, husbands, lovers, and friends. It was a venture intended to peer deeper into a tangled saga, many of the details and nuances of which I believed were lost in the story's original telling. This book was about Bich-Ha Pan. It was also about Hann, Felix, and Jennifer Pan. But that one night's violence spread far beyond that family alone, causing heartbreak in many other homes. Mothers and fathers lost their sons; siblings their brothers, and children their fathers, now in jail serving twenty-five-year sentences. Eric Carty, Lenford Crawford, Daniel Wong, and David Mylvaganam are loved, and their presence in the lives of family and friends will also be missed. The book is also about them and should anyone in this book ever choose to speak, I would welcome those conversations.

My retelling of this tragic crime might dredge up bad memories for those involved. For that I apologize. I hope some good comes from it, and that more than one line of communication between parents and children is opened as a result.

I should point out, too, that because of the nature of this crime, a number of the names in this book have been altered to protect people's identities.

I HAVE ONE more story to tell, one that was far less publicized. Up until April 2016, I had never been to 238 Helen Avenue. But I knew — although there was very little chance he'd speak — that I had to meet Hann Pan eventually. I wasn't successful. Walking up to the home that he and Bich had worked so much of their lives to buy, I first noticed its decrepit appearance — the two wooden pillars at the front and the two false windows up top were rotting.

Knowing how much violence had been brought to bear on this unsuspecting family gave the home an eerie feel. Having been immersed in what occurred there for much of the past two years left me emotional, and I shivered as I strode up. As I got closer, the feeling became more intense, growing almost too much to handle. My stomach churned, much like Jennifer's might have done in the police station. As a matter of fact, my stomach turns as I write this. Perhaps the most frightening detail lying before me was the front door's sheer curtains that blocked my view of the inside of the home my eyes strained to witness. The lower centre portion of one curtain was stained black and permanently wrenched to the side. I imagined a frightened Hann repeatedly peeling it back to see who was at the door, whether journalists, television cameras, or well-wishers. When no one answered my knocking, I ventured to the back of the home on Dodds Gate and the alley behind. My eyes immediately looked up to what would have been Jennifer's window, imagining her sitting there as her alleged decisions became reality. I then left a note for Hann in the mailbox.

Fate brought me back to that door on April 10, 2016, when I randomly found myself nearby, the second and last time I was in the neighbourhood. At the front door my emotions betrayed me once again as I lost my nerve, not wanting to bother this poor man. After twisting to walk away, I steadied myself, turned back, lifted my arm to knock and noticed what I figured were Hann's outdoor shoes and a potted plant to my right. I knocked, expecting the door to be slammed in my face if it opened. Instead, a short man with one of the widest grins I've ever seen answered the door. We spoke briefly. He told me he was Bich's brother and that he was living at the house. By the end of the conversation, he still maintained the huge grin on his face, so I remarked on it. "You smile a lot," I said with a grin of my own.

"They call me Smiler," he replied with a giggle.

I asked Smiler to inform Hann of my request to speak with him, thanked him, and went on my way. Two days later, Sandy Luong, twenty-three, went missing at 2:30 p.m. On April 15 her sister, Tracy (Jennifer's cousin), along with police, were in front of cameras pleading for her return.

"We love her very much," Tracy said. "Sandy's the type of person who's soft-spoken. She loves to read. She's very kind and very caring. She's the type of person that, if she only had $1, she'd rather give it to someone else to help them."

A man cried in the background, his face covered by one hand as he wept. When the broken man glanced up and spoke to the camera, the frown on his face was remarkable in its despair — it was Smiler. He talked quickly in a thick accent to the cameras. "Sandy, if you hear this, call me," he said before shrinking away from the cameras almost immediately.

Two days later Jennifer Pan's cousin and Smiler's daughter, Sandra Luong, who had been living at 238 Helen Avenue where her aunt had been gunned down just years earlier, was found dead — a suicide.